Year 10

Life processes and living things
Supplying the cell
Control in animals and plants
Ecology
Concept map
Exam questions

Materials and their properties
Equations and rates of reaction
Energy in chemistry
Rocks and metals
Concept map
Exam questions

Physical processes
Waves in action
Energy in the home
Forces and motion
Concept map
Exam questions

2 Supplying the cell

The basics of life

Cells – the building blocks of life

All living things are made of cells. The cells are so tiny that you can only see them using a microscope.

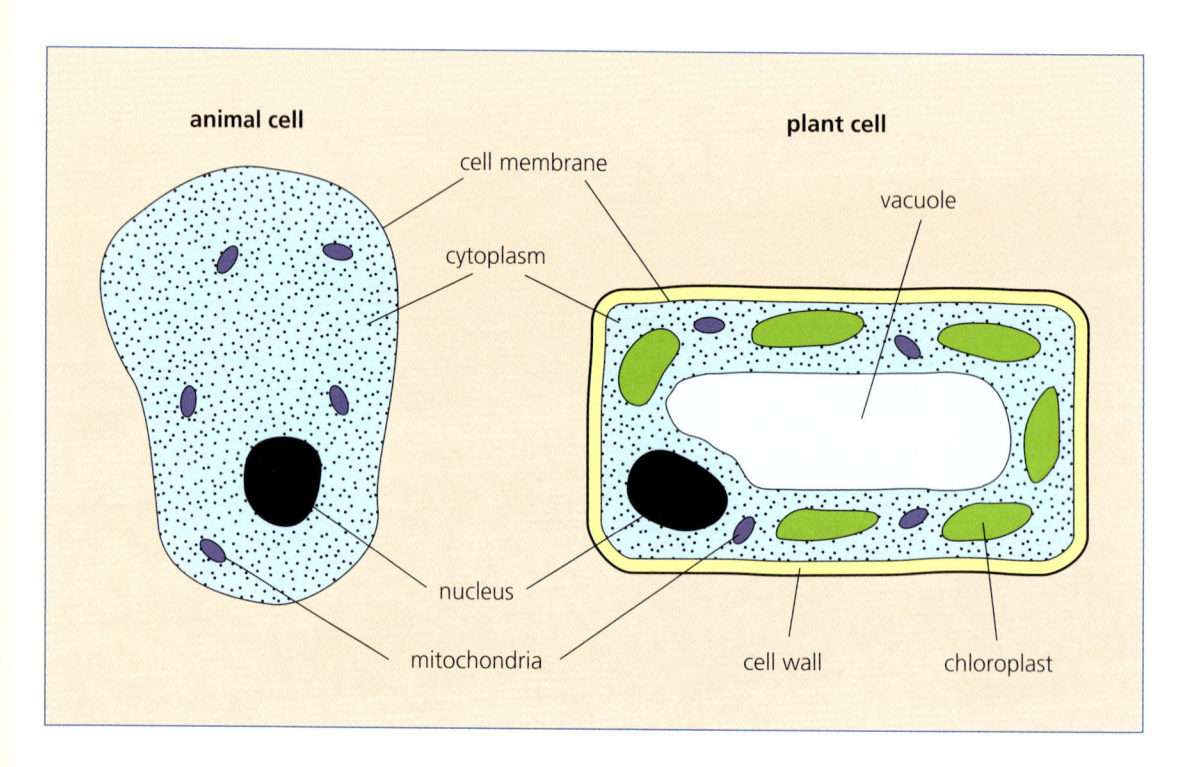

Cells contain:

- a **nucleus** to carry the genetic information and control everything a cell does
- **cytoplasm** – a watery jelly in which most of the cell's chemical reactions occur
- a **cell membrane**, which controls what goes in and out of the cell
- **mitochondria**, which release energy from food (respiration).

Plant cells also have a few extras:

- a **cellulose cell wall** to help support the plant – think of the size of tall trees, and remember they don't have any bones to hold them up
- **chloroplasts** to contain the chlorophyll needed for photosynthesis
- large **cell vacuole**, a space filled with a fluid called cell sap which helps to provide support.

The main chemical in cells is water.

The right cell for the job

Cells contain the same basic parts, but they also have important differences. They are specialised to do different jobs. These are examples:

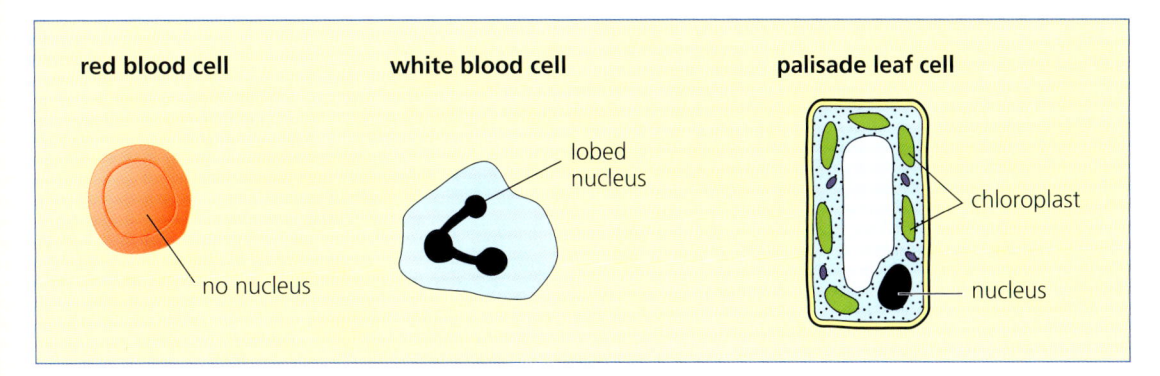

red blood cell — no nucleus

white blood cell — lobed nucleus

palisade leaf cell — chloroplast, nucleus

Red blood cells carry oxygen. They have no nucleus, to make more space for haemoglobin to carry more oxygen.

They have a small size to make them flexible enough to pass through small blood vessels. Their biconcave disc shape provides a large surface area to take in and release oxygen.

White blood cells fight infection, and they can change their shape to engulf microbes. Palisade leaf cells near the surface of leaves are long and thin with lots of chloroplasts to trap light for photosynthesis.

How most materials move in and out of cells

As a consequence of the random movement of individual particles, there is an overall movement of particles from an area of high concentration to an area of low concentration. This process is called **diffusion**. Therefore, inside the lung tissue, where the oxygen concentration is higher in the alveoli than in the blood capillaries, there is an overall movement of oxygen by diffusion from the alveoli to the red blood cells within the blood capillaries, thereby re-oxygenating the blood.

Questions

1. Which part of a plant cell
   a. is needed for photosynthesis
   b. controls what moves in and out of the cell
   c. supports the plant?
2. A red blood cell is peculiar because it does not have a nucleus. Why?

4 Supplying the cell

Digestion

The food you eat has to reach all your cells to release the energy needed to keep you alive. Food also provides the raw materials for growth and maintenance.
So that it reaches the cells, food has to be broken down into small enough pieces to be carried in the blood to the cells. This breaking down is called **digestion**, and it occurs in the **digestive system**.

Digesting what you eat

This is what happens:

- **digestion** is the breakdown of large, insoluble pieces of food into small, soluble pieces
- digestion is helped by the production of **digestive juices** by parts of the digestive system
- digestive juices contain special chemicals, called **enzymes**, which speed up digestion
- there are many different enzymes. Each one has its own type of food to break down
- **bile** is produced in the liver and stored in the **gall bladder**. It is *not* an enzyme. It helps to break down lipids (fats) by **emulsifying** them. This means breaking large droplets of fat into much smaller droplets, thereby increasing the surface area for the enzyme, lipase, to attack
- bile is alkaline, and therefore helps to neutralise the acids coming out of the stomach.

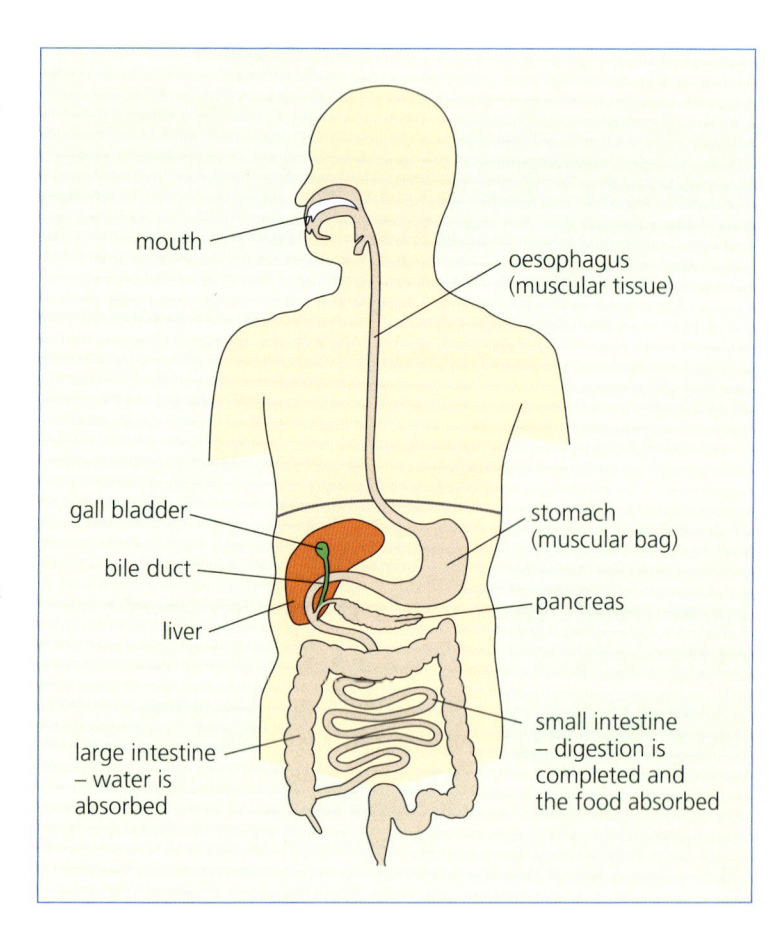

Digestive juices

The stomach makes an enzyme to digest certain foods. This enzyme needs acid conditions for it to work well. Therefore the stomach also makes an acid to provide the enzyme with the right conditions to work well. An added bonus is that the acid kills any germs on the food!

The pancreas makes other enzymes which digest food. These enzymes are released into the small intestine together with juices from the liver. These juices neutralise the acid from the stomach so that the enzymes from the pancreas can work.

Enzymes are proteins which speed up (**catalyse**) reactions in living things. They will only work at the correct pH, and are also affected by temperature:

- too cold, movement is slow – the enzyme and food do not collide often enough for a fast reaction
- too hot – enzymes are destroyed (**denatured**).

At extremes of pH or high temperatures, enzymes are denatured. This means they change shape irreversibly and so can no longer work.

Absorption and the small intestine

The small intestine has lots of finger-like projections called **villi**, which increase the surface area for the absorption of digested food.

The small intestine is adapted for food absorption:

- it is very long
- the villi give a huge surface area
- the walls are very thin and permeable
- it has a good blood supply to transport digested food.

Peristalsis

Food is squeezed through the digestive system by the muscles in the walls of the oesophagus, stomach and intestines. This squeezing action is called **peristalsis**.

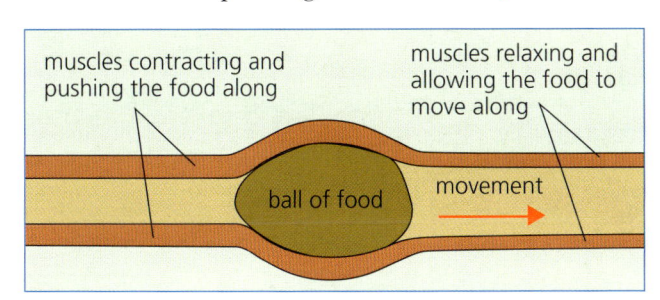

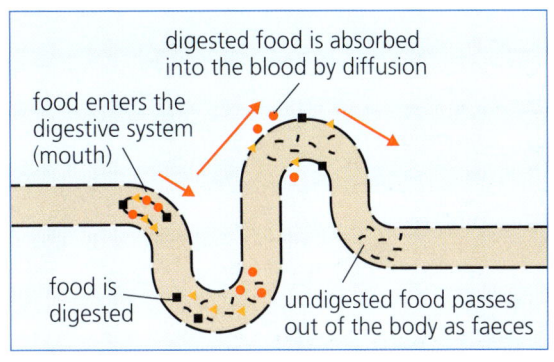

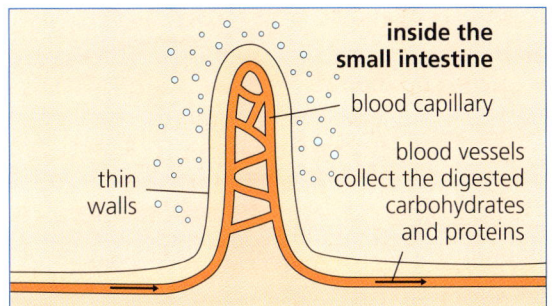

one villus
lots of villi

Questions

1. Explain what digestion is.
2. Where in the body is bile produced, and what does it do in the digestive system?
3. Explain how enzymes help with digestion.
4. Give **two** uses of stomach acid.
5. Name **two** parts of the digestive system that produce enzymes.
6. Explain how all enzymes are affected by temperature.
7. Explain how the small intestine is adapted for the absorption of food.
8. What is peristalsis, and why is it so important?

6 Supplying the cell

Breathing

You breathe in air to take oxygen into your body to be used in respiration (to release energy from your food). Releasing energy from food produces carbon dioxide, which needs to be removed from the body. Therefore **breathing** is **gas exchange**. Gas exchange occurs in the **lungs**, which are in the chest, protected by the **ribs**.

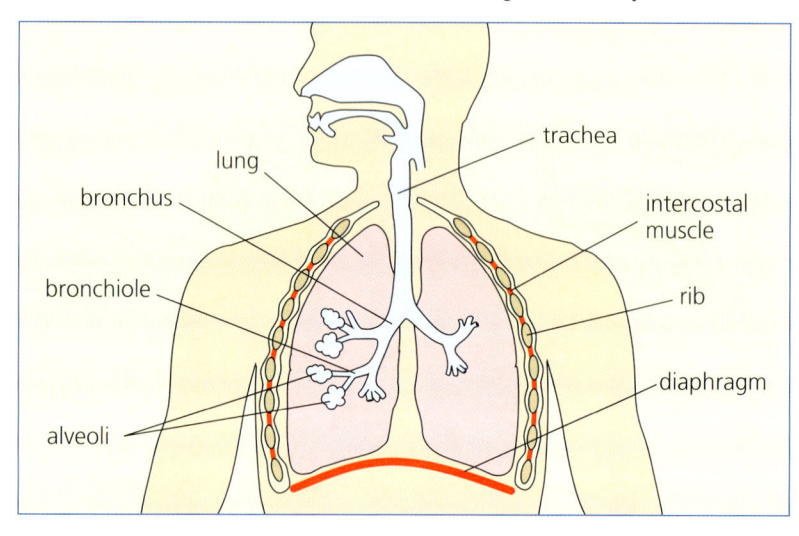

Gas	Air in	Air out
O_2	21%	16%
CO_2	0.04%	4%
N_2	78%	78%
H_2O vapour	variable	saturated

Gas exchange

The **bronchus** and **bronchioles** carry air into the lungs. At the end of the bronchioles are lots of little air sacs called **alveoli**. The alveoli are where gas exchange occurs.

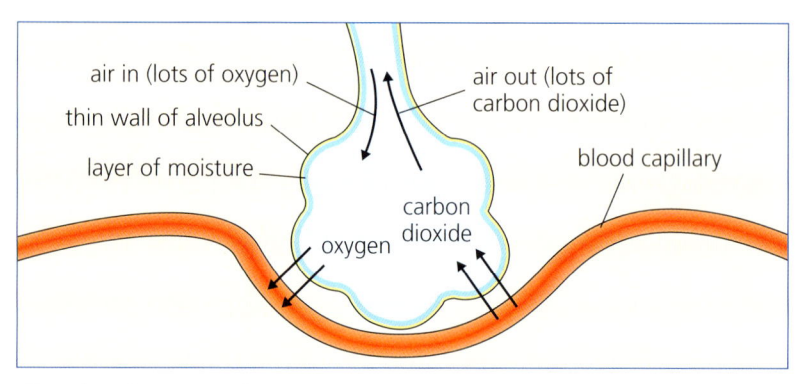

one alveolus
lots of alveoli

The alveoli are good at gas exchange because they have:
- a large surface area (there are thousands of alveoli)
- moist surfaces which make diffusion faster
- thin, permeable walls, which make diffusion faster
- lots of blood capillaries to carry the gases.

In the alveolus oxygen moves from a high concentration (lots of oxygen) through the thin wall into the blood capillary where there is a low concentration of oxygen (very little oxygen). Movement from a high to a low concentration like this is called **diffusion**. There is a high concentration of carbon dioxide in the blood, so carbon dioxide diffuses out of the blood into the alveolus.

Breathing in and breathing out

When we breathe in (inhale), the lung volume increases and therefore the air pressure decreases. When we breathe out (exhale) the lung volume decreases and the air pressure increases. Therefore the air pressure in the lungs is continuously changing. The bronchi and larger bronchioles have pieces of cartilage in their walls to support them and prevent them from collapsing as the air pressure changes.

Breathing in (side view)
- air sucked in
- volume of chest increases
- intercostal muscles contract
- rib cage moves up and out
- diaphragm contracts and flattens

Breathing out
- air squeezed out
- volume of chest decreases
- intercostal muscles relax
- rib cage moves down and in
- diaphragm relaxes

Keeping the lungs clean

Air often contains germs and dust. To help keep the lungs clean the trachea produces a sticky **mucus** to trap invaders. It also has small hairs called **cilia** which beat together to move the mucus away from the lungs.

Smoking stops the cilia beating. This allows germs and mucus into the lungs. The germs increase the risk of infection, e.g. bronchitis. The mucus irritates the lungs causing coughing, e.g. smokers' cough. Chemicals in the smoke destroy alveoli. This makes gas exchange more difficult and may cause the disease emphysema. Some of the chemicals cause lung cancer.

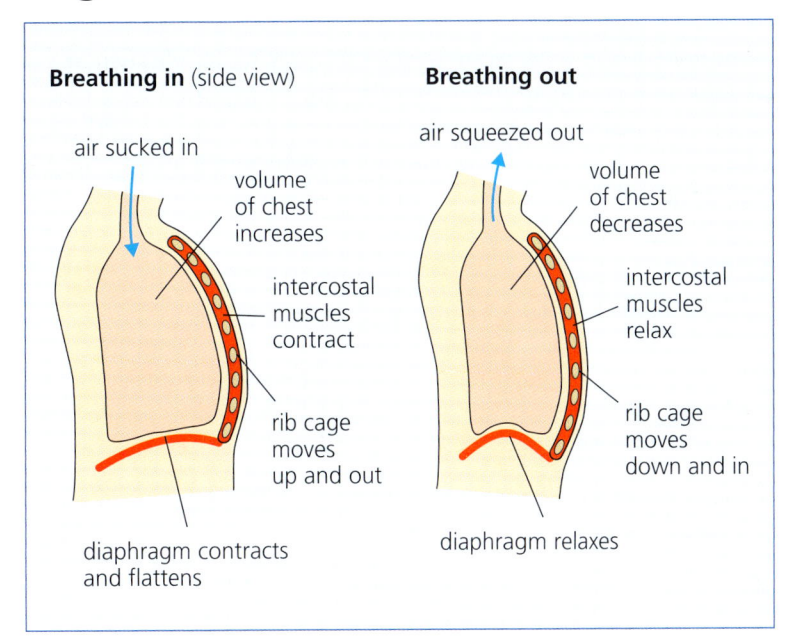

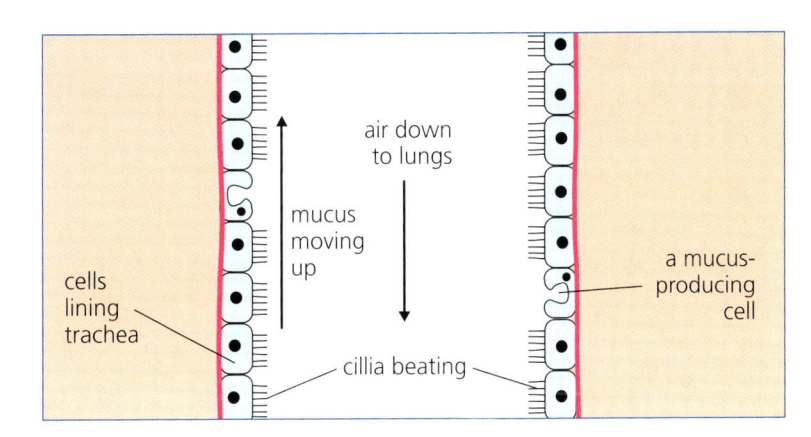

- air down to lungs
- mucus moving up
- cells lining trachea
- cillia beating
- a mucus-producing cell

Questions

1. Why do we need oxygen?
2. Explain why oxygen diffuses from the alveoli into the blood.
3. Give **three** ways in which alveoli are adapted for gas exchange.
4. Describe the changes in the position of the ribs and diaphragm that cause inhalation and exhalation.
5. Explain why the bronchi and larger bronchioles contain pieces of cartilage.
6. Explain the link between irritating chemicals in cigarette smoke and lung damage.

8 Supplying the cell

Circulation and transport

Your body needs a transport system to carry materials such as oxygen and food to all the body cells. The transport system has three main parts: **blood** to carry the materials; a network of tubes called **blood vessels** for the blood to pass through; and a pump called the **heart**.

Blood

Blood is made up of the following components:

- **plasma** is a watery fluid, which transports digested foods, water, antibodies, hormones and waste products such as urea and carbon dioxide

- **white blood cells** defend the body against disease

- **platelets** help with blood clotting

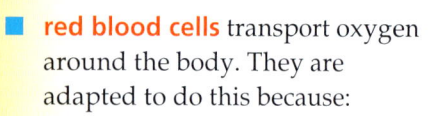

- **red blood cells** transport oxygen around the body. They are adapted to do this because:
  1. they do not contain a nucleus and therefore there is more room inside them
  2. they have a large surface area
  3. they contain haemoglobin, which combines reversibly with oxygen.

$$\text{oxygen} + \text{haemoglobin} \rightleftharpoons \text{oxyhaemoglobin}$$

In areas where there is lots of oxygen, e.g. the lungs, oxyhaemoglobin is formed, but in areas where there is little oxygen, e.g. actively respiring cells, oxyhaemoglobin breaks down to release the oxygen.

Blood vessels

Blood is carried throughout the body in blood vessels. There are three different types of blood vessel.

Arteries
Carry blood at high pressure away from the heart.

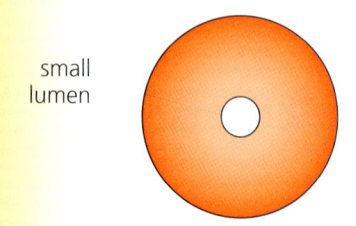

small lumen

Thick elastic muscular wall to withstand high blood pressure.

Capillaries
Link arteries and veins, allowing materials to be exchanged with surrounding tissues.

Walls only one cell thick to allow materials to diffuse in and out. Materials moving out form tissue fluid.

Veins
Carry blood at a lower pressure back to the heart.

wide lumen

Thin muscular walls because the blood is no longer at high pressure. Contain valves to prevent blood flowing backwards.

Double circulatory system

A double circulatory system means that one blood cell passes through the heart twice on each complete trip around the body.

The advantage is that oxygenated blood returns to the heart so it can be sent out around the body at higher pressure. This means a greater rate of flow of blood around the body to all tissues.

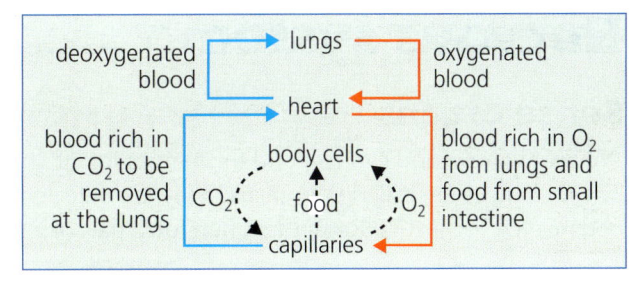

Heart

Blood has to be pumped around the body, and this is the job of the heart. The heart is made of muscle. It has four chambers and four valves.

The four chambers are the **right** and **left atria**, which collect incoming blood from the veins, and the very muscular **right** and **left ventricles**, which contract to squirt blood out into the arteries at high pressure. It needs the pressure because some of the blood has a long way to go!

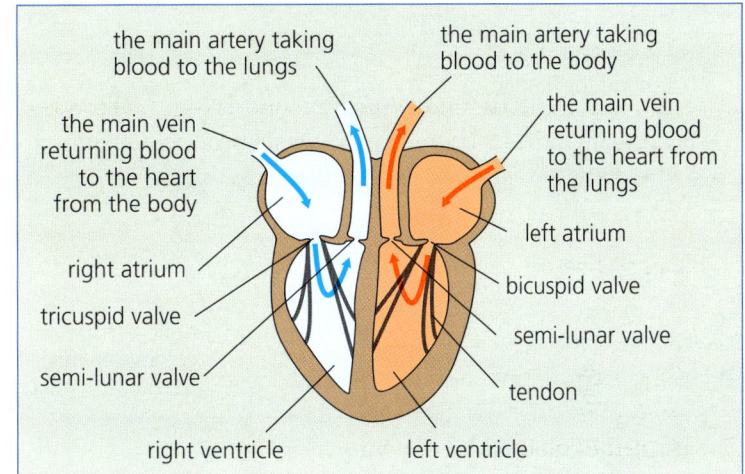

Look at the arrows in the heart. They show the direction the blood flows. The **valves** stop the blood flowing backwards. The valves that stop blood flowing back into the atria from the ventricles are called the **bicuspid** and **tricuspid valves** – the bicuspid valve has two cusps and the tricuspid valve has three. The other valves are called the semi-lunar valves. These are named after their shape. They guard the entrance to the arteries leaving the heart and they are the shape of a half moon.

Questions

1. Name **three** materials transported by plasma.
2. Explain how red blood cells are adapted to transport oxygen.
3. Where do the following materials enter and leave the blood: oxygen, carbon dioxide, food?
4. The formation of oxyhaemoglobin is reversible. Why is this important?
5. Give **two** differences between an artery and a vein.
6. What is the advantage of a double circulatory system?
7. Name the thick muscular chambers of the heart.
8. a Why is it necessary to have valves between the chambers of the heart?
   b Name **one** other part of the body where there are valves, and explain their function.

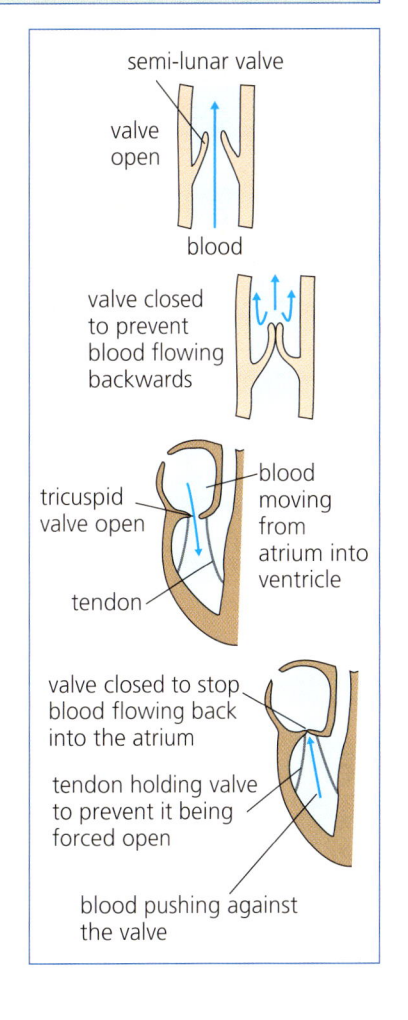

10 Control in animals and plants

Nervous system

Sense organs

We are aware of and can respond to changes in our surroundings. These changes are called **stimuli** and they are detected by parts of the body called **receptors**. Receptors often form part of a **sense organ**.

The eye

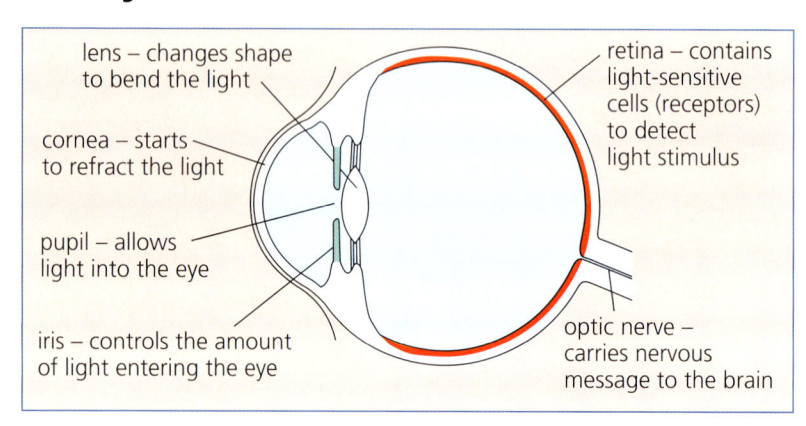

- lens – changes shape to bend the light
- cornea – starts to refract the light
- pupil – allows light into the eye
- iris – controls the amount of light entering the eye
- retina – contains light-sensitive cells (receptors) to detect light stimulus
- optic nerve – carries nervous message to the brain

The iris is the coloured bit of your eye.

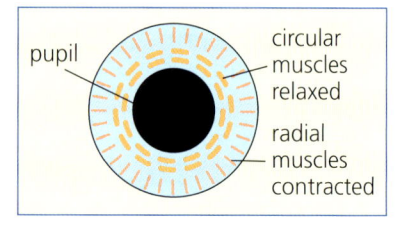

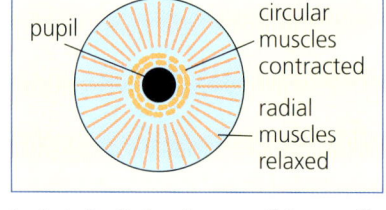

- pupil
- circular muscles relaxed
- radial muscles contracted

- pupil
- circular muscles contracted
- radial muscles relaxed

In dim light the pupil is large and the iris becomes smaller. This allows more light in.

In bright light the pupil is small and the iris becomes larger. This prevents too much light damaging the retina.

The nervous system

To enable us to respond to stimuli quickly, the receptors and sense organs need to be able to communicate with other parts of the body. This is the job of the **nervous system**. The nervous system is made up of two parts:

1. the **central nervous system**, which is the spinal cord and brain
2. the **peripheral nervous system**, which is the network of nerve cells (**neurones**) connecting all parts of the body to the central nervous system.

Sending a message

There are two types of neurones and they are named after the impulses they carry. Impulses come into the central nervous system from receptors via neurones called sensory nerve cells or **sensory neurones**. Neurones carrying impulses away from the central nervous system are called **motor neurones**.

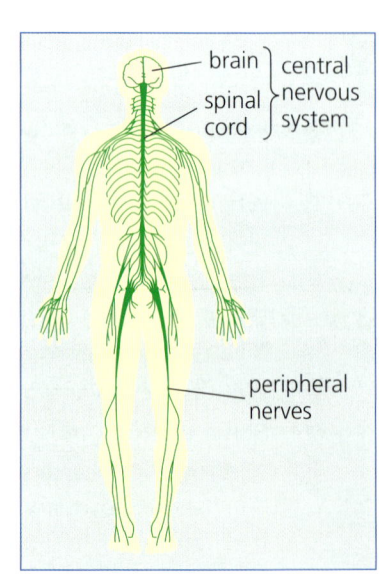

- brain
- spinal cord
- central nervous system
- peripheral nerves

The nervous system

The diagram shows the structure of a motor neurone. Neurones are well adapted to their function by being long, having an insulating sheath and with branched endings.

The end of one neurone is not connected to the next one. There is a little gap between them. This is called the **synapse**. Impulses passing along a neurone are electrical but when they reach the synapse they release a chemical which diffuses across the synapse and spreads the impulses to the next neurone. Only one side of the synapse can make the chemical messenger. So nervous impulses only go in one direction.

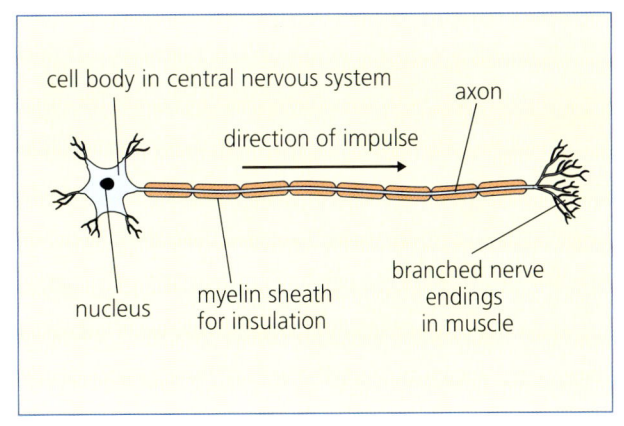

A motor neurone

Reflex actions

What happens when you touch something hot?

1. Temperature receptors detect the hot stimulus.
2. The receptors send the impulse along a sensory neurone to the central nervous system.
3. The central nervous system sends the impulse along a motor neurone to a muscle (an **effector**).
4. The muscle contracts, moving your hand away from the hot object.

> stimulus → receptor → sensory neurone → central nervous system → motor neurone → effector (muscle) → response (hand moves)

This is called a **reflex action**.

Reflex actions are:
- fast
- automatic (without thinking)
- protective.

Examples include blinking, swallowing and sneezing.

Voluntary responses are under the conscious control of the brain. Although reflex actions are automatic, relay neurones in the central nervous system do inform the brain of what is going on.

Questions

1. What are the functions of the following parts of the eye: retina, iris, optic nerve and lens?
2. Describe how the muscles in the iris change to prevent too much light damaging the retina.
3. Give **three** ways in which motor neurones are adapted to do their job.
4. What is a synapse? Suggest one advantage of synapses.
5. Describe the path taken by a nervous impulse in the reflex action resulting from a dog biting your hand.

Hormones

Alongside the nervous control in your body, some activities are also controlled by **hormones**. These are chemical messengers produced by groups of cells called **glands**. Hormones travel in the blood plasma and work on groups of cells in the body. Each hormone acts in a particular way, on a particular group of **target cells**.

Controlling sugar (glucose) levels

All cells need glucose for energy. But you need to have the right amount of glucose available in your blood. Too much or too little can be fatal.

The hormone that controls the amount of glucose is called **insulin**. This is produced by the pancreas. When there is too much glucose in the blood, the pancreas releases insulin. Insulin lowers the level of glucose by:

- making cells take up more glucose
- making **liver** cells change glucose to **glycogen**. This is then stored in the liver.

Some people do not make any insulin, or do not make enough. This means they suffer from **diabetes**. In these cases the level of glucose in the blood can go up and down wildly. Many people with diabetes control their blood glucose level by injecting themselves with insulin. The amount of insulin depends on their diet and activity.

Controlling sexual development

The changes which take place during adolescence (the stage of children growing into adults) are controlled by hormones.

As girls grow older their ovaries start to produce the hormone **oestrogen**. Oestrogen causes a number of changes in girls. They:

- start their menstrual cycle (have periods)
- develop breasts
- grow pubic and underarm hair
- grow taller.

These are called **secondary sexual characteristics**.

In boys, the development of secondary sexual characteristics is controlled by the hormone **testosterone**, which is produced by the testes. The effect is that boys:

- grow taller
- develop a longer penis and produce sperm
- grow pubic, underarm and facial hair
- develop a deeper voice.

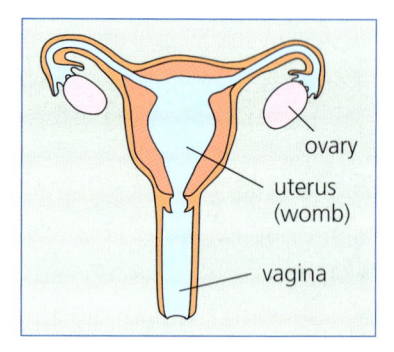

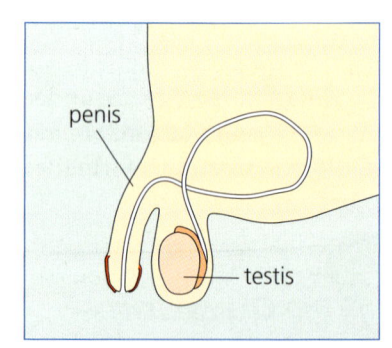

Questions

1. Give **three** female secondary sexual characteristics.
2. Explain why hormones (chemical messages) are likely to take longer to affect the body than nervous impulses.

Controlling the menstrual cycle

Two hormones control a woman's menstrual cycle, **oestrogen** and **progesterone**.

What these hormones do:
- oestrogen repairs the uterus wall
- progesterone keeps the uterus wall thick and in position
- oestrogen and progesterone together control **ovulation** (ovaries releasing eggs).

Preventing pregnancy ...
Hormones can be used in **contraceptive pills** to prevent ovulation and mimic pregnancy. This means that a woman will not release eggs and therefore cannot get pregnant.

... and helping pregnancy
Some women have difficulty in getting pregnant. Hormones can be used to help them produce more eggs, which will increase their chances of getting pregnant.

Controlling growth

Growth is controlled by **growth hormone**. This is produced by the **pituitary gland** in the brain. Too little growth hormone causes **dwarfism**. This is when a person does not grow enough. Too much growth hormone produces a giant. This is when a person grows too much.

Fight or flight

The hormone adrenaline prepares the body for action. It is produced by the two **adrenal glands**. It makes the heart beat faster. This forces blood around the body more rapidly, delivering more oxygen and glucose to the muscles to release more energy.

Blood is also diverted away from the skin to the muscles, which may make you look pale.

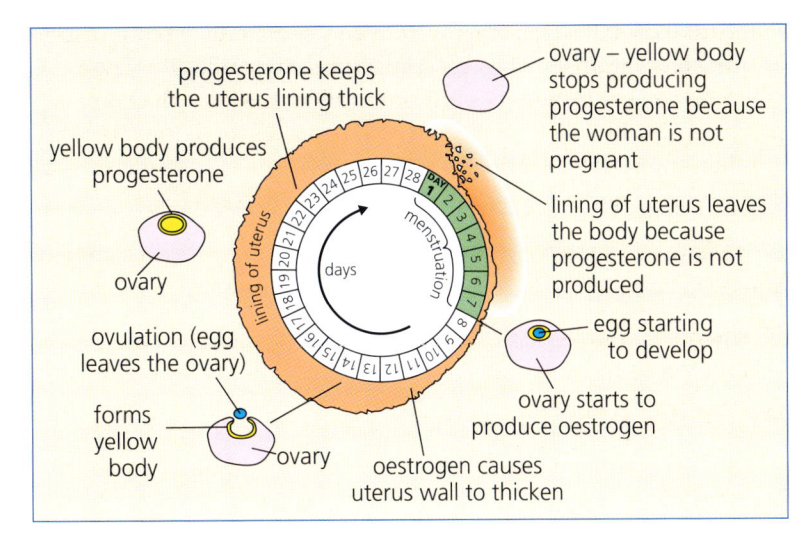

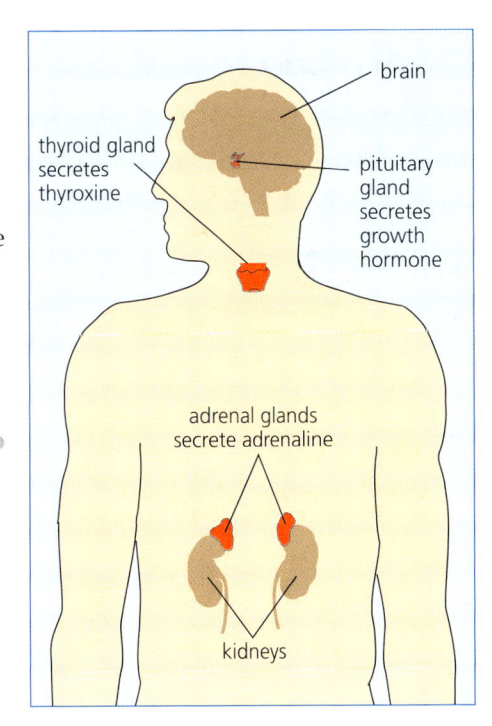

Questions

1. Explain why a pregnant woman will not menstruate.
2. How do contraceptive pills work?
3. What part does oestrogen play in the menstrual cycle?

Control in plants

Plants do not have a nervous system and so usually cannot respond as quickly as animals. They react to stimuli more slowly. Their reactions are controlled by hormones called **auxins**, which are produced in shoot and root tips. The auxins dissolve in water and are then transported through the plant.

Auxins regulate cell growth and development to control:
- growth of shoots and roots
- flowering
- ripening of fruit.

How do plants grow?

The shoots of a plant always grow towards the light. They do this because leaves need the light to make the food needed for plants to grow. They make their food by photosynthesis (see page 80).

Growing towards the light is called **phototropism**. 'Photo' means light and 'tropism' means growth.

Plant roots always grow downwards in the direction of gravity (**geotropism**). They need to do this to find the water the plant needs, and to anchor the plant in the ground.

Auxins control the direction plants grow by making different parts grow at different speeds. To make a shoot grow towards the light, auxins make its shaded side grow faster, resulting in the tip bending over towards the light. To make a root grow downwards, auxins make the top side of the root grow faster, resulting in the tip curving downwards.

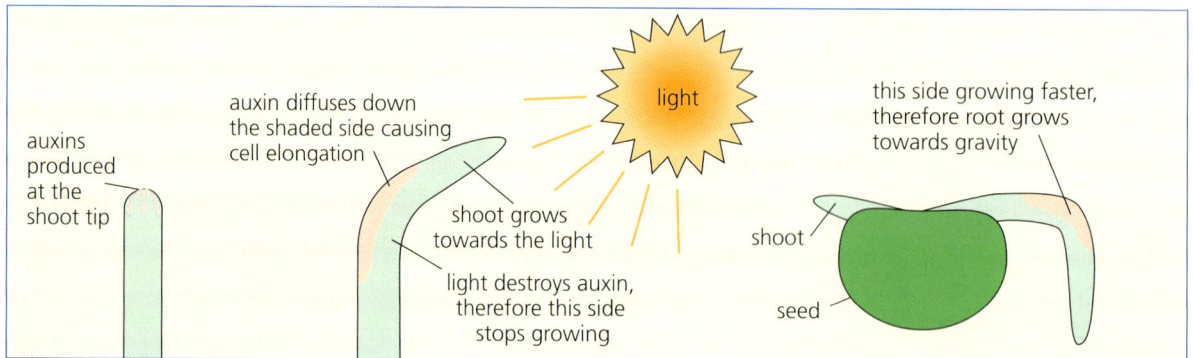

I don't understand I turn it round ... every week!

Questions

1. Give **two** uses of auxins in plants.
2. Explain how auxins travel around a plant.
3. Name **two** stimuli plants respond to. Explain why it is important that plants can respond to these stimuli.
4. Explain how a bulb planted upside down manages to grow.

Using plant hormones

We use synthetic auxins to trick plants and make them behave in ways which are more convenient for us.

Making more plants

It can take some time for plants to produce young new plants naturally. Cutting shoots off plants and dipping them in auxins makes them grow roots. Gardeners use auxins, known as rooting powder, to make new plants.

Ripening fruit

Auxins can also be used to slow down fruit ripening. This is useful for farmers who have a long way to take their fruit to the shops. If they treat it in this way it stops the fruit getting overripe before it gets to the customers.

Selective weedkillers

Selective weedkillers contain auxins which speed up the growth of selected plants. This makes them grow too fast and die. For example, if there are weeds with broad leaves growing in a lawn, a weedkiller can be used which will kill only those weeds and not the grass.

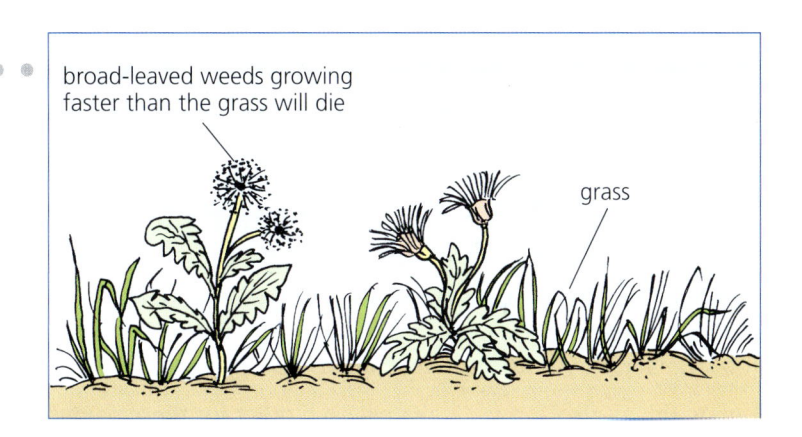

broad-leaved weeds growing faster than the grass will die

grass

Control of dormancy

Many seeds show dormancy, which means that they do not start to grow at once. In the wild, this would prevent seeds produced in autumn trying to grow during the cold winter months. They would lie dormant until the better conditions arrived in the spring. This would improve their chances of growing into plants. Dormancy is controlled by inhibitory plant hormones within the seeds. When we grow seeds we sometimes have to use plant growth hormones to overcome this inhibitory effect. Otherwise we would be in for a very long wait!

Questions

1. Describe **two** commercial uses of auxins in agriculture.
2. Explain what is meant by a 'selective' weedkiller.

Ecology

Populations and adaptations

There are a number of ways to find out what populations live in a habitat and how many members each has.

1. You can count the plants on a piece of land by using a metal or wooden frame called a **quadrat**. For example, if you wanted to know the number of daisies in a field, you put the quadrat on the ground and count the number of daisies inside it. You multiply this number by how many quadrats would cover the whole field. This gives you a rough estimate of the size of the daisy population on the field.

2. You can collect insects and other very small creatures by sweeping a net through the undergrowth and then sucking them into a special jar called a **pooter**. This gives you some idea of the animals living in the habitat and a rough idea of their numbers.

3. You can collect small nocturnal animals by digging small **pitfall traps** and covering them over. The animals which fall in can be identified and released the next day.

With all three methods the sample size affects the accuracy of the estimate and it is always possible that the samples are unrepresentative of the population. It is very important to sample randomly to try to ensure a thorough sampling of the area under investigation.

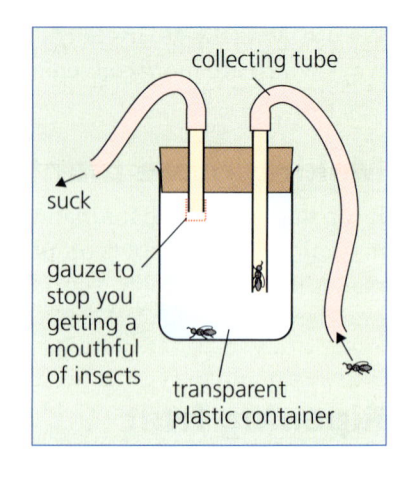

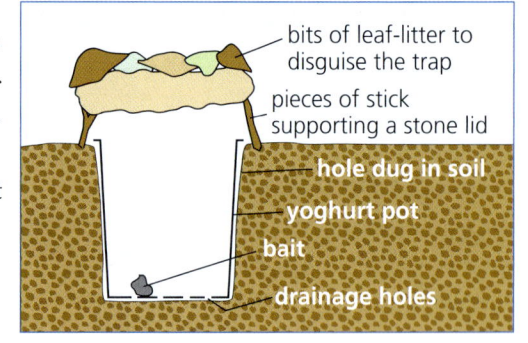

Surviving in the environment

Living things need water, space, light, minerals, food and shelter. The size of each population in a habitat depends on how much of all these resources is available. When a population becomes too large for the resources in its habitat, it stops growing.

Living things also **compete** against each other for these resources. The size of a population of one species often depends on how well it competes against other populations for what it needs. Sometimes a newly introduced species thrives, e.g. grey squirrels have out-competed the native British red squirrel because they are bigger and more aggressive. In Australia, rabbits have become a real nuisance because they have no natural predator and are therefore breeding unchecked.

> If wheat is planted closely, the farmer can increase the yield because more wheat can be fitted into the field. But if the plants are too close together they compete for space, water and light, and do not grow as well. This results in a reduced yield.

Adapting to survive

Each population is **adapted** to survive in its particular habitat. For example:

Polar bear – very cold habitat
- thick coat of fur to keep body heat in
- large body means it loses less heat to the air.

Camel – an arid habitat
- long thin legs
- does not sweat very much
- no layer of fat under the skin
- hump of stored fats can be broken down to provide water.

Fish – water
- streamlined to move easily through the water
- waterproof scales
- fins for swimming
- gills for 'breathing'.

Plants are also adapted to survive. For example, small plants on woodland floors flower very early before the leaves grow on trees and block the light from the Sun. Many plants also have to protect themselves against animals to survive. They use spines, stings or poisons to avoid being eaten.

Can't live without you

Parasites are living things that can only survive as long as their hosts are available. For example, a cat flea needs a cat to provide it with food in the form of blood. The flea may live in the fur of the cat where it can feed whenever it needs to. If the flea leaves the cat, either to lay its eggs or whilst the cat is cleaning itself, it is unable to feed again until it returns to a cat. Starving cat fleas have been known to try a human host, but they prefer the real thing.

Some parasites live inside their hosts, for example the tapeworm, and they have to ensure that they do not overfeed on their host or they would both die.

Other living things may have a relationship called **mutualism**. In this type of relationship, two organisms live together and both benefit from the arrangement. For example, some bacteria can live in the soil and change nitrogen into nitrates. Certain soil predators eat these bacteria. Plants need nitrates in order to grow. To make sure they get enough nitrates, some plants (**leguminous plants**) allow these bacteria to live in their roots inside root nodules. The bacteria supply the plants with the nitrates they need, and in return the plants protect the bacteria from soil predators.

Predator and prey relationships

Predators are animals which eat other animals (their **prey**). Predators are more likely to catch their prey if they:

- are **camouflaged** and difficult to see, like a polar bear in the snow
- have large teeth, claws, sting or poison to kill their 'food'
- have good senses – sight, hearing or smell – to find the 'food'.

Prey try to escape being caught by:

- camouflage that makes them hard to see, e.g. a stick insect
- colours which warn that they are unpleasant to eat, e.g. yellow and black wasps
- tasting horrible – predators soon learn which caterpillars are tasty.

Predators depend upon prey, so if the numbers of prey in a habitat go down, then some predators will starve and the number of predators will also go down.

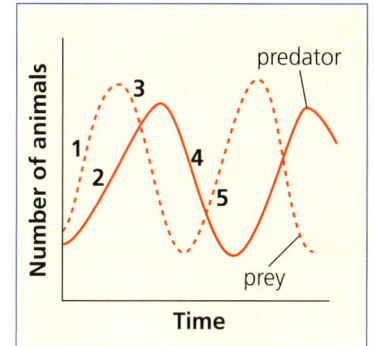

1 Prey has plenty of food, so breeds and increases in number.
2 More prey means more food for predators, so predators breed and their numbers increase.
3 More predators eating more prey means prey numbers decrease.
4 Fewer prey, therefore some predators starve.
5 Fewer predators, therefore not so many prey eaten and prey numbers start to increase again.

Questions

1. What populations would you sample using:
   a a pooter   **b** a quadrat   **c** a pitfall trap?

Ecology

Food chains

Feeding relationships

Green plants make their own food (glucose and starch) using energy from the Sun. They are called **producers** because they convert the light energy from the Sun into chemical energy (food), which is stored in organic compounds such as glucose and starch. Other living things are called **consumers** because they have to get their food by eating (consuming) green plants or other animals.

All animals rely on plants, even if they do not eat them directly. Animals may eat other animals but there is always an animal which eats only plants (a **herbivore**) at the start of the line. Animals which eat only meat are called **carnivores**. Animals which eat plants and meat are called **omnivores**.

Feeding relationships can be drawn as a **food chain**.

Some of the energy captured from light by plants is passed down the food chain as plants and animals are eaten. The Sun is the source of energy for all food chains.

Each feeding level is called a **trophic level**. The first trophic level contains the producers, the second trophic level the herbivores or primary consumers, and subsequent trophic levels contain all the carnivores. Because most living things eat more than one type of food, a food chain is usually changed into a **food web** in which all the feeding relationships are shown.

Pyramid of numbers

Another way of showing feeding relationships is as a **pyramid of numbers**. Here, each trophic level is represented by a block. The size of the block represents the number of individuals.

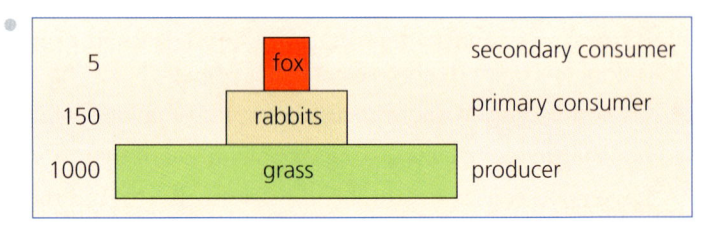

5	fox	secondary consumer
150	rabbits	primary consumer
1000	grass	producer

But it does not always work, for example:

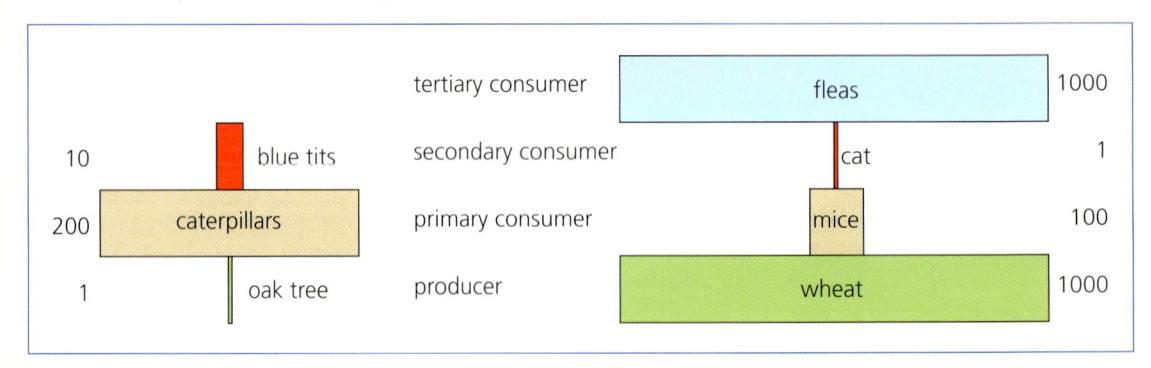

		tertiary consumer	fleas	1000
10	blue tits	secondary consumer	cat	1
200	caterpillars	primary consumer	mice	100
1	oak tree	producer	wheat	1000

Don't be put off – always put the producer at the bottom and arrange the other feeding levels above it, keeping to the order in which they appear in a food chain.

Pyramid of biomass

A more accurate way of representing feeding relationships is to produce a **pyramid of biomass**. Here the size of the block represents the mass of the animals and plants feeding at that level, rather than the number. Samples of the plants and animals are heated in an oven to remove their water content and then their dry mass is recorded. The dry mass is used to construct the pyramid. A pyramid of biomass for the oak tree example is shown.

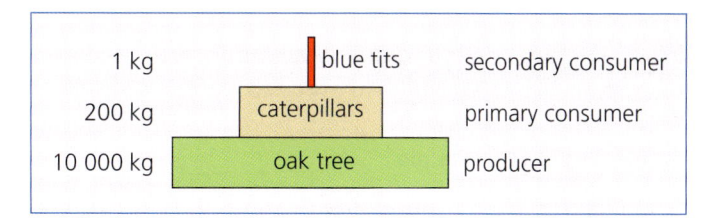

1 kg	blue tits	secondary consumer
200 kg	caterpillars	primary consumer
10 000 kg	oak tree	producer

As you move along a food chain, energy is lost from each trophic level. Some is lost as heat energy, some as waste materials (excretion), and some through death. This can be shown pictorially:

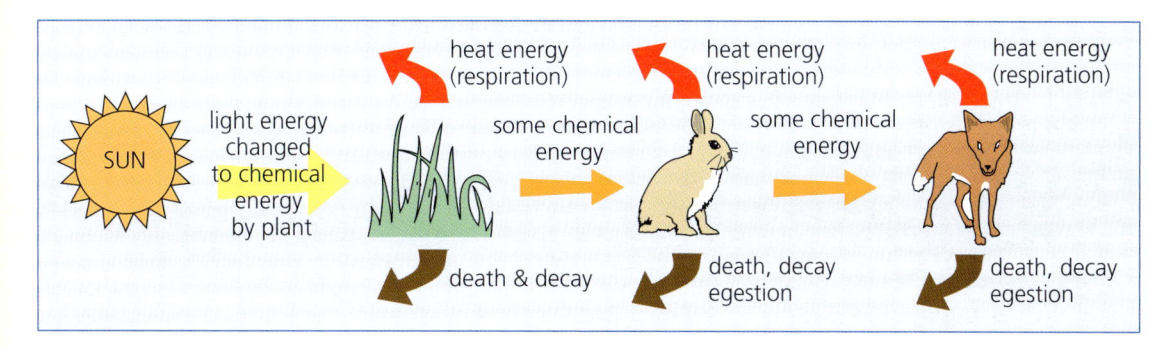

Therefore there is less energy available at each step of the food chain. This is why a pyramid of biomass gets progressively smaller as it moves along the food chain.

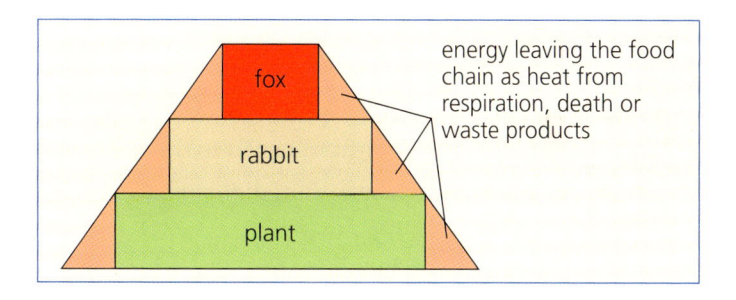

Questions

1. On a moorland the main plant is heather, which is the food for lots of animals, including rabbits, grouse, bees and deer. There are also several fox families and a pair of eagles, which survive by hunting the grouse and rabbits.
   a Name **one** moorland producer, **one** primary consumer and **one** predator.
   b Draw **two** food chains using some of the living things mentioned in the passage.
   c Draw pyramids of numbers based on your food chains.

2. In what form does energy enter the environment?

3. What is the difference between a food chain and a food web?

4. Explain why a pyramid of biomass is a more accurate representation of an ecosystem than a pyramid of numbers.

5. Explain why most food chains are restricted to only four trophic levels.

Ecology

Cycling and decay

What happens to all the dead bodies and waste produced by organisms in a food chain? In every ecosystem there are living things called **decomposers** which feed on dead plants and animals and their waste materials.

Some **bacteria** and **fungi** are decomposers. They make dead things **decay** so that the useful substances these things contain can be used again by other living things. One of these useful substances is carbon, which is part of all living things because it is present in all proteins, carbohydrates and fats. Decomposers return carbon to the atmosphere as carbon dioxide, and plants remove it from the atmosphere to convert it into carbohydrates during photosynthesis. Therefore a cycle is produced.

Decomposers are living things and therefore have the same needs as other living things. They need:

- food – the material they are going to decompose
- moisture
- oxygen
- warm temperatures.

The more suitable the conditions for microbial respiration, the faster the decomposers will grow.

The carbon cycle

In the carbon cycle:

- Soil bacteria and fungi release carbon dioxide into the air as they respire; they also return minerals to the soil
- plants and animals release carbon dioxide into the air as they respire
- carbon dioxide is used by plants for photosynthesis
- energy in some decomposing materials becomes trapped as fossil fuels, e.g. coal, oil
- burning fossil fuels releases carbon dioxide
- burning all organic materials, including wood, paper and animal tissues, releases carbon dioxide.

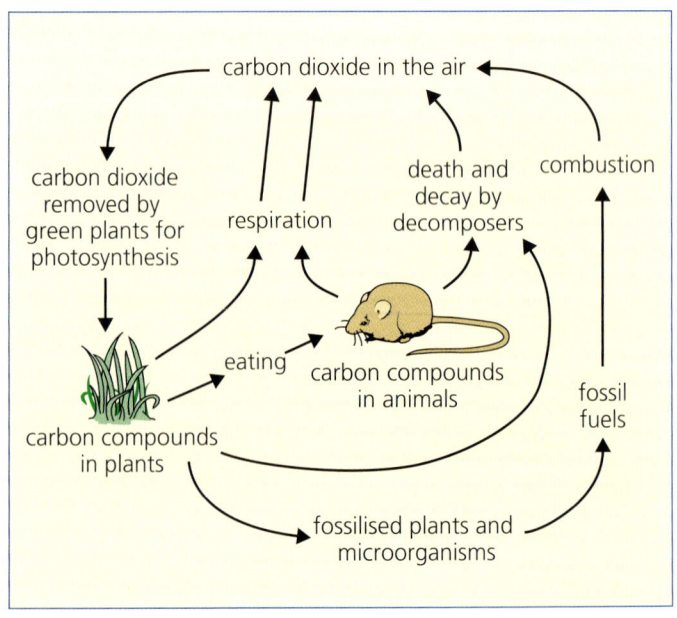

The nitrogen cycle

In addition to carbon, nitrogen is vital to living things. It is needed to make proteins, which animals and plants need to grow. Although the atmosphere contains a large amount of nitrogen, atmospheric nitrogen must be changed into soluble nitrates and nitrites before it can be used by most living things.

The nitrogen cycle at work

- Nitrogen-fixing bacteria convert atmospheric nitrogen into amino acids and proteins. Some of these bacteria are free living in the soil and others live in the root nodules of leguminous plants, e.g. clover, beans, peas.
- Lightning converts atmospheric nitrogen into nitrates.
- Plant roots absorb nitrates from the soil and convert them into amino acids and proteins.
- Decay bacteria convert proteins and urea into ammonia.
- Nitrifying bacteria add nitrates to the soil by converting ammonia into nitrates.
- Farmers artificially boost the nitrate content of soil by adding fertilisers.
- Farmers can also boost the nitrate content of soil by ploughing plant remains, especially leguminous plant remains, back into the soil so they can decay.

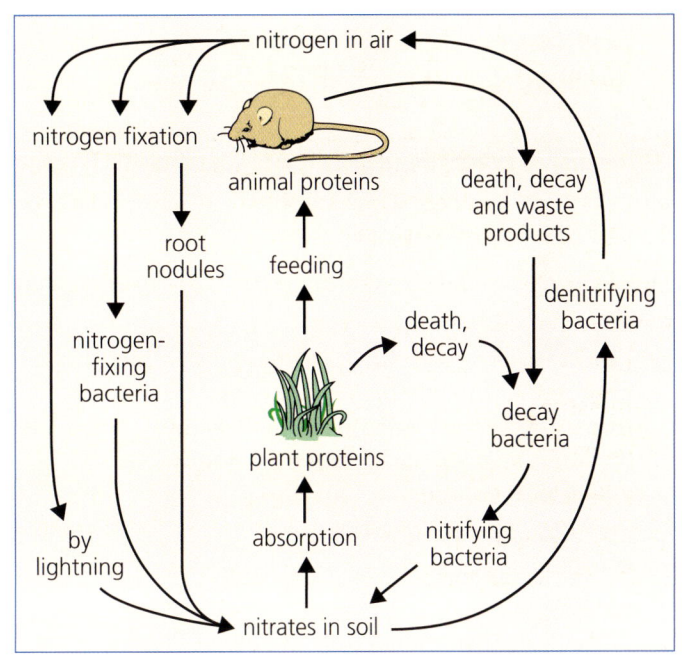

Questions

1. Name **two** groups of living organisms which can act as decomposers.
2. Explain why decomposers are so important within an ecosystem.
3. a Explain why a moist piece of bread left in a warm room was covered in mould after two days, whereas an identical piece of bread left in a cold room had very little mould in the same time period.
   b Suggest what you would expect to find if:
   i the piece of bread was dried and then left at the higher temperature
   ii the piece of bread was sealed in a plastic bag and left at the higher temperature.
4. Describe **three** ways in which human activities are in danger of upsetting the carbon cycle.
5. State the main way in which carbon dioxide is removed from the atmosphere.
6. The nitrogen cycle involves nitrogen-fixing bacteria, denitrifying bacteria and nitrifying bacteria. Explain the **three** different roles they have in the cycle.
7. Explain why traditional farming techniques include crop rotation, in which every five years a field is planted with beans and, instead of cropping the beans, the farmer ploughs them back into the soil.

Ecology

Human influence on the environment

Producing more food

The human population is growing exponentially (very rapidly). In order to feed the growing population, farmers can produce more food if they use:

- **herbicides** to kill weeds which compete with their crops
- **pesticides** to kill pests which eat their crops
- **fertilisers** to provide extra nitrates and minerals to grow a bigger crop
- **intensive practices** such as rearing animals indoors so that they get fatter and meatier more quickly and do not use up as much energy in keeping warm.

However, these methods can cause harm to the environment and to health.

- Pesticides may kill animals that are not pests, either directly by poisoning or through the food chain. In the food chain illustrated here, if all the ladybirds are killed, then the blue tits will starve and the greenfly population will become enormous because there are no ladybirds left to eat them.

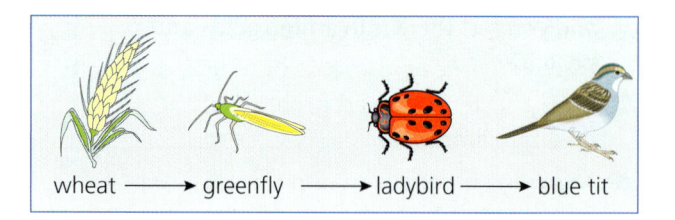

wheat → greenfly → ladybird → blue tit

- Some pesticides are not broken down by the body and are able to accumulate within a food chain.

small water living plants (.001 ppm pesticide) → small water living animals (.01 ppm) → small fish (0.1 ppm) → big fish (1.0 ppm) → human (10.0 ppm)

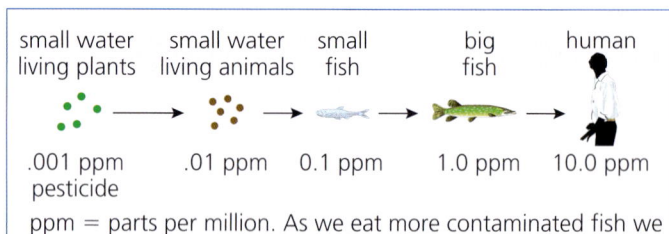

ppm = parts per million. As we eat more contaminated fish we increase the amount of pesticide inside us.

- Intensive farming of animals means they are unable to move around or behave naturally. Some people see this as cruel to the animals and call for more free-range farming.

Biological control

Biological control is the use of a natural predator to control the populations of pests. Ladybirds are sometimes used to control greenfly numbers in greenhouses, reducing the need for pesticide use.

Feature	Biological control	Pesticide control
time to take effect	slow	fast
length of time it lasts	for a long time	for a short time, and usually needs repeating
cost	relatively cheap	expensive
pollution dangers	none	considerable
development of pest resistance	none	likely to occur

Environmental problems

An exponentially (rapidly) growing human population means the limited global mineral and fossil fuel reserves are even more in demand and their use leads to increasing pollution.

- Sulphur dioxide dissolves in rainwater to form acid rain, which kills plants and attacks some buildings.
- CFCs from aerosol sprays and old fridges are depleting the ozone layer in the upper atmosphere, allowing harmful ultraviolet light through.
- Carbon dioxide is a **greenhouse gas** and causes heat to be trapped in the atmosphere leading to **global** warming. The possible consequences of this are melting ice caps, rising sea levels and loss of low lying-habitats.

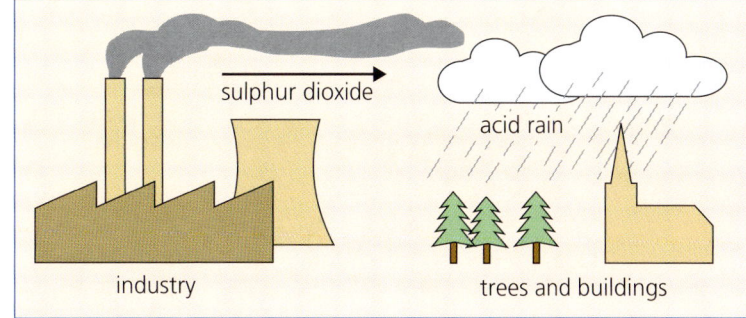

The way forward

In order to survive we must aim for **sustainable development** which doesn't do irreversible damage to wildlife habitats and doesn't deplete the limited resources of the world.

- Woodlands are a renewable resource and, if replanted as used, will continue to provide us with fuel, timber and many other useful products.
- For many years we have over-fished our coastal waters. Now we need to set fishing quotas to enable sufficient fish to remain in the waters to breed and restock the populations. We also need to use nets with larger holes to avoid the young fish being caught before they can breed.
- We need to educate people to set a level of selective harvesting of food and materials, so that no more is removed than can be re-grown.

Endangered species

Some species in Britain are endangered and need protection. Examples are the red kite and red squirrel. There are various steps we can take to try and help our endangered wildlife:

- Education – encourage people to become involved in local wildlife projects and ensure that people are aware of what is happening to many of our native species.
- Protected sites – there are over 4000 sites of special scientific interest nationally and it is the responsibility of local authorities to ensure that these are not damaged in any way.
- Legal protection – some species are protected by law, making it illegal to kill or harm them. For example, if you have bats living in your roof space it is illegal to attempt to kill or remove them.

Questions

1. Why do farmers use pesticides and herbicides?
2. Seeds were often dipped in the pesticide dieldrin before sowing. In the 1950s, large numbers of birds of prey were found dead or dying, poisoned by high levels of dieldrin in their bodies. Explain how this could have happened.
3. Suggest how regular replanting and careful management of a woodland may protect its resident population of red squirrels.

Life processes and living things

Concept map

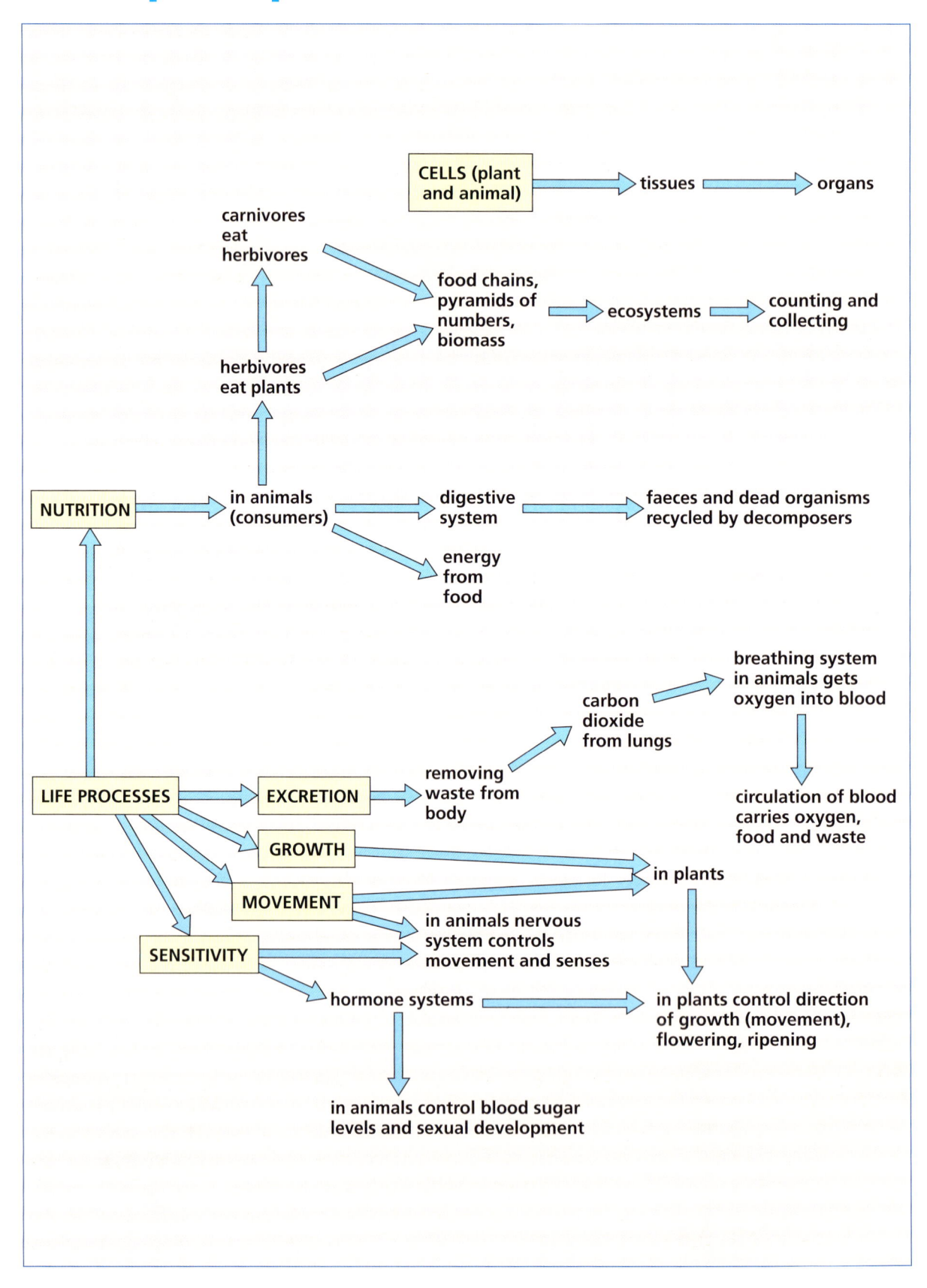

CELLS (plant and animal) → tissues → organs

carnivores eat herbivores ↗
↘ food chains, pyramids of numbers, biomass → ecosystems → counting and collecting
herbivores eat plants ↗

NUTRITION → in animals (consumers) → digestive system → faeces and dead organisms recycled by decomposers
→ energy from food

LIFE PROCESSES →
- **EXCRETION** → removing waste from body → carbon dioxide from lungs → breathing system in animals gets oxygen into blood → circulation of blood carries oxygen, food and waste
- **GROWTH**
- **MOVEMENT** → in plants
- **SENSITIVITY** → in animals nervous system controls movement and senses
  → hormone systems → in plants control direction of growth (movement), flowering, ripening
  → in animals control blood sugar levels and sexual development

Exam questions

1 This question is about digestion. Enzymes in the mouth, stomach and small intestine help to digest food.
   a What do enzymes do to food during digestion? [1]
   b Bile also helps to digest food. Which food type does bile help to digest? [1]
   c How does bile help to digest this food type? Explain as fully as you can. [2]
   d When food has been digested it is then absorbed. This occurs in the small intestine. Write down **two** ways the small intestine is adapted to absorb digested food. [2]
   [6 marks]

2 Look at the drawing. It shows a section through an alveolus.

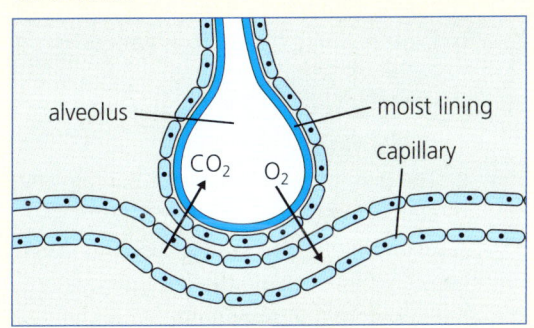

[Diagram showing alveolus with moist lining, capillary, CO_2 and O_2 exchange]

   a An alveolus is adapted for efficient gaseous exchange. Explain **three** ways in which the alveolus is adapted for oxygen uptake. [3]
   b The alveoli are connected to the trachea by a system of tubes called the bronchioles and bronchi. Like the trachea, many of these contain pieces of cartilage in their linings. Write down what these pieces of cartilage are used for. [2]
   [5 marks]

3 This question is about blood.
   a Red blood cells contain a chemical substance that carries oxygen.
      i Write down the name of this chemical substance. [1]
      ii Write down a word equation for the reaction between this substance and oxygen. [1]
      iii This reaction is reversible. Write down where in the body this reaction works in reverse. [2]
   b Blood is carried in arteries, veins and capillaries. Complete the following table. [5]

Blood vessel	Function	Adaptation
	to carry blood at high pressure	
capillary		walls only one cell thick
	to carry blood at low pressure back to the heart	

   [9 marks]

4 Look at the drawing. It shows a person frightened by a charging bull.

Adrenaline is released in the body of the person. It travels round the body in the bloodstream, preparing the body for action.
   a Write down the name given to chemical messengers like adrenaline. [1]
   b How does adrenaline prepare the body for action? Explain as fully as you can. [4]
   [5 marks]

5 This question is about the plant hormone auxin. Auxin is produced in the tip of the shoot. Auxin causes shoots to grow towards the light.
   a Write down the name of this response to light [1]
   b Suggest why this response is beneficial for plants. [2]
   c Explain as fully as you can how auxin causes shoots to bend towards the light. [3]
   [6 marks]

Exam questions

6 By accident, Martin trod on a drawing pin. He moved his foot away very quickly. This is called a reflex action.
  a Describe the nerve pathway which allows this reflex action to happen. [3]
  b Write down **two** other examples of reflex actions. [2]
  c Nerve cells, or neurones, are well adapted for carrying impulses. Write down **two** of these adaptations. [2]
  [7 marks]

7 In America some farmers keep their pigs in indoor pens. The floors of these pens are metal slats which allow urine and waste to drop through into a reservoir. In some areas, nitrate-rich material from these reservoirs has seeped out into local waterways, causing widespread nitrate pollution. Explain fully what effect nitrate pollution can have on a waterway. [4]
  [4 marks]

8 The diagram shows some different types of cells.

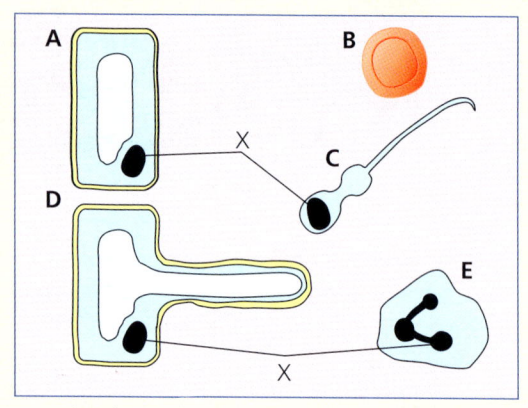

  a Write down the name of structure X and its function? [2]
  b Cell **B** does not contain structure X. Suggest a reason for this. [1]
  c Cell **C** contains lots of mitochondria.
     i What is the function of mitochondria? [1]
     ii Why is it an advantage for this cell to contain lots of mitochondria? [1]
  d Name **one** chemical which is made in cell **A** and is found in a high concentration in cell **B**. [1]
  e Name **one** chemical which is taken up by cell **D** and transported to cell **A**. [1]
  f Write down **two** of the cells which are plant cells, and give a reason for your choice. [3]
  [10 marks]

9 Look at the diagram. It shows a model gut.

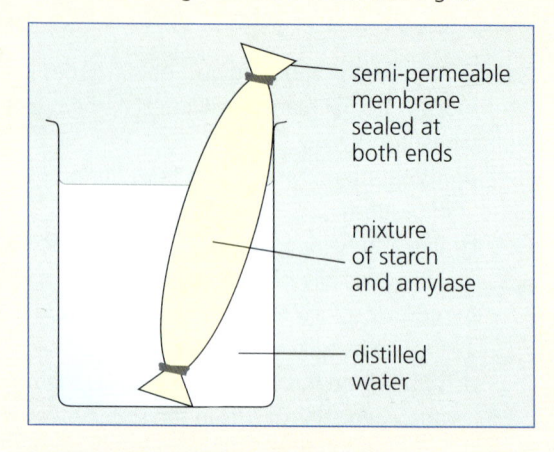

  a Inside the model gut are enzymes. What do enzymes do in your digestive system? [2]
  At the start of the experiment the model gut was filled with starch and enzyme. After 30 min the distilled water was tested and found to contain glucose.
  b Explain where the glucose has come from. [2]
  c What does the distilled water represent in the model gut? [1]
  d The distilled water does not contain any starch. Suggest a reason for this. [1]
  A second model gut was set up with starch and enzyme, but this time the enzyme was boiled for 5 min before the experiment.
  e What would you expect to find in the distilled water after 30 min and why? [3]
  [9 marks]

10 Here is a section through an eye.

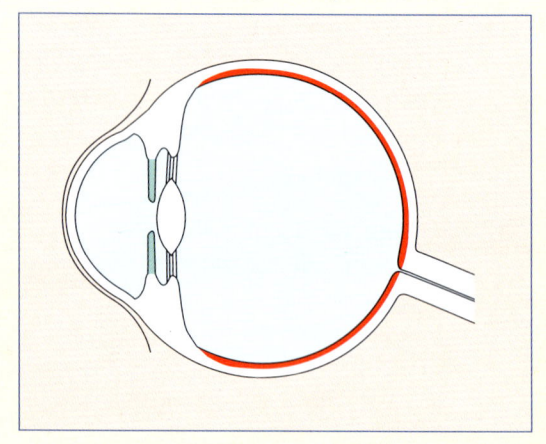

  a On the diagram label the cornea, retina and lens. [3]
  b What is the function of these parts of the eye? [3]

c Briefly describe how the muscles in the iris control how much light enters the eye. [4]
d What is the name given to this type of reaction? [1]
e Suggest **one** advantage of it to the body. [1]
[12 marks]

11 This question is about the menstrual cycle.

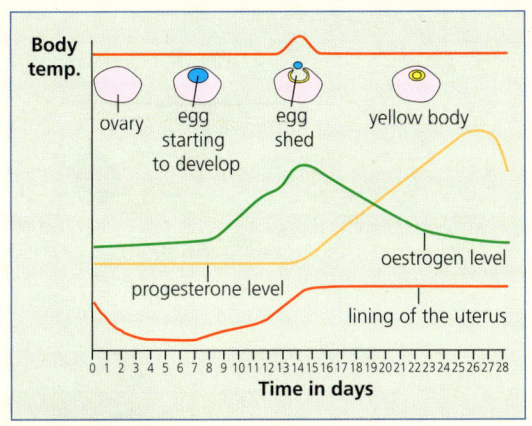

The figure shows the changes which occur during the menstrual cycle.
a What happens during days 1–7 of the cycle? [1]
b What is the main function of the hormone oestrogen? [1]
c On which day does ovulation occur? [1]
d If fertilisation occurs, explain what you would expect to happen to the progesterone level. [2]
e Some women use their body temperature as a form of birth control. Suggest one reason why this might not be very reliable. [1]
[6 marks]

12 Kim wanted to find out which species lived in a small wood near to his home. He wanted to sample the plants and the animals living in the wood. Explain how he could use each piece of apparatus to sample the wood.
a A quadrat. [3]
b A sweep net and pooter. [3]
c A pitfall trap. [3]
[9 marks]

13 Look at the food web of a pond.

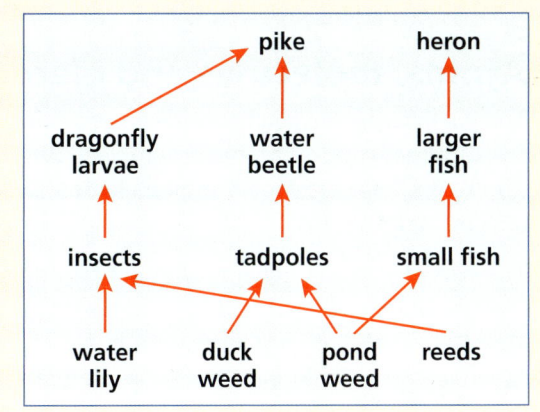

a Draw **two** different food chains from the food web. [3]
b What do the arrows in the food chain represent? [1]
c Explain why most food chains are limited to only four trophic levels. [2]
d Write down a possible food chain which would result in organisms moving from the pond food chain to a terrestrial food chain. [3]
[9 marks]

14 The figure shows a simplified nitrogen cycle.

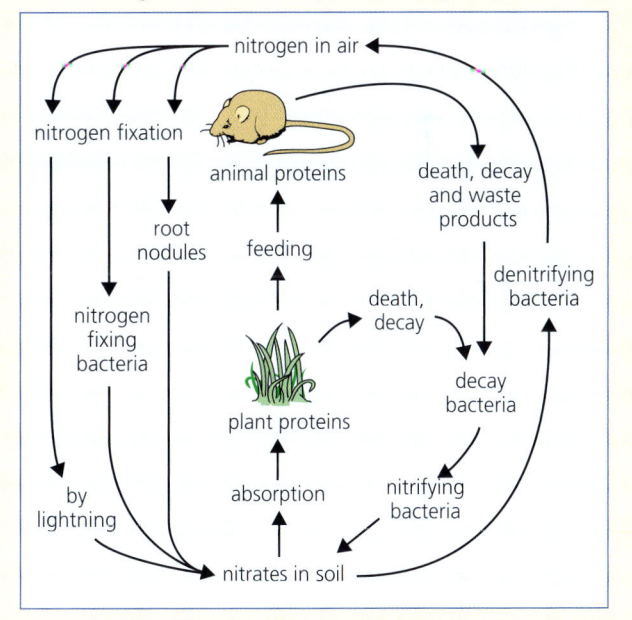

a Why do living things need nitrogen? [1]
b Explain why most living things cannot use the nitrogen in the air. [2]
c What does nitrogen fixation mean? [1]
d Give two ways in which farmers can increase the nitrogen content of their fields. [2]
[6 marks]

Equations and rates of reaction

Atoms, elements, compounds and formulae

Atoms, molecules and elements

The particles inside all chemicals are made from **atoms**. There are 104 different types of atom known. Each different type of atom is a different **element**. Some common elements are hydrogen, carbon, oxygen, sulphur, iron.

The particles inside a chemical might be single atoms on their own, or they might be made from groups of atoms. A small group of atoms combined together is called a **molecule**. Molecules can be made from atoms of one element, or from atoms of several different elements.

Enormous groups of atoms are called **giant structures** – you will come across these later.

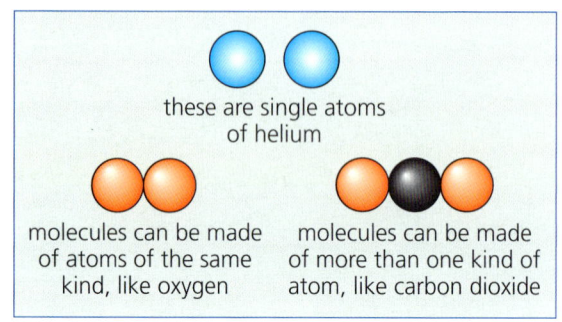

these are single atoms of helium

molecules can be made of atoms of the same kind, like oxygen

molecules can be made of more than one kind of atom, like carbon dioxide

Compounds and chemical bonds

Atoms of different elements can join together to make **compounds**. Compounds are always made from more than one element. The atoms inside a compound are held to each other by **chemical bonds**.

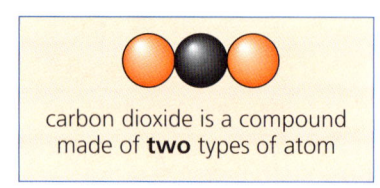

carbon dioxide is a compound made of **two** types of atom

Symbols for the elements

- Elements have symbols of either one or two letters.
- If the symbol has one letter, that letter must be a capital.
- If the symbol has two letters, the first letter is a capital and the second letter is a little letter, e.g. Fe.

Formulae for compounds

The formula for a compound tells us which elements are inside the compound. It also tells us how many atoms of each element are in the compound.
- The formula of a hydrogen molecule is H_2.
- It is made of *two* atoms of hydrogen bonded together.
- The formula of hydrogen chloride is HCl.
- It is made of *one* atom of hydrogen and *one* atom of chlorine bonded together.

Formula	Displayed formula
H_2	H—H
HCl	H—Cl

If the molecule of a compound contains different numbers of atoms inside it, we write the numbers of each element in small figures after each symbol in the formula.
- The formula of water is H_2O.
- It has *two* atoms of hydrogen and *one* atom of oxygen bonded together. See how the '2' comes after the 'H' in H_2O.

Formula	Displayed formula
H_2O	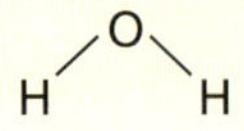 H—O—H

The formula Be(OH)$_2$ looks more complicated.

There are *two* of everything inside the bracket, so it is made of *one* atom of Be, *two* atoms of O and *two* atoms of H.

(NH$_4$)$_2$SO$_4$ obeys the same rules. It is made of *two* atoms of N, *eight* atoms of H, *one* atom of S and *four* atoms of O.

You must know these names and formulae.

General	Compounds of sodium (Na) and potassium (K)	Compounds of calcium (Ca), Iron (Fe), Magnesium (Mg), Zinc (Zn) and Copper (Cu)
H$_2$ hydrogen	NaCl sodium chloride	ZnCl$_2$ zinc chloride
O$_2$ oxygen	NaNO$_3$ sodium nitrate	Zn(NO$_3$)$_2$ zinc nitrate
H$_2$O water	NaOH sodium hydroxide	Zn(OH)$_2$ zinc hydroxide
CO$_2$ carbon dioxide	Na$_2$SO$_4$ sodium sulphate	ZnSO$_4$ zinc sulphate
NH$_3$ ammonia	Na$_2$CO$_3$ sodium carbonate	ZnCO$_3$ zinc carbonate
HCl hydrochloric acid	Na$_2$O sodium oxide	ZnO zinc oxide
H$_2$SO$_4$ sulphuric acid	Potassium compounds follow the same pattern, e.g. KCl, K$_2$SO$_4$	The other elements follow the same pattern e.g. CaCl$_2$, MgCl$_2$, CuCl$_2$, FeCl$_2$
HNO$_3$ nitric acid		

Questions

1 Which are compounds in the following list:
hydrogen, hydrogen sulphide, oxygen, sugar, nitric acid, carbon?

2 Copy and complete this table for the following compounds:
HCl, H$_2$O, CH$_4$, AlCl$_3$, H$_2$SO$_4$, Cu(NO$_3$)$_2$, (NH$_4$)$_2$Cr$_2$O$_7$

Formula	Number of atoms in the formula	Number of different elements

3 Write down the formula of the hydrogen sulphide molecule shown in this diagram:

H—S—H

4 Write down the formula of ammonia shown in this diagram:

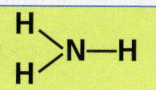

H
 \N—H
H /

Equations and rates of reaction

Chemical equations

Chemical reactions

When substances react chemically they turn into completely new substances. Sodium (a metal) and chlorine (a poisonous green gas) turn into common salt when they react together. Hydrogen and oxygen (both colourless gases) turn into water. Salt is a compound of sodium and chlorine; water is a compound of hydrogen and oxygen.

Chemical reactions are very difficult to undo.

Chemical reactions usually involve a temperature change. If you put iron filings into copper sulphate solution, the solution gets warm – this is one sign that a chemical reaction has happened.

What is a chemical equation?

A chemical equation tells us what happens in a chemical reaction. It tells us what chemicals we start with (**reactants**) and what the chemicals turn into (**products**).

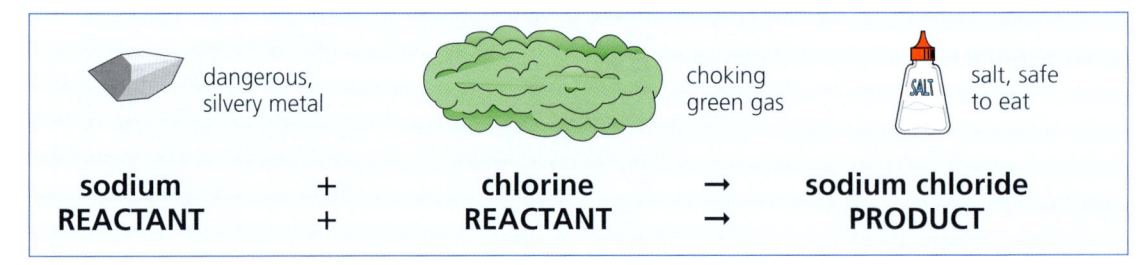

dangerous, silvery metal		choking green gas		salt, safe to eat
sodium	+	chlorine	→	sodium chloride
REACTANT	+	REACTANT	→	PRODUCT

In this reaction, two chemical reactants have turned into one chemical product. All the atoms inside the two reactants are now inside the chemical product.

magnesium	+	hydrochloric acid	→	magnesium chloride	+	hydrogen
REACTANT	+	REACTANT	→	PRODUCT	+	PRODUCT

In this equation, two chemical reactants have turned into two chemical products. All the atoms that made up the reactants are now inside the two chemical products.

Questions

1. Copy out these equations and label each substance as either a reactant or a product:
   a. hydrogen + oxygen → hydrogen oxide
   b. carbon + iron oxide → carbon dioxide + iron
   c. propane → hydrogen + propene

2. In a chemical reaction, the reactants are sodium and water, and the products are sodium hydroxide and hydrogen. Write this as a word equation.

Balancing equations

All the atoms inside the reactant molecules end up inside the product molecules, so equations always have the same number of atoms on each side of the equation sign.

> You can only change the numbers *in front* of a formula. Never change any other numbers in the equation!

For example, hydrogen gas and chlorine gas will react with each other.

hydrogen + chlorine → hydrogen chloride

The symbol equation *might* look like this

$H_2 + Cl_2 \rightarrow HCl$ ✗

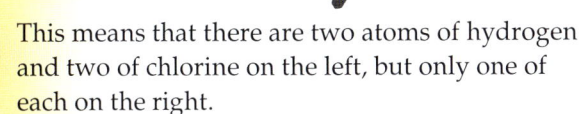

This means that there are two atoms of hydrogen and two of chlorine on the left, but only one of each on the right.

To balance this up we make sure that all the atoms of hydrogen and chlorine are used.

$H_2 + Cl_2 \rightarrow 2HCl$ ✓

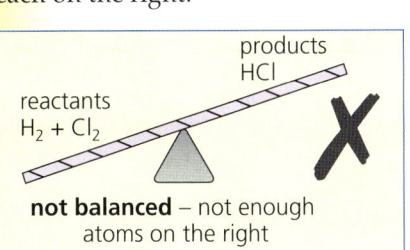

not balanced – not enough atoms on the right

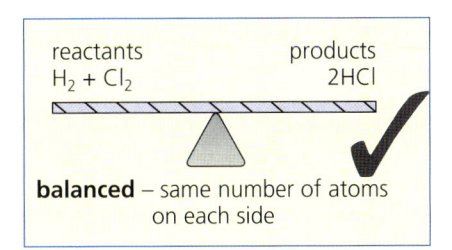

balanced – same number of atoms on each side

Remember to always count up the atoms of each element on the left, then see if the numbers are the same on the right.

$HCl + MgO \rightarrow MgCl_2 + H_2O$ ✗

$2HCl + MgO \rightarrow MgCl_2 + H_2O$ ✓

Not enough atoms of hydrogen and of chlorine on the left.

The same rules apply even if there are brackets.

$CuO + HNO_3 \rightarrow Cu(NO_3)_2 + H_2O$ ✗

$CuO + 2HNO_3 \rightarrow Cu(NO_3)_2 + H_2O$ ✓

Not enough H and NO_3 on the left.

Questions

1. Copy each equation, then write down all the atoms of each element on **a** the reactant side **b** the product side.
   State whether the equation balances.

   $Mg + O_2 \rightarrow 2MgO$ $CH_4 + 2O_2 \rightarrow CO_2 + 2H_2O$

2. Copy and complete these equations – there is a line for each missing number.

   a $H_2 + Cl_2 \rightarrow$ ___HCl

   b $Mg +$ ___$HCl \rightarrow MgCl_2 + H_2$

   c $C_3H_8 + 5O_2 \rightarrow$ ___$CO_2 +$ ___H_2O

   d $C_2H_4 +$ ___$O_2 \rightarrow$ ___$CO_2 +$ ___H_2O

   e $FeCl_2 +$ ___$NaOH \rightarrow Fe(OH)_2 +$ ___$NaCl$

Rates of reactions

Chemical reactions happen at different speeds. You can see some of them around you. Rusting is a slow chemical reaction. Burning is a fast chemical reaction. Explosions are even faster! The speed of a reaction is called its **rate**.

Speeding up reactions

Reactions happen when reactant particles collide and turn into products. Most ways of speeding up reactions make the particles collide more often – there are more collisions per second; the frequency of the collisions increases. There are several ways of making a reaction go faster.

- Increase the **temperature**. Reactant particles hit each other harder because they have more energy, so there are more effective collisions. Also, there are more collisions per second.

Sodium thiosulphate solution ('thio') goes cloudy with dilute acid. If you warm the liquids the reaction will go faster.

- Increase the **concentration**. This only works with a solution! Increasing the concentration makes the particles closer together, so the collision frequency increases.

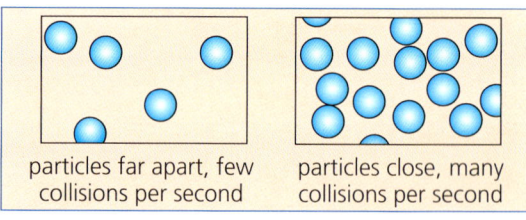

'Thio' goes cloudy more quickly when it is more concentrated.

- If one of the reactants is a solid, you can break it down into smaller lumps. This increases the **surface area**, giving more places for reactions to happen. The collision frequency increases.

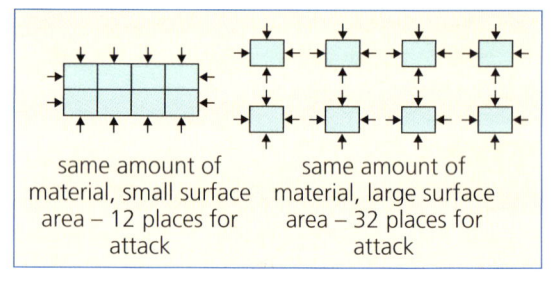

Large marble chips react slowly with acid. If you use smaller marble chips with acid the reaction will go faster.

- Use a **catalyst**. Catalysts speed up a reaction. They are only needed in small amounts and are not used up by the reaction. Catalysts are unchanged at the end, they can be re-used. Different reactions need different catalysts to speed them up.

Hydrogen peroxide slowly breaks down into water and oxygen:

> hydrogen peroxide → water + oxygen
> $2H_2O_2 \rightarrow 2H_2O + O_2$

To speed this up you can add manganese dioxide as a catalyst.
All the manganese dioxide is left in the beaker at the end, and it can be used again.

look down here (wearing goggles)
thio and acid go cloudy
mark on paper disappears

particles far apart, few collisions per second   *particles close, many collisions per second*

same amount of material, small surface area – 12 places for attack   *same amount of material, large surface area – 32 places for attack*

Questions

1. Give **three** ways of speeding up the reaction between an acid solution and a solid carbonate.
2. Which methods will still work for a reaction between an acid solution and a carbonate solution?

Measuring the rate

The easiest way to measure the speed of a reaction is to find out how fast one of the products is made.

For example, when marble chips react with acid you can measure the amount of carbon dioxide gas given off every minute. You can do this with a large syringe, or by catching the gas in a test tube.

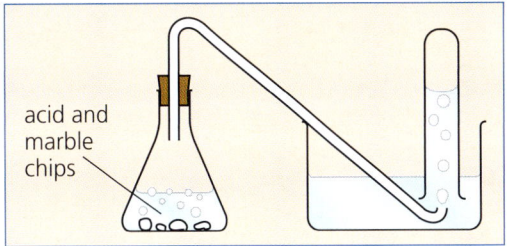

Reactions always start fast, and then slow down as the reactant chemicals are used up.

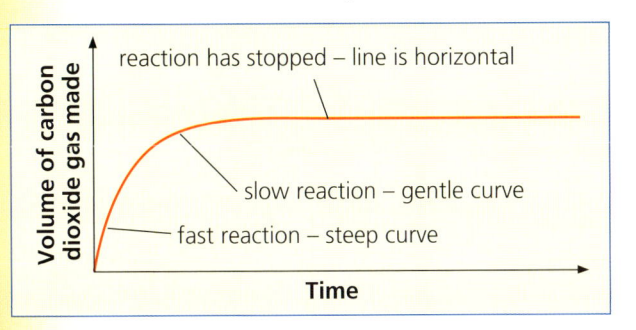

reaction has stopped – line is horizontal
slow reaction – gentle curve
fast reaction – steep curve

Reactions carry on until one of the reactants runs out.

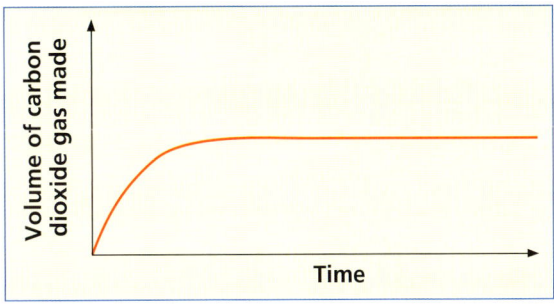

This reaction started with less reactants. The graph does not go up as high – less product has been made.

Making more product?

Increasing the speed of a reaction will not make more product. It just means that the reaction finishes more quickly. The only way to make more product is to use more reactants.

Calculating a rate of reaction from a graph

The slope of the graph tells us the rate. In this reaction we want to know the rate at the **start** of the reaction, so we draw a tangent line to measure the slope more easily.

5 grams of product is made in 20 seconds, so the rate of reaction is 5/20 = 0.25 grams per second.

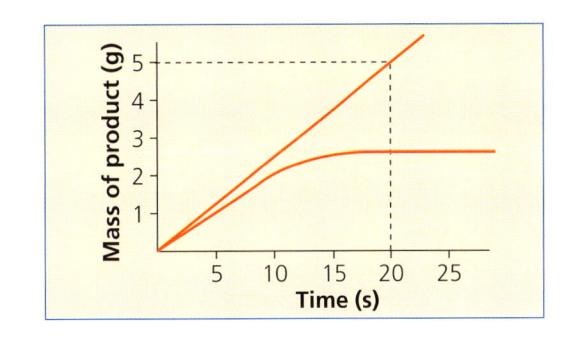

> You must be able to continue the line of a graph to show you understand the trend. You must be able to read points off a graph.

Questions

1. This graph shows the way the mass of marble chips changes during a reaction with acid.

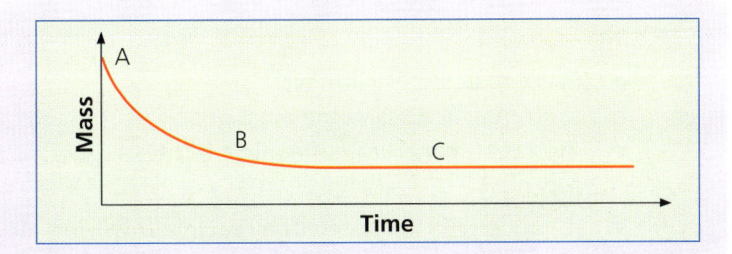

   a Which letter shows where the reaction is fastest? Explain why.

   b Which letter shows where the reaction has stopped?

Catalysts and enzymes

- All living things contain enzymes.
- Enzymes are biological catalysts.

Enzymes are proteins. Proteins have complicated shapes. The part of the enzyme that catalyses the reaction is called the **active site**.

Enzymes are highly specific – the shape of the active site works for specific reactions only.

Enzymes are very delicate – the shape of the active site is easily changed. When this happens, the enzyme stops working. It has been **denatured**.

Enzymes and temperature

Enzymes work best at one particular temperature, the **optimum temperature**.

- Too cold – the reaction is slow. As the temperature gets hotter, there are more energetic particles. The reaction goes faster.
- Too hot – enzymes are denatured.

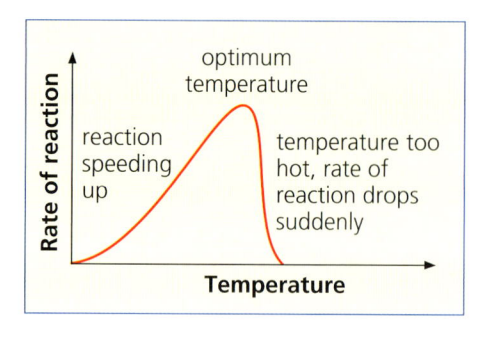

Enzymes and acidity

Enzymes work best at one particular pH – the **optimum pH**.

Too much acid or alkali affects the shape of the active site in the enzyme. The enzyme is denatured, and the reaction stops.

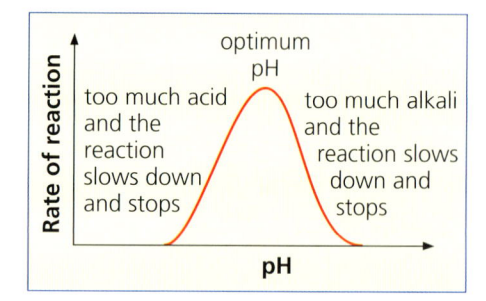

Questions

1. A student has three enzymes, A, B and C. She does an experiment to find which will make the best catalyst for a particular reaction.

   Which enzyme made the reaction go most quickly?

2. The student used two more enzymes, X and Y.
   a. Which reaction was fastest?
   b. Which reaction made the most product?
   c. This experiment was not really a fair test. Why not?

3. What happens to the speed of a reaction involving an enzyme:
   a. if you start to heat it up?
   b. if you heat it further?

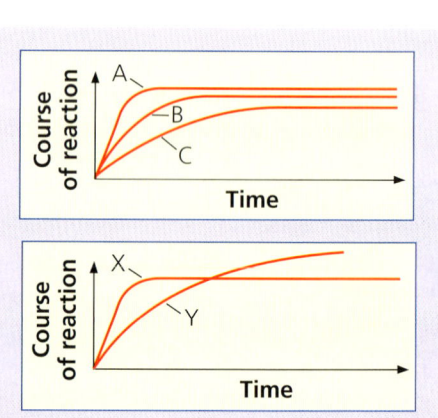

Using enzymes

Fermentation is important in the baking and brewing industries. During fermentation, sugar is converted into alcohol and carbon dioxide. Yeast contains enzymes which act as a catalyst for this reaction.

$$\text{sugar (glucose)} \rightarrow \text{alcohol (ethanol)} + \text{carbon dioxide}$$
$$C_6H_{12}O_6 \rightarrow 2C_2H_5OH + 2CO_2$$

Yeast is a living organism, so it needs water for fermentation to work. No air must be present, otherwise ethanoic acid (vinegar) is made instead of alcohol. It also needs warmth – high temperatures denature the enzymes and kill the yeast; low temperatures slow down the reaction.

Conditions for fermentation
- warm (25–55 °C)
- water
- enzymes from yeast
- no air

Baking
Sugar and yeast are added to bread dough. Fermentation produces bubbles of carbon dioxide and alcohol. The carbon dioxide makes the dough rise. The high temperature of the cooking kills the yeast and drives off the carbon dioxide and the alcohol.

Brewing
Yeast is added to grape juice to make wine, and barley to make beer. Sugars in the grapes and the barley ferment to produce alcohol. The carbon dioxide bubbles out of the liquid.

Other uses for enzymes

Dairy industry
Rennet is an enzyme which makes milk curdle and turn into cheese.

Soft-centred chocolates
Chocolates with soft centres are totally solid when they are first made. The 'soft' centre contains solid sugar, a little water and an enzyme. The enzyme breaks the sugar molecules into simpler sugars which dissolve in the water. This makes the mixture soft and runny.

Washing powders
Biological washing powders contain enzymes which break down substances such as proteins and fats in stains on clothing.

Genetic engineering
Genetic engineering is a way of transferring useful genes from one living thing to another. Particular genes are cut out using special enzymes called restriction enzymes.

Penicillin
Bacterial enzymes are used to convert penicillin into other forms, such as ampicillin.

Questions
1. When yeast ferments it converts sugar into **two** chemicals. What are they?
2. Look at the note box on this page. What do you think might be the optimum temperature for the enzymes in yeast?

Energy in chemistry

Energy and reactions

Most chemical reactions transfer energy. The energy can be transferred in different ways: heat and light when something burns; electricity from the chemicals inside a battery; you can even hear the sound when marble reacts with acid.

Exothermic and endothermic reactions

Reactions which get hot are **exothermic**; they are giving out energy. A few reactions take energy in, which makes them feel cold. These are **endothermic**.

Measuring the energy

You can tell how much energy has been transferred in an exothermic reaction by using the reaction to heat up some water.
- Put fuel in a spirit burner and weigh.
- Measure water into a copper calorimeter (copper conducts heat from flame to water).
- Burn the fuel to heat the water – measure the temperature rise.
- Re-weigh the spirit burner to find the mass of fuel used.

Fuels can be compared by burning the same mass of fuel every time and seeing which gives the greatest temperature rise. A better way is to calculate the actual amount of energy transferred to the water using the formula

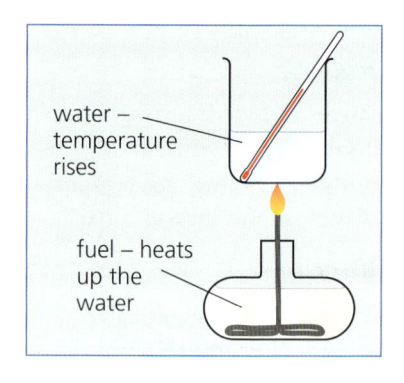

energy transferred = mass × specific heat capacity × temperature change

Remember that the mass, specific heat capacity and temperature change are all for the substance to which you are transferring the energy – the water in the container.

Energy is measured in joules J and kilojoules kJ. There are 1000 joules in a kilojoule.

Worked example

Q 3 g of fuel raised the temperature of 500 g of water in a metal container from 20 °C to 36 °C.
Calculate the energy transferred by one gram of fuel.
(The specific heat capacity of water is 4.2 J/g°C.)

A Temperature rise = 36 − 20   = 16 °C
Total energy transferred = 500 × 4.2 × 16   = 33 600 J
Energy transfer per gram of fuel = 33.6 ÷ 3 = 11.2 kJ

Energy per gram = $\frac{\text{energy supplied}}{\text{mass of fuel burnt}}$

Fair testing

- Always use the same mass of water in the copper can.
- Always start with the water at about the same temperature.
- Burn enough fuel to give the same temperature rise each time (similar heat losses).
- Calculate the energy for the same mass of fuel each time, i.e. energy transfer per gram of fuel.

Bond making and breaking

When compounds react the first thing that they do is to split into their atoms. Then the atoms join together again to make new compounds. To pull the atoms away from each other, bonds have to be broken. When the atoms join back together, new bonds are made.

Energy has to be put in to break the bonds – this part is endothermic. Energy is given out when bonds are made – this part is exothermic.

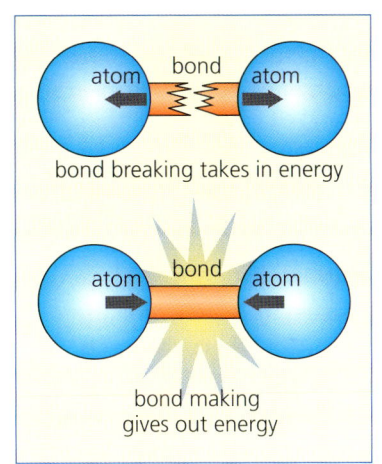

If more energy is given out than is taken in, the whole reaction is exothermic. If more energy is taken in than given out, the whole reaction is endothermic.

ΔH is the symbol for change in chemical energy.

bond breaking takes in energy

bond making gives out energy

- Exothermic reactions give out energy, chemical energy turns into heat, so **ΔH is negative**.
- Endothermic reactions take in energy, heat turns into chemical energy, so **ΔH is positive**.

Why burning methane gives out heat

When methane burns:

$$CH_4 + 2O_2 \rightarrow CO_2 + 2H_2O$$

Bonds which break	Bonds which are made
4 × C—H	2 × C=O
2 × O=O	4 × O—H

More energy is given out when the bonds are made than is taken in when the bonds are broken.

Checklist for choosing a fossil fuel
- Energy value – how much energy does it transfer?
- Availability – you need to be able to get the fuel to where you want to use it.
- Storage – some fuels, are difficult and dangerous to store.
- Cost – how much do different fuels cost for the same energy?
- Toxicity – crude oil is often poisonous.
- Pollution – all fossil fuels give off carbon dioxide (greenhouse gas); many fossil fuels give off sulphur dioxide (acid rain).
- Ease of use – it is not easy to use coal-fired cars! Power stations can burn low-grade oil but cars can't.

Questions

1. Which bonds are broken and which bonds are made in this reaction?

   $$CH_4 + Cl-Cl \rightarrow CH_3-Cl + H-Cl$$

2. Calculate the energy transferred by 2.5 g of fuel if it will raise the temperature of 400 g of water by 4.5 °C. (The specific heat capacity of water is 4.2 J/g °C.)

Energy in chemistry

Oil as a fuel

Crude oil is mostly a mixture of **hydrocarbons**. Hydrocarbons are molecules made of hydrogen and carbon only. Some hydrocarbons are very important as fuels.

Separating oil products

Crude oil is a mixture of liquids which boil at different temperatures. These liquids can be separated by **fractional distillation**. The crude oil is boiled and the mixture of vapours sent up the fractionating column. The column gets cooler nearer the top. As each vapour reaches the part of the column that is just below its own boiling point, that vapour will condense. The highest boiling point liquids condense low down the column where it is hottest, and the lowest boiling point liquids rise up to the cooler part. The column has an exit point for each liquid. The gas that comes out at the top of the column contains propane and butane. It is liquefied and sold as LPG (liquified petroleum gas).

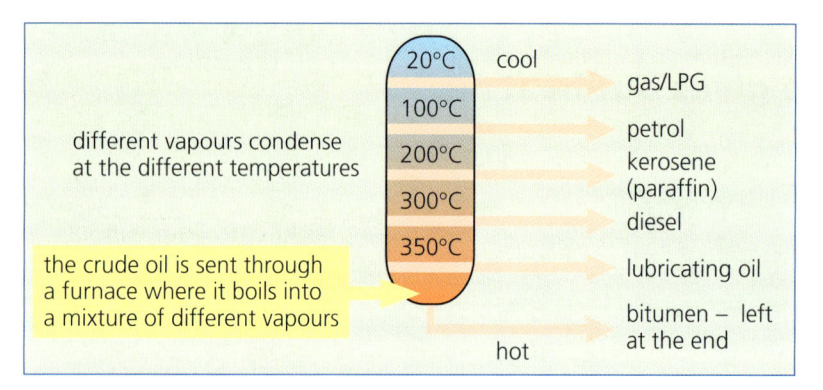

different vapours condense at the different temperatures

- 20°C cool → gas/LPG
- 100°C → petrol
- 200°C → kerosene (paraffin)
- 300°C → diesel
- 350°C → lubricating oil
- hot → bitumen – left at the end

the crude oil is sent through a furnace where it boils into a mixture of different vapours

The boiling points of larger molecules are higher because they have more weak forces between them. It takes a higher temperature to overcome these forces and boil the liquid.

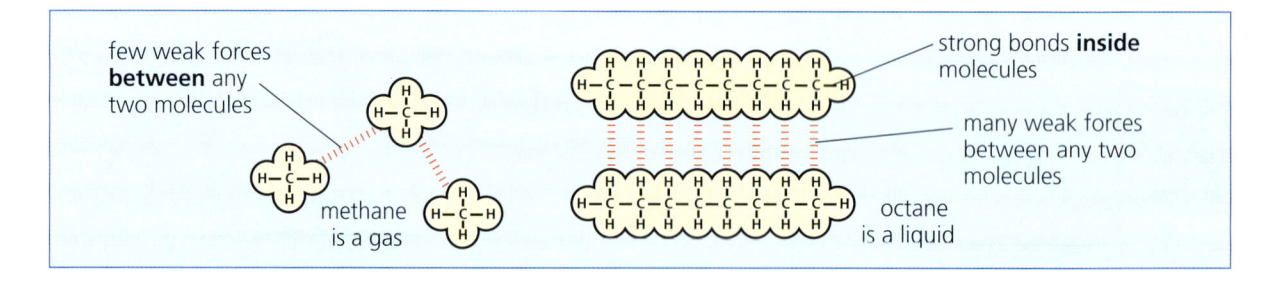

As the hydrocarbon molecule gets bigger, there are more weak forces between the molecules. The melting points and boiling points of the hydrocarbons increase as they get bigger.

few weak forces **between** any two molecules

methane is a gas

strong bonds **inside** molecules

many weak forces between any two molecules

octane is a liquid

Questions

1. Why does petrol leave the fractionating column higher up than kerosene?
2. Why does diesel have a higher boiling point than petrol?

Burning alkanes

One group of hydrocarbons is called the **alkanes**. Here are the first five alkanes.

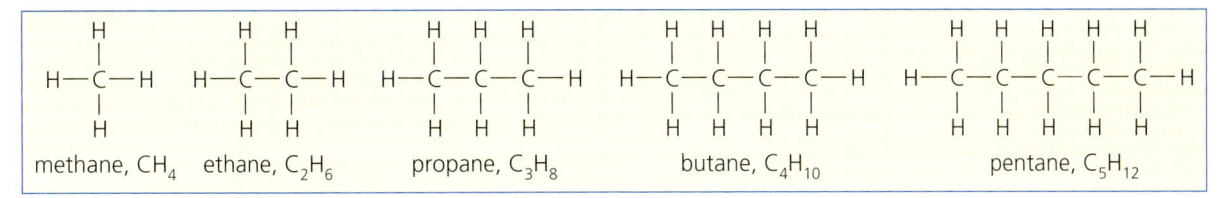

methane, CH_4 ; ethane, C_2H_6 ; propane, C_3H_8 ; butane, C_4H_{10} ; pentane, C_5H_{12}

Some hydrocarbons are used to make other substances such as plastics, but most are burned as a fuel because they transfer a lot of energy.

- Methane is natural gas – used for heating, cooking and in Bunsen burners.
- Propane and butane are used for heating and for camping gas stoves.
- Paraffin is used for heating and for lamps.
- Petrol and diesel are used as fuels for transport.

What happens in burning – oxidation

When something reacts with oxygen to make an oxide we say that it has been **oxidised**. This is an **oxidation** reaction.

When a hydrocarbon burns with plenty of oxygen
- the hydrogen atoms form water
- the carbon atoms form carbon dioxide.

The reaction for methane burning in a gas cooker is:

$$CH_4 + 2O_2 \rightarrow CO_2 + 2H_2O$$
methane + oxygen → carbon dioxide + water

Beware If there is not enough oxygen in the room, the hydrogen part of the methane molecule reacts as normal but the carbon forms carbon monoxide instead of carbon dioxide. Carbon monoxide is poisonous and will kill you. Gas cookers and some gas fires are only safe if the room is well ventilated.

$$CH_4 + 1\tfrac{1}{2}O_2 \rightarrow CO + 2H_2O$$
methane + oxygen → carbon monoxide + water

A better way of writing this is

$$2CH_4 + 3O_2 \rightarrow 2CO + 4H_2O$$

If the oxygen levels drop further, the hydrogen atoms in the methane still react to make water but the carbon stops burning. It forms soot.

$$CH_4 + O_2 \rightarrow C + 2H_2O$$

If the methane doesn't burn properly, not only are the products poisonous but the reactions don't give out as much heat!

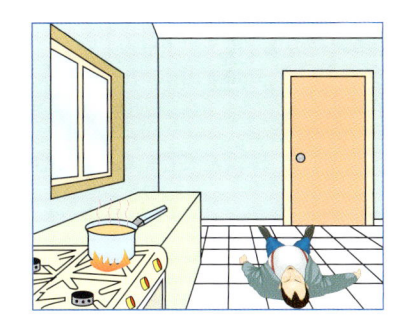

Questions

1. Propane is a hydrocarbon. Write a word equation to show what happens when propane burns in oxygen.

2. Propane has the formula C_3H_8. Write a balanced symbol equation to show what happens when propane burns in oxygen.

3. Pentane has the formula C_5H_{12}. Write a balanced symbol equation to show what happens when pentane burns in oxygen.

Energy in chemistry

Air, oceans and the carbon cycle

Air is a mixture of gases

Oxygen is one of the two most important gases in air, but it does not make up the largest amount of the air. The air is made of approximately

- 78% nitrogen – which does very little
- 21% oxygen – a most important gas
- small amounts of other gases, including
- 0.035% carbon dioxide – the other important gas, even though there is only a very small amount of it.

The atmosphere also contains large amounts of water vapour, but the amount changes with the weather.

The amounts of carbon dioxide and oxygen are approximately constant because they are being made at about the same rate as they are being used up. We think that carbon dioxide levels are increasing very slowly, because it is being made slightly faster than it is being used up.

Human influences on the air
- Deforestation – less photosynthesis; less oxygen provided; less CO_2 removed
- Energy consumption – more fossil fuel burnt; more CO_2 released
- Pollution caused by fossil fuels – carbon dioxide (greenhouse gas); sulphur dioxide (acid rain); unburnt hydrocarbons (greenhouse smog).

The human population causes all of the above!

What affects carbon dioxide levels in the air?

- **Photosynthesis** – green plants turn carbon dioxide into sugars.

| carbon dioxide | + | water | → | glucose | + | oxygen |
| $6CO_2$ | + | $6H_2O$ | → | $C_6H_{12}O_6$ | + | $6O_2$ |

Photosynthesis:
- takes carbon dioxide out of the air
- puts oxygen into the air.

Photosynthesis takes in energy from the Sun – it is **endothermic**.

- **Respiration** – all living things respire – they react sugar to give energy.

| glucose | + | oxygen | → | carbon dioxide | + | water |
| $C_6H_{12}O_6$ | + | $6O_2$ | → | $6CO_2$ | + | $6H_2O$ |

Respiration:
- takes oxygen out of the air
- puts carbon dioxide into the air.

Respiration gives out energy – it is **exothermic**.

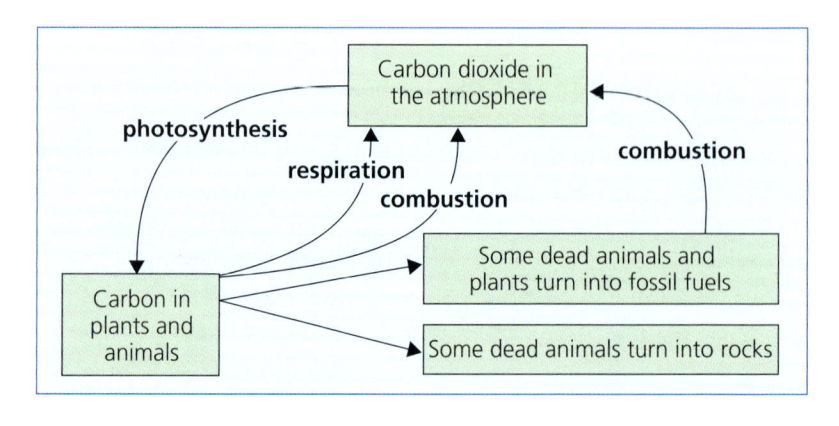

Where did the air come from?

Billions of years ago there was no oxygen in the Earth's atmosphere. Life did not exist. We think that the atmosphere was formed by volcanoes, which were producing ammonia, methane, carbon dioxide and water.

Three billion years ago the first simple plant life appeared. The plants turned the carbon dioxide and water into food and oxygen – photosynthesis had started. At the same time ammonia was being converted into unreactive nitrogen gas.

The amount of oxygen in the atmosphere increased, and the different types of living things increased, until the living things were using up the oxygen as fast as it was being made. This now keeps the amount of oxygen constant.

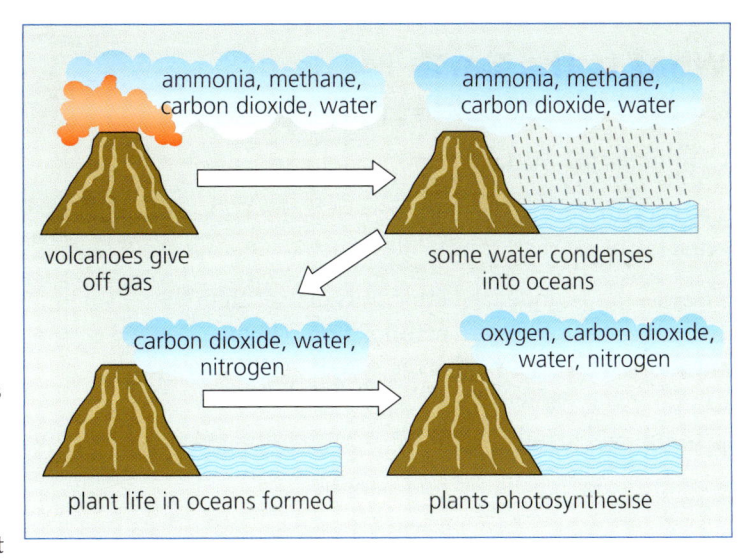

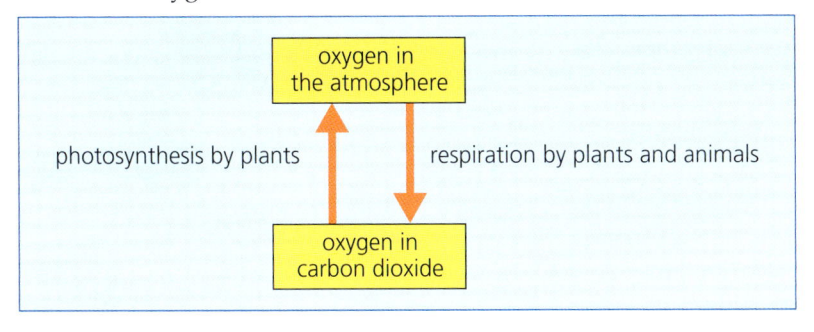

Where did the oceans come from?

When the Earth formed there was steam coming out of volcanoes. As the Earth cooled the steam condensed and turned into rain, which formed the oceans. The water dissolved chemicals out of the rocks, so sea water contains a mixture of different salts dissolved in it.

Questions

1. What are the **two** main processes that put carbon dioxide into the atmosphere?
2. What is the main process that takes carbon dioxide out of the atmosphere?
3. Copy and complete the following sentences:

   The atmosphere is made of _____% nitrogen, _____% oxygen and _____% carbon dioxide. Plants produce _____ gas during photosynthesis; it is needed for respiration and things burn in it. Respiration is similar to burning because they both produce _____ gas. The amounts of carbon dioxide and oxygen in the atmosphere stay fairly constant because the rate of photosynthesis is balanced by _____ and _____.

Rocks and metals

The Earth's crust

What is the Earth made of?

The top layer of the Earth is a thin rocky **crust**.

Continents are made of **continental crust**.

The rock under the oceans is **oceanic crust**. Oceanic crust is denser than continental crust.

The **mantle** is under the crust. It is denser than the crust and has a different composition. The mantle is solid at the top, but nearer the core it gets hotter and can flow very slowly.

In the middle of the Earth is the **core**. The Earth's core contains iron. It is liquid and very hot.

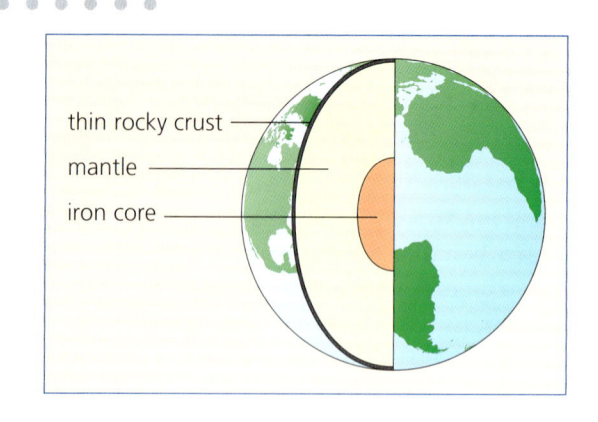

Plate tectonics

The shapes of the continents of Africa and South America fit together like a jigsaw. They have similar rocks and fossils on the coasts that face each other. This is because they were once joined together.

The thin rocky crust and the top part of the mantle make up the **lithosphere**. The lithosphere is made up of large sections called **plates** which, because they have a lower density, float on top of the mantle. Heat from the core creates **convection currents** within the mantle. These currents move the plates slowly across the Earth's surface. Plates travel a few centimetres each year.

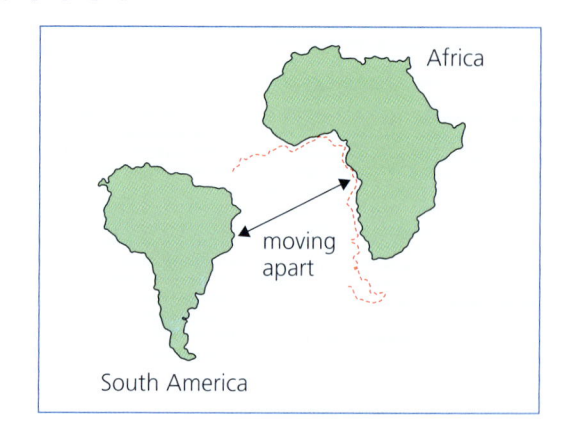

The plates may be moving away from each other, or into each other. The forces created where the plates move against each other are so strong that the edges of the plates are marked by earthquakes, volcanoes and mountain ranges.

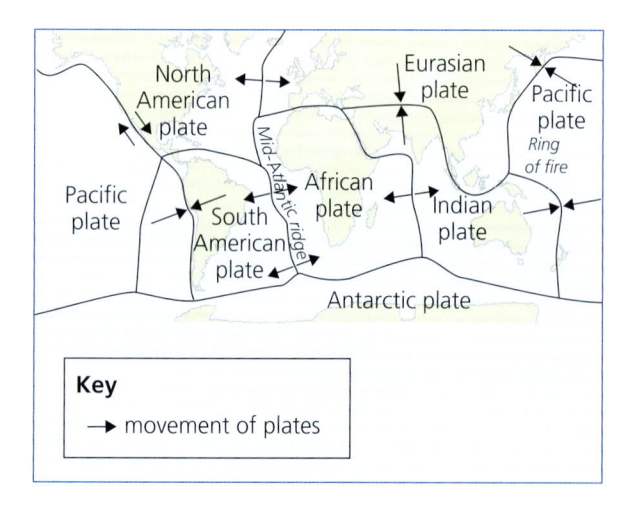

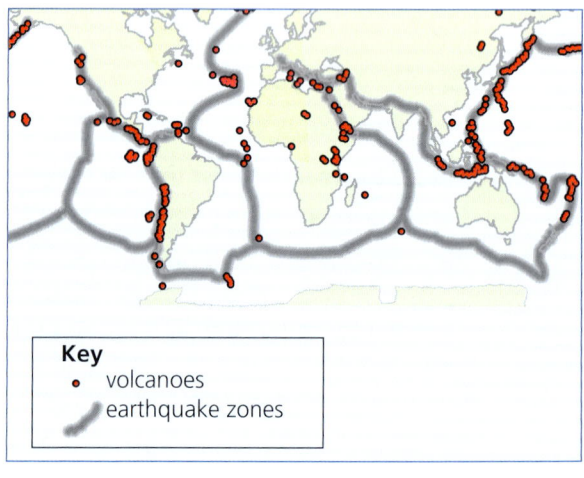

What happens when plates move together?

Oceanic colliding with continental

Oceanic plates are denser than continental plates. The light continental plate rides on top and the dense oceanic plate goes down into the mantle. This is called **subduction**. As the oceanic plate goes down, the rock partially melts. The enormous forces make the continental plate buckle, forming mountains and volcanoes.

Continental colliding with continental

When this happens both plates stay on the surface. The plates buckle, fold and fault, forming mountains.

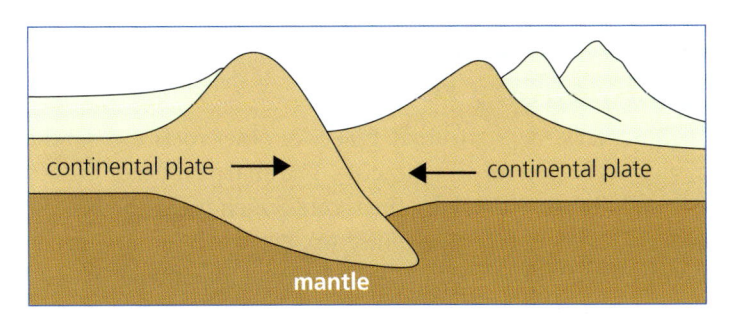

What happens when plates move apart?

The Atlantic Ocean is getting wider by at least a centimetre every year. This is because the plates under the ocean are moving apart, leaving a gap down the centre of the ocean floor. Magma flows into the gap, making a ridge of new igneous rocks. This is called **sea floor spreading**. There are earthquakes and sometimes volcanoes.

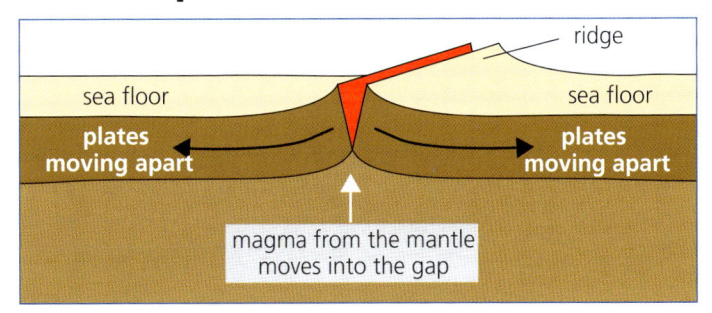

Scientists first realised that the sea floor was spreading when they found out that as you go further from the ridge the rocks get older.

Questions

1. The Pacific Plate is surrounded by a ring of volcanoes called 'The ring of fire'.
   a. Find the volcanoes on the map.
   b. How far are the volcanoes from the edges of the plates?
   c. How far are the earthquake zones from the edges of the plates?

2. When two plates push into each other, one plate stays on the surface and the other plate disappears.
   a. Where does this plate go?
   b. What happens to the rocks of the plate that disappears?

3. What happens to the age of the rocks as you move away from a place where the sea floor is spreading?

Rocks

There are three types of rock – igneous, sedimentary and metamorphic.

Igneous rocks

Igneous rocks are made from magma which has cooled down and solidified. It usually forms interlocking crystals of different **minerals**. Cooling underground is slow. This produces a rock with large crystals, e.g. granite. Cooling at the surface is rapid. This produces a rock with small crystals, e.g. basalt.

Sedimentary rocks

Sedimentary rocks are small pieces of older rock, e.g. sand or mud, which settle and form sediments. The sharp edges of these pieces are usually worn away by the rivers which bring them down to the sea. As layers of sediment build up, the lowest sediments are compressed by the weight of the layers above them, which helps turn the lowest layers into solid rock.

Fine grains will only settle in water if the conditions are very still, so a fine grained sedimentary rock tells us how it was formed. Large pebbles in the rock tell us that the water was still moving fast when the layer formed, i.e. the water had lots of energy.

The lowest layer of rock is usually the oldest – it is the first to form. If dead animals are covered in the sediment as the layer is forming, the animals may form fossils. The fossils can tell us how old the rock is.

The rock layers are not always totally flat. They may have ripple marks in them if they were in shallow water. We might even see evidence of such things as the sloping edges of sand dunes (cross-bedding).

Metamorphic rocks

Metamorphic rocks are rocks which have changed after they were originally formed. The changes are usually caused by high temperature or by pressure from other rocks. Grains may have re-crystallised; fossils might have been distorted or even destroyed. The amount of metamorphic rock might be quite small, such as that immediately next to an igneous intrusion where the temperature is very high. The amount could also be very extensive, for example large areas changed by the huge forces created by a moving tectonic plate.

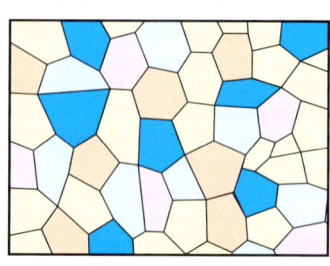

igneous – slow cooling large interlocking crystals

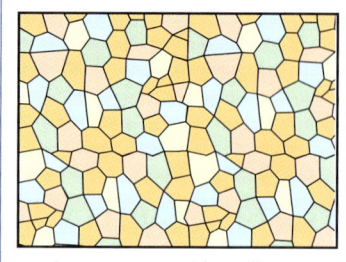

igneous – rapid cooling small interlocking crystals

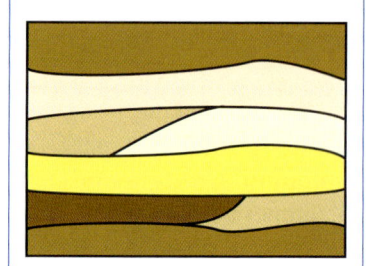

sedimentary – cross-bedding caused by sand dunes for example

What to look for
- Igneous – look for interlocking crystals, or glassy rock.
- Sedimentary – look for layers, bits of older rock grains and pebbles; some types may have fossils in them.
- Metamorphic – look for distorted grains, or distorted fossils.

What happened when?

If the rock is in layers it is usually sedimentary rock, with the oldest layer lying at the bottom.

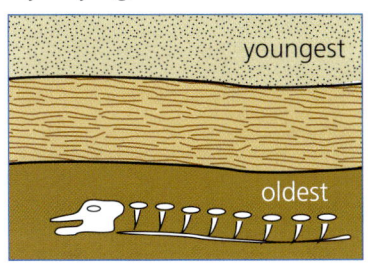

Solving the puzzle

Enormous forces can cause the rock to fault and fold.

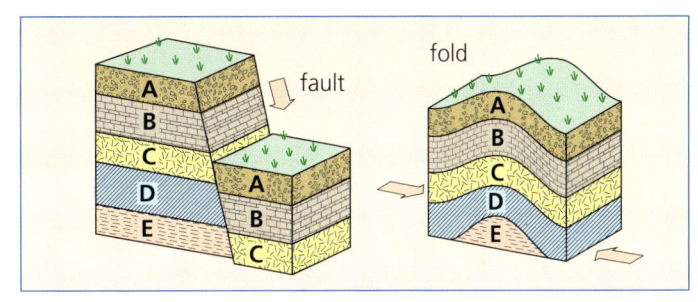

Faulting and folding happened after rock layer A was formed.

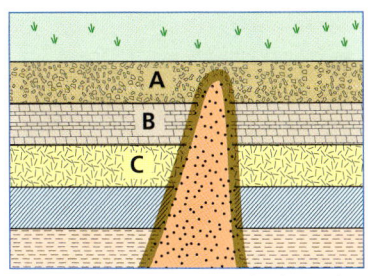

An intrusion

Sometimes an intrusion of igneous rock might have happened after the sedimentary rock has formed.

The igneous intrusion happened after sedimentary layers A, B and C formed. The igneous rock is the youngest.

The sedimentary rocks around the edge of an intrusion are changed by the enormous temperature of the igneous rock. An area of metamorphic rock is now formed.

Useful substances from rocks

We can dig some rocks out of the ground and use them straight away.

Minerals and ores

Most rocks can't be used straight away. The useful part of the rock, the **mineral**, is usually mixed in with other bits of rock that we don't want. The combination of mineral and other rock is called an **ore**. Sometimes the mineral is the metal element itself, such as gold, but usually the mineral is a metal combined with other elements such as oxygen or sulphur. For example, iron oxide is the mineral in some types of iron ore.

Substance	Obtained from
pottery	clay
cement	limestone (calcium carbonate)
glass	sand (silicon oxide)
chlorine and sodium hydroxide	salt (sodium chloride)
aluminium	bauxite (aluminium oxide)
iron	haematite (iron oxide)

A lump of iron ore

Questions

1. Copy and complete the following sentences:

   Granite rock is made from magma which cools underground. This means that it will have _____ size crystals. It is an _____ type of rock. If rocks are then put under great pressure or temperature they will change to _____ rock.

2. Copy and complete the following sentences:

   Rocks on the surface are slowly broken into small pieces. The pieces are carried to the sea where they settle and turn into _____ rock. If that rock is put under great pressure or temperature it will change into _____ rock.

Getting metals from minerals – reduction

If the mineral is a compound, the useful element is combined with other elements. The mineral haematite is the compound iron oxide. It is made of iron chemically bonded to oxygen. We have to break the chemical bonds to get the iron and the oxygen apart.

> Removal of oxygen is called **reduction**. If a metal is *not* very reactive it is easy to **reduce** the oxide. Reactive metals form stronger bonds with oxygen so it is difficult to reduce them.

Sodium, calcium, magnesium and zinc are all very reactive. They will all bond tightly with oxygen from the air, they all give off hydrogen with water and with acids. Sodium and calcium are so reactive that it is too dangerous to put them with acids!

Less reactive metals such as copper and gold don't react with water or acids, so copper is used to make water pipes and gold is used for jewellery.

Metals reacting with other compounds

Aluminium is more reactive than iron, so it can steal oxygen out of iron oxide. It reduces iron oxide.

aluminium + iron oxide → aluminium oxide + iron

Carbon is more reactive than iron and zinc, so carbon will take oxygen out of iron oxide and also out of zinc oxide. Carbon reduces iron oxide and zinc oxide.

Zinc is more reactive than copper, so it can steal the sulphate out of copper sulphate solution and leave the copper behind. This is called **displacement**.

zinc +	copper sulphate	→	zinc sulphate	+ copper
grey metal	blue solution		colourless solution	red metal

Reactivity series
most reactive
sodium
calcium
magnesium
aluminium
carbon
zinc
iron
hydrogen
copper
silver
gold
least reactive

Metals like aluminium are so reactive that when they bond with oxygen, the bond is very hard to break. We use electrolysis to break bonds as strong as these.

Questions

1. Copy and complete the following equation:

    zinc + copper oxide → _____ + _____

2. Which of these will hydrogen react with? iron oxide, copper oxide, silver oxide.
   What will be formed in the cases that do react?

3. Metal C will take the oxygen from the oxide of metal A.
   Metal B will take the oxygen from the oxide of metal D.
   Metal A will take the oxygen from the oxide of metal B.
   Put the metals in order of reactivity, starting with the most reactive.

Carbon as a reducing agent

Carbon is a very useful substance for taking oxygen away from (reducing) metal oxides. It is more reactive than iron and copper, which we have to extract in very large quantities. This means that carbon can take copper out of copper ore and also iron out of iron ore. Carbon also has the advantage of being fairly cheap.

Extracting iron

Iron ore contains haematite which is iron oxide. Iron is extracted from iron oxide using carbon in a blast furnace. The carbon is converted into carbon monoxide inside the blast furnace and it is the carbon monoxide which actually causes the reduction.

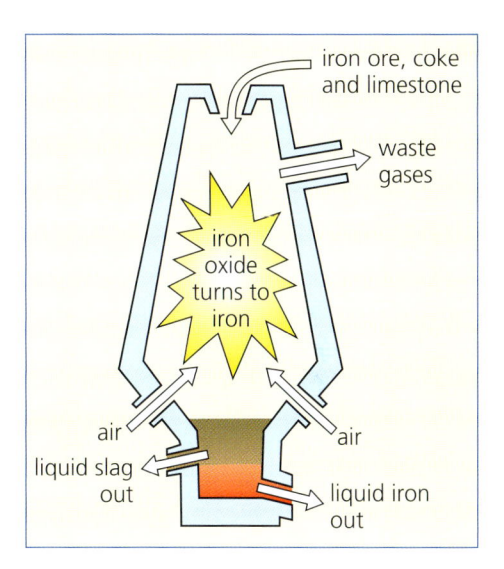

Iron ore and coke are put in through the top of the furnace and a blast of hot air is fed in though the holes at the side. So much heat is given out in this reaction that the temperature reaches more than 1000 °C. The iron melts and collects at the bottom of the furnace. Limestone is used to react with impurities in the iron ore and turn them into liquid slag. The slag floats on top of the iron and is drained out of the furnace before the liquid iron is run out.

Carbon and oxygen form carbon monoxide:

$$2C + O_2 \rightarrow 2CO$$
carbon + oxygen → carbon monoxide

Carbon monoxide reduces the iron oxide:

$$3CO + Fe_2O_3 \rightarrow 2Fe + 3CO_2$$
carbon monoxide + iron oxide → iron + carbon dioxide

It is this last stage, which is the reduction stage. The iron oxide has lost its oxygen, leaving iron.

Oxidation and reduction: 1
- *oxidation = gaining oxygen*
- *reduction = losing oxygen*

Questions

1. aluminium + iron oxide → aluminium oxide + iron
   Which substance has been reduced?
   Which substance has been oxidised?
2. What do we call the reaction that takes oxygen away from something?
3. Carbon will take oxygen from copper oxide. Write a word equation for this reaction.
4. a Which would you expect to corrode in air more quickly, iron or zinc?
   b Explain why.

Rocks and metals

Atoms, ions and electrolysis

Atoms

An atom consists of a tiny positive nucleus surrounded by shells of electrons.

Atoms are neutral – their negative and positive charges cancel out. This means that the number of electrons must be the same as the number of protons.

Name	Charge	Where found
proton	+1	inside the nucleus
neutron	0	inside the nucleus
electron	–1	outside the nucleus, in shells

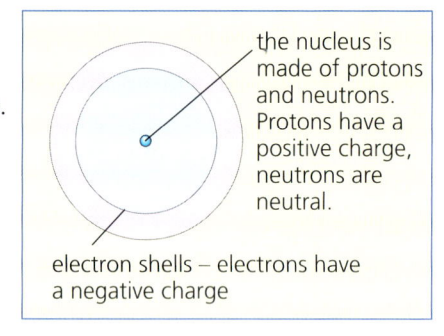

the nucleus is made of protons and neutrons. Protons have a positive charge, neutrons are neutral.

electron shells – electrons have a negative charge

Ions

An atom can become electrically charged, but as soon as this happens it is called an **ion**. Atoms turn into ions by gaining electrons or by losing electrons. They do this in order to end up with a stable outer shell of electrons – a noble gas configuration (see page 113).

A chlorine atom gains one electron, forming a chloride ion $\quad Cl + e^- \rightarrow Cl^-$
An oxygen atom gains two electrons, forming an oxide ion $\quad O + 2e^- \rightarrow O^{--}$
A sodium atom gives away one electron, forming a sodium ion $\quad Na \rightarrow Na^+ + e^-$
A calcium atom gives away two electrons, forming a calcium ion $\quad Ca \rightarrow Ca^{++} + 2e^-$

Ionic compounds and electric current – electrolysis

Ionic compounds do not conduct electricity when they are solid but they will conduct electricity if they are melted or dissolved. Ionic solids don't conduct electricity because the particles in a solid are held in one place. In liquids the ions can move, so they can carry the charge through the liquid. Ionic liquids are called **electrolytes**.

Ions are attracted by the oppositely charged electrode. The **cathode** is negative; it attracts positive ions. When the positive ions reach the cathode they pick up electrons from the cathode and turn into neutral atoms. If a substance gains electrons, it has been reduced.

The **anode** is positive; it attracts negative ions. When negative ions reach the anode they usually give their extra electrons to the anode and turn into neutral atoms. If a substance loses electrons, it has been oxidised.

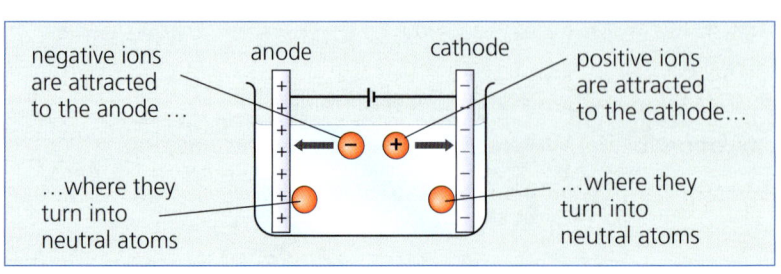

If an atom gains electrons it becomes a negative ion. Negative ions are called anions.
If an atom loses electrons it becomes a positive ion. Positive ions are called cations.

negative ions are attracted to the anode …
…where they turn into neutral atoms
positive ions are attracted to the cathode…
…where they turn into neutral atoms

Using electrolysis to extract aluminium

Aluminium ore contains aluminium oxide. Aluminium is very reactive (it bonds tightly to oxygen), so carbon isn't reactive enough to take the oxygen away from the oxide. Instead we melt the aluminium oxide and then electrolyse it. Aluminium oxide melts at a high temperature, so the process requires a lot of electrical energy.

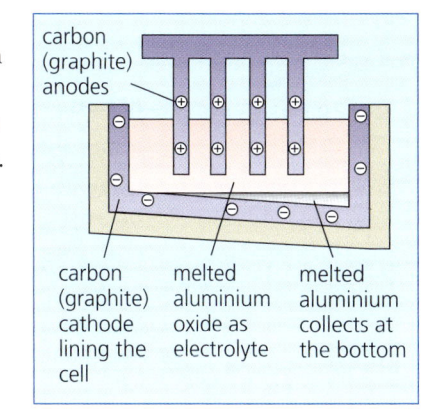

The sides and the bottom of the tank are lined with graphite. The graphite lining is connected to an electricity supply to make the cathode. The anodes are also made of graphite. They are lowered into the molten aluminium oxide.

Aluminium ions are positive, so they are attracted to the negative cathode and are neutralised. Molten aluminium collects at the bottom of the tank. Oxygen is formed at the carbon anodes and then reacts with the anodes to make carbon dioxide.

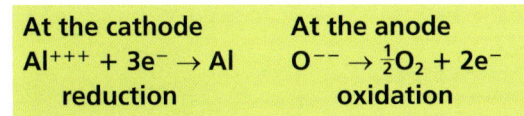

At the cathode	At the anode
$Al^{+++} + 3e^- \to Al$	$O^{--} \to \frac{1}{2}O_2 + 2e^-$
reduction	oxidation

The overall equation is:
aluminium oxide → aluminium + oxygen
$2Al_2O_3$ → $4Al$ + $3O_2$

Using electrolysis to purify or extract copper

The anode is the impure copper. The cathode is a pure copper plate. During electrolysis the copper dissolves from the impure anode and plates onto the cathode. The pure copper cathode becomes thicker as more copper plates onto it.

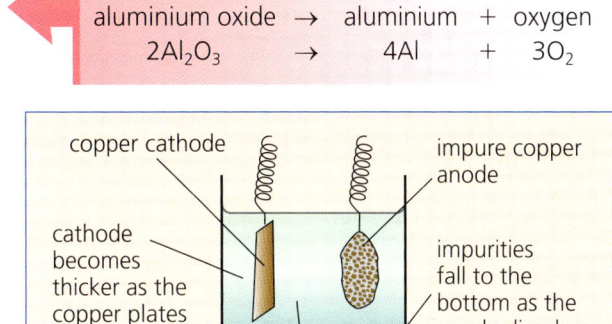

At the cathode	At the anode
$Cu^{++} + 2e^- \to Cu$	$Cu \to Cu^{++} + 2e^-$

Copper is sometimes extracted from boulders by this method. The impure copper boulder is the anode, a pure copper rod is the cathode.

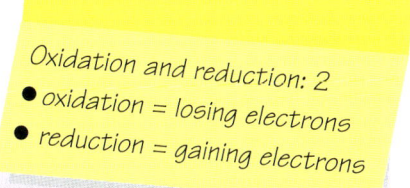

Oxidation and reduction: 2
- *oxidation = losing electrons*
- *reduction = gaining electrons*

Questions

1. Metals give away electrons. What sort of charges do their ions have?
2. Some non-metals can gain electrons. What sort of charges do their ions have?
3. Magnesium atoms lose two electrons. Write the symbol for a magnesium ion.
4. Solid sodium chloride is ionic. Why doesn't it conduct electricity?
5. Which electrode will metals go towards during electrolysis?
6. What is the charge on a an anode? b a cathode?
7. Look at the equation:

    $2Al_2O_3 \to 4Al + 3O_2$

    a Has the aluminium in the aluminium oxide been oxidised or reduced?
    b How can you tell?

Materials and their properties

Concept map

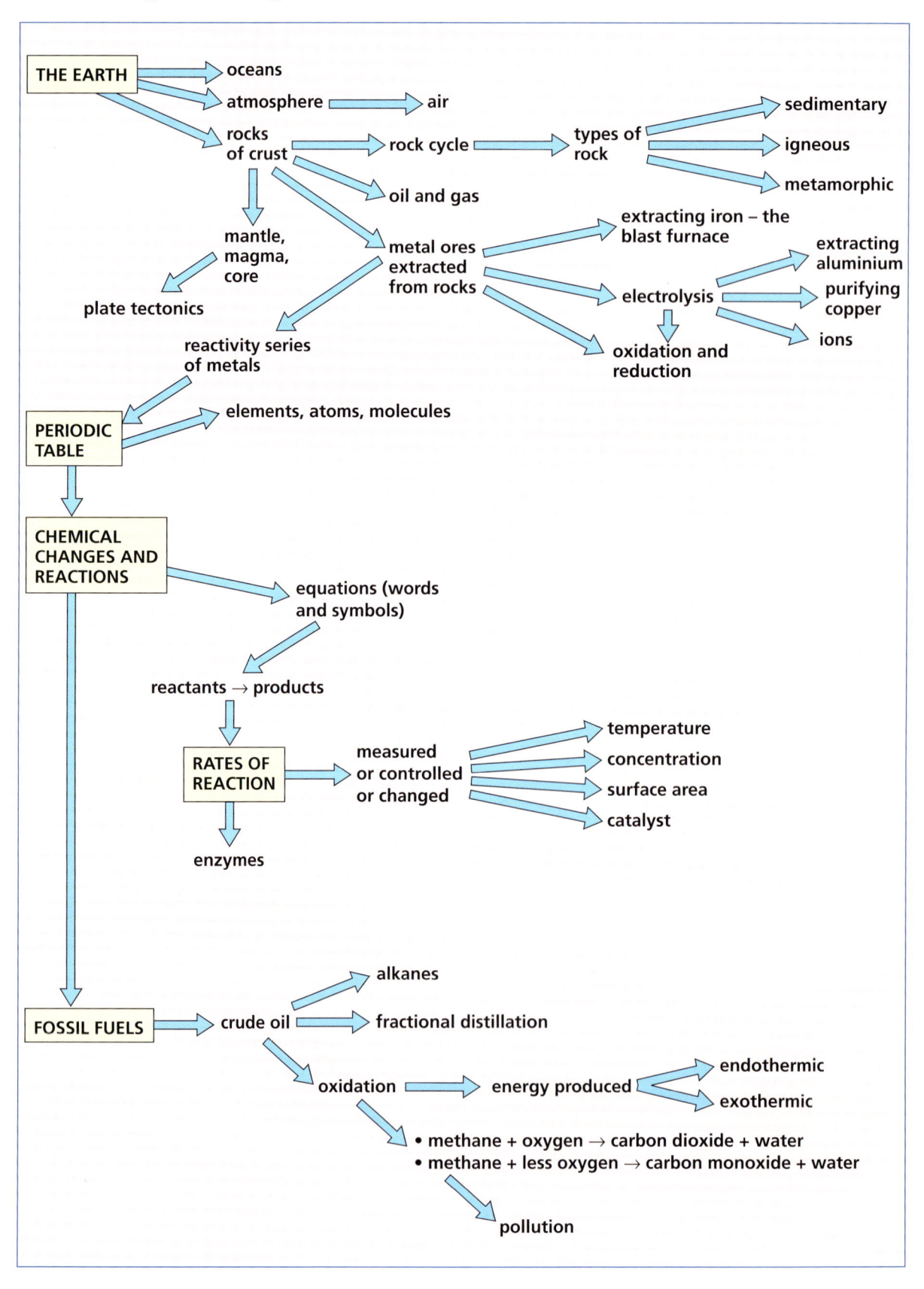

- **THE EARTH**
  - oceans
  - atmosphere → air
  - rocks of crust
    - rock cycle → types of rock
      - sedimentary
      - igneous
      - metamorphic
    - oil and gas
    - mantle, magma, core → plate tectonics
    - metal ores extracted from rocks
      - extracting iron – the blast furnace
      - electrolysis
        - extracting aluminium
        - purifying copper
        - ions
      - oxidation and reduction
    - reactivity series of metals

- **PERIODIC TABLE** → elements, atoms, molecules

- **CHEMICAL CHANGES AND REACTIONS**
  - equations (words and symbols)
  - reactants → products
    - **RATES OF REACTION**
      - measured or controlled or changed
        - temperature
        - concentration
        - surface area
        - catalyst
      - enzymes

- **FOSSIL FUELS** → crude oil
  - alkanes
  - fractional distillation
  - oxidation → energy produced
    - endothermic
    - exothermic
  - methane + oxygen → carbon dioxide + water
  - methane + less oxygen → carbon monoxide + water
  - pollution

Exam questions

1 Calcium forms calcium oxide, CaO, when you heat it in air.
  a Write a word equation for this reaction. [2]
  b Write a balanced chemical equation for this reaction. [2]
  [4 marks]

2 Crude oil is a mixture of alkane molecules. We can separate these molecules by fractionation (fractional distillation).

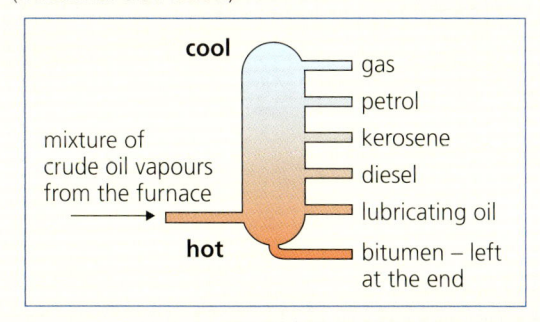

  a Different hydrocarbons have different boiling points. Explain why. [2]
  b Alkanes are made of carbon and hydrogen. When the alkanes such as methane, CH_4, burn they react with oxygen in the atmosphere.
   i What do we call reactions where chemicals combine with oxygen? [1]
   ii Name two chemicals that are made when methane is burnt in a plentiful supply of air. [2]
   iii Write a balanced equation for this reaction. [2]
   iv Name two chemicals that are made when methane is burnt in a reduced supply of air. [2]
   v Write a balanced equation for this reaction. [2]
  [11 marks]

3 Geologists think that a particular type of rock from South America was made from molten magma which came to the surface and quickly cooled.
  a What do we call rocks formed when molten magma solidifies? [1]
  b What can you see in the diagram that shows you that both these rocks were formed when molten rock cooled? [2] 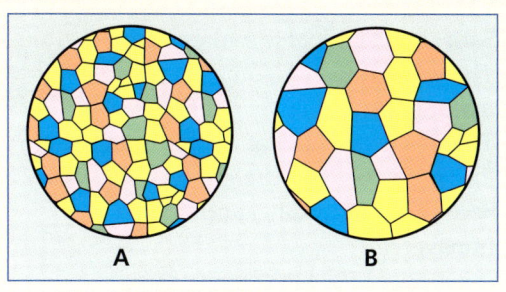
  c Which of the rocks in the diagram could have cooled quickly? Explain how you can tell. [1]
  d There is an identical type of rock in Africa. Geologists think that the two rocks were formed very close to each other. Use ideas about plate tectonics to explain why they are so far apart. [2]
  [6 marks]

4 Aluminium is produced by the electrolysis of aluminium oxide. Aluminium oxide is made up of Al^{3+} and O^{2-} particles.
  a What do we call Al^{3+} and O^{2-} particles? [1]
  b Explain why melted aluminium oxide will conduct electricity but the solid won't. [1]
  c The sides and the bottom of the electrolysis cell are lined with carbon. This is connected to an electricity supply to make the negative electrode. Positive carbon electrodes are dipped into the liquid. 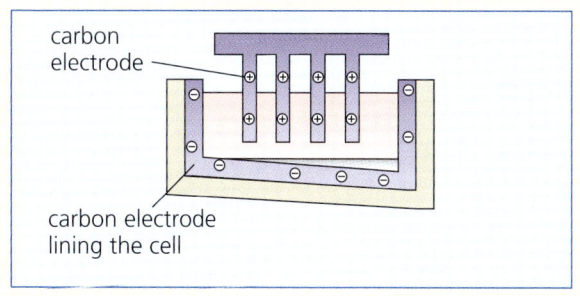
   i What do we call a positive electrode? [1]
   ii What do we call a negative electrode? [1]
   iii What happens to the Al^{3+} particles when the current is switched on? [2]
  [6 marks]

Waves in action

Making waves

Jo throws a brick at Sam. The brick (made from **matter**) transfers some **energy** from Jo to Sam.

Sam shouts at Jo. He makes a **sound wave**. The wave transfers some energy to Jo by making the air between them vibrate. There is no transfer of matter from Sam to Jo. There are two different types of wave. Sound is longitudinal and light is transverse.

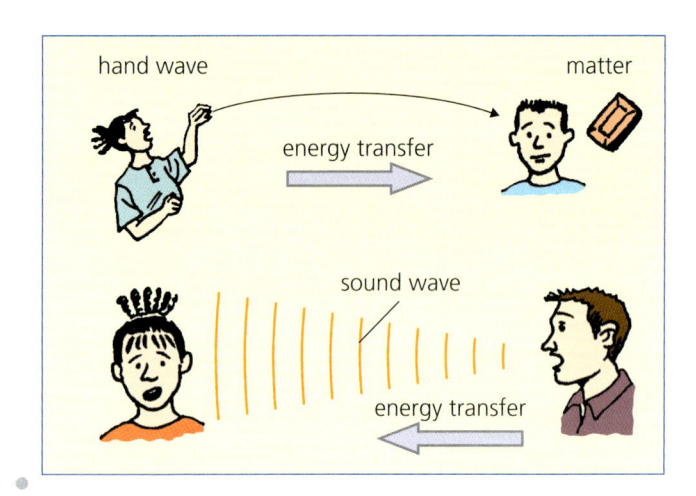

Longitudinal waves

Sound is a **longitudinal wave**. It is caused by **vibrations** which squeeze and stretch the air. The pattern of high and low pressure travels through the air as a wave, carrying energy away from the source of the vibrations. The high-pressure regions are called **compressions**. The low-pressure regions are called **expansions** or **rarefactions**.

The **frequency** (in hertz (Hz)) of the wave is the number of vibrations per second. So if the source vibrates 1000 times in 5 s, the frequency is 1000/5 = 200 Hz.

The **wavelength** (in metres (m)) of the wave is the distance from one compression (or expansion) to the next. So if there are 20 compressions in 60 m, the wavelength is 60/20 = 3 m.

This diagram shows a longitudinal wave moving along a spring. Each coil vibrates back and forth in the same direction as the flow of energy. The compressions and rarefactions move from left to right.

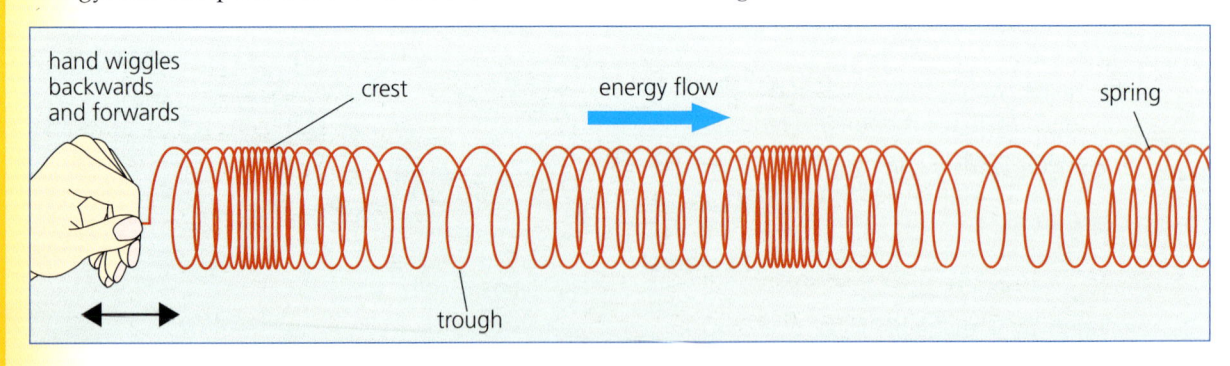

Transverse waves

Jo transmits a **transverse** wave to Sam along a stretched rope. As the wave travels from left to right, it makes each bit of the rope vibrate up and down. The **amplitude** of the wave is the maximum distance each part of the rope moves from its rest position. There are lots of different transverse waves, for example water waves, light waves and radio waves.

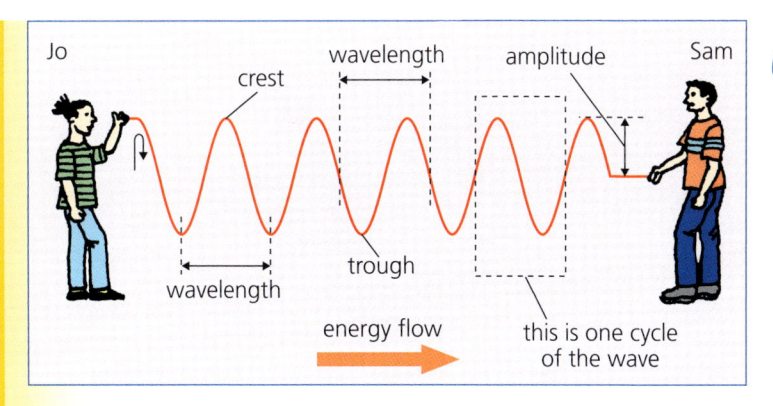

Speed, frequency and wavelength...

The speed of a wave is linked to its frequency and wavelength with this formula.

speed = frequency × wavelength   v = fL

You must know this one by heart

Symbol	Meaning	Units of measurement
v	speed	metres per second or m/s
f	frequency	hertz or Hz
L	wavelength	metres or m

Worked example

Q Sound has a speed in air of 300 m/s. Calculate the wavelength of a 1200 Hz sound wave in air.

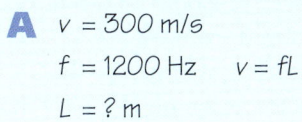

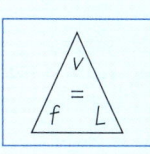

A v = 300 m/s
f = 1200 Hz   v = fL
L = ? m

$$L = \frac{v}{f}$$

$$? = \frac{300}{1200} = 0.25 \text{ m}$$

List the data...
write the formula...
draw the triangle...
change the formula...
insert the data.

Questions

1. Calculate the frequency of a wave whose source makes 12 000 vibrations in 6 s.
2. Calculate the wavelength of a wave which has 25 compressions in 100 m.
3. Copy and complete the following sentences.

    Sound is created by _____. These create regions of high pressure (_____) and low pressure (_____) which move through the air. The number of vibrations per second is the _____ of the wave, measured in _____. The distance between compressions is the _____ of the wave, measured in _____. Sound is a _____ wave. It makes the air vibrate in the same direction as the _____ _____.

4. a Calculate values for the number of cycles, the wavelength and the amplitude of this wave in a stretched rope.
   b Explain why you can tell that the wave is a transverse one.

5. State the formula linking speed, wavelength and frequency of a wave.
6. A wave in water has a frequency of 6 Hz and a wavelength of 4 m. Calculate its speed.
7. A radio wave has a speed of 300 000 000 m/s. If it has a frequency of 6 000 000 Hz, what is its wavelength? If its wavelength is 500 m, what is its frequency?

Waves in action

Using light waves

Reflection

Light waves travel in straight lines. These are drawn as **rays**.

When light rays reflect off a shiny surface, the **angle of reflection**, r, is the same as the **angle of incidence**, i. Both angles are measured from the **normal**. This is a line at right angles to the reflector at the point where the ray hits it.

Light reflected from a flat mirror appears to come from behind the mirror. If you look at the reflected light, you see an **image** of the **object** which produced the light. The distance from the image to the mirror is the same as the distance from the object to the mirror.

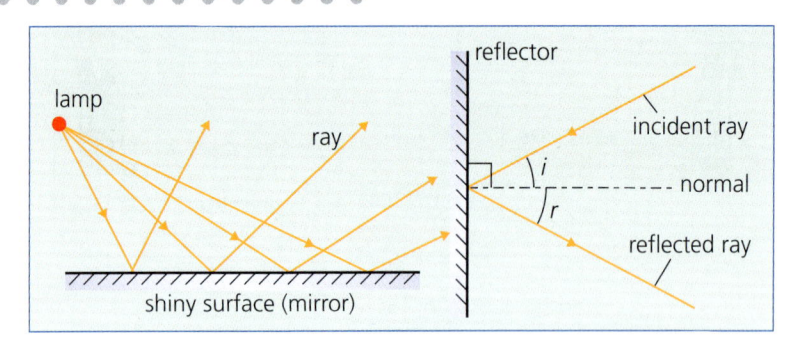

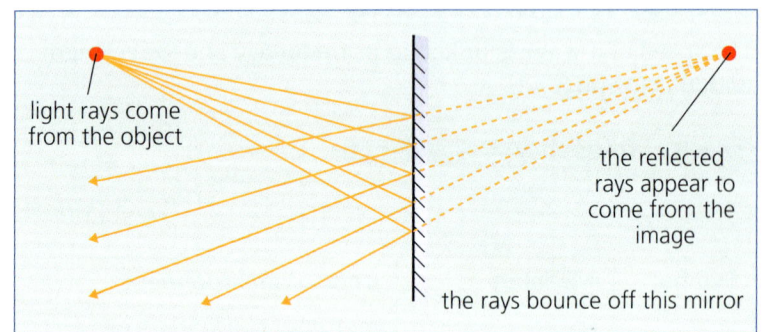

Refraction

When light goes from air into a transparent material (such as glass) it changes direction. It is **refracted**.

On the way into the material the angle of refraction is always smaller than the angle of incidence. Both angles are measured from the normal.

On the way out of the material the angle of refraction is always larger than the angle of incidence.

If the angle of incidence is large enough, rays of light will not refract out. They are **totally internally reflected**. This is used in optical fibres. Light which goes in at one end has to reflect off the edge of the fibre until it gets to the other end.

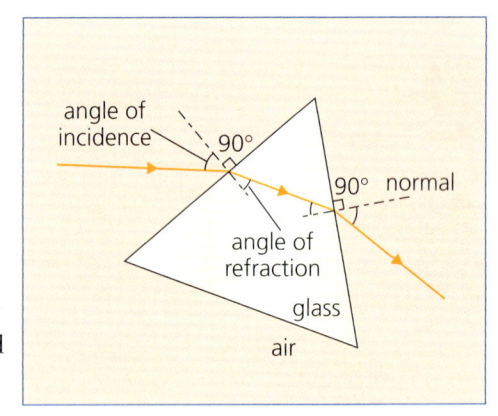

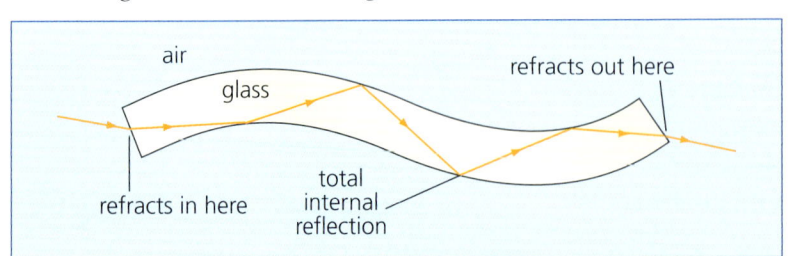

Lenses use refraction to make images. Parallel light rays entering a lens are focussed to a point. Cameras and eyes have a light-sensitive surface at the focus point.

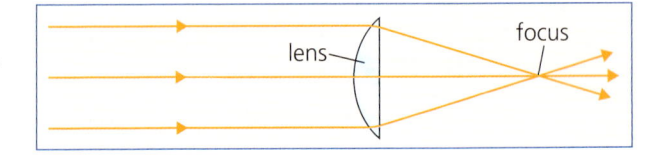

Diffraction

Light is **diffracted** when it goes through a gap which is small enough. The light emerges from the gap with a range of directions. The light is diffracted more as the size of the gap is reduced.

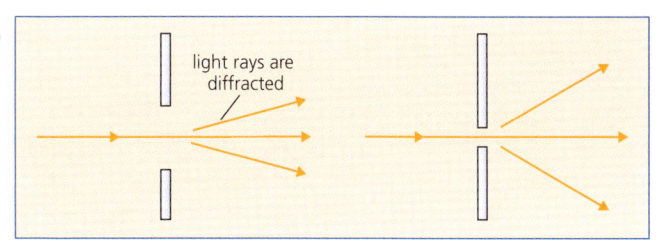

Doctors use **endoscopes** to look inside your stomach. A bundle of optical fibres carries light into the stomach. Another bundle carries the image of the reflected light so that it can be seen by the doctor.

Glass prisms can make perfect mirrors. Light will totally internally reflect off the long face. A **periscope** uses two 45° prisms to form an image of an object which you can't see directly.

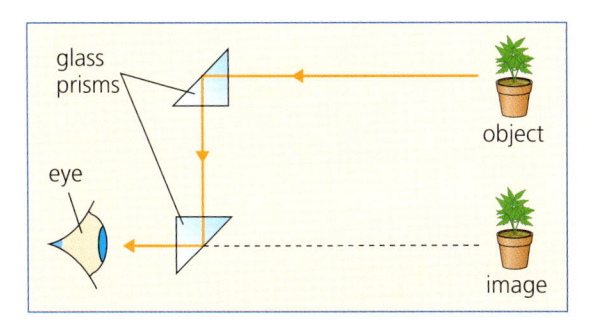

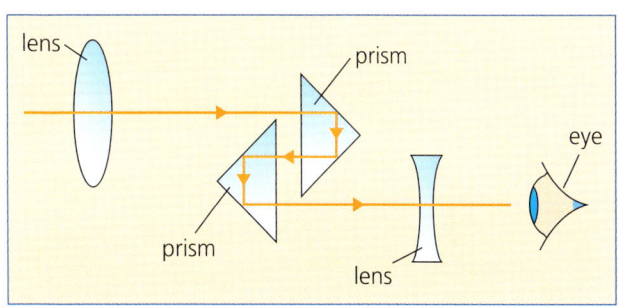

Binoculars use total internal reflection in two prisms to shorten the distance between the two lenses. Although the light is reflected four times, none of it is lost.

Bicycle reflectors use an array of small prisms to totally internally reflect light which hits them. The light reflects twice from each prism and ends up going backwards.

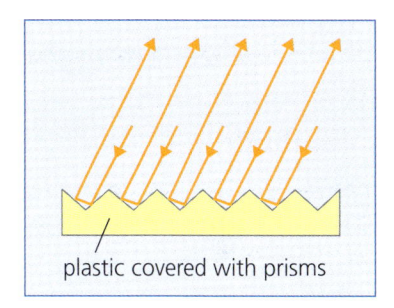

Questions

1. What are the values for the angles of incidence and reflection for these rays of light?

2. What are the values of the angles of incidence and refraction for this ray of light?

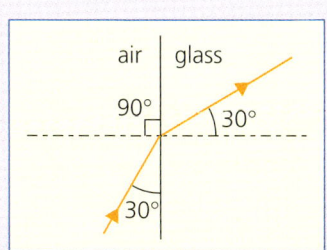

3. Draw a diagram to show how light gets from one end of an optical fibre to another.
4. Describe **two** uses of optical fibres.
5. Describe **three** uses of prisms to reflect light.

Waves in action

Ultrasound

The highest frequency sound that humans can hear is about 20 000 Hz (or 20 kHz). Sound with higher frequency than 20 kHz is called **ultrasound**. It is very useful. For example, ultrasound is used in industry to clean small objects such as rings. The object is suspended in water and ultrasound vibrates the dirt loose.

Ships use **pulses** of ultrasound to detect what is underneath them. Each pulse **reflects** off solid objects in the water. A special microphone under the ship listens for these **echoes**. The time delay between the pulse and its echo is used to calculate the distance to the solid reflector.

Sound travels at 1500 m/s in water. So a time delay of 0.1 s means that the pulse travelled $1500 \times 0.1 = 150$ m. The reflector must therefore be $\frac{1}{2} \times 150 = 75$ m below the ship.

Ultrasound can also be used to look inside the human body without the need for surgery. Pulses of ultrasound are fed in through the skin. Each time a pulse passes from one organ into another, some of it is reflected back to the skin.

These echoes can be used to form a picture of what lies under the skin. Ultrasound is often used to scan babies before they are born.

Kidney stones can be shaken into small pieces by ultrasound. This avoids the need for surgery which would involve cutting the patient open to remove the stones.

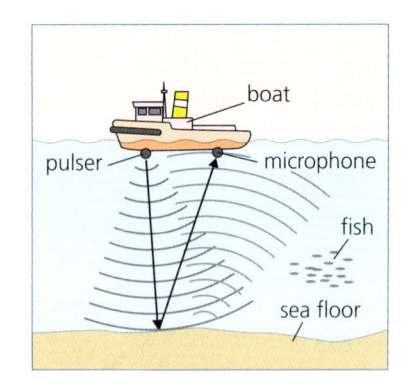

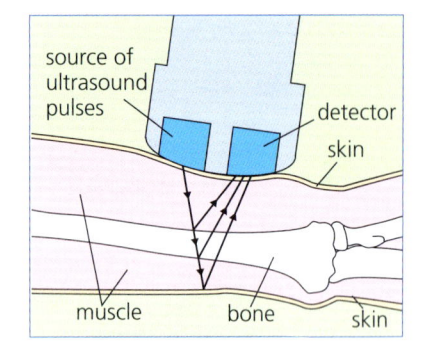

Seismic waves

Earthquakes produce two different low-frequency waves which travel through the Earth:

- **p-waves** are longitudinal and can therefore travel through both solids and liquids
- **s-waves** are transverse and can therefore only travel through solids.

The Earth has a liquid core which s-waves cannot pass through. The size of this core can be found by finding those places which receive only p-waves from an earthquake.

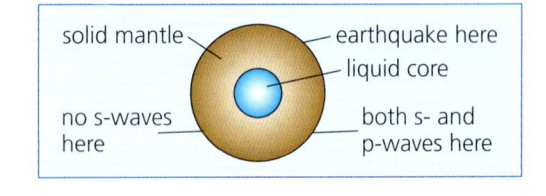

Questions

1. Describe the differences between s-waves and p-waves.
2. Here are the frequencies of five different sound waves. List them in order of increasing frequency. Which of them will be ultrasound?

    12 000 Hz   24 kHz   47 Hz   50 000 Hz   900 Hz

3. A submarine sends out pulses of ultrasound. Echoes arrive back 0.05 s after each pulse. Sound in water has a speed of 1500 m/s. How far away is the source of the echoes?
4. Describe a use of ultrasound in medicine.

Electromagnetic waves

The **electromagnetic spectrum** is a family of waves which can pass through empty space at the colossal speed of 300 000 000 m/s.

We use electromagnetic waves in many different ways. The energy delivered by an electromagnetic wave increases with decreasing wavelength.

Radio waves are used to carry information about sound (music and speech) as well as pictures (TV). Radio waves create alternating currents of electrons in electrical conductors.

Microwaves can be made into beams by curved reflectors. As well as being used to communicate with satellites in space, pulsed microwaves are used to detect aircraft and ships. Microwaves with one particular wavelength are strongly absorbed by water and can be used to heat up food.

Infra-red waves carry heat energy. They are emitted by hot objects, such as the Sun. They can also carry information down optical fibres and allow hand-held remote controls to communicate with TVs and video recorders. Infra-red waves can set whole atoms and molecules vibrating.

Ultraviolet waves damage living cells and can cause skin cancer. Dark skin will absorb ultraviolet waves and protect the living cells underneath. Ultraviolet waves can damage living cells and knock electrons out of metals.

X-rays pass through flesh but are strongly absorbed by bone. They allow photographs to be made of the inside of the body. X-rays also kill living cells and can cause cancer.

Gamma rays can pass through steel and concrete. They are very dangerous, but can be used to destroy cancer cells. Gamma rays are emitted by radioactive atoms. A short-lived radioactive substance can act as a tracer when it is injected into someone – the gamma rays emitted by the tracer can be picked up outside the body, showing the passage of the tracer through the person.

Gamma rays from a source outside the body are used to treat cancer. The rays are focussed on the tumour, and the source is rotated around the body. This means that the tumour is damaged more than the rest of the body, so that its cells die.

X-rays and gamma-rays can knock electrons out of atoms and kill living cells.

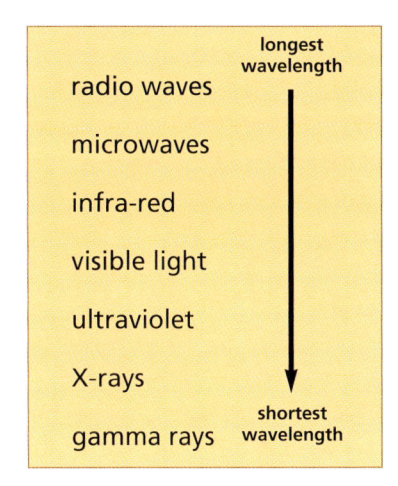

radio waves	longest wavelength
microwaves	
infra-red	
visible light	
ultraviolet	
X-rays	
gamma rays	shortest wavelength

Questions

1 Write down the seven parts of the electromagnetic spectrum in order of increasing wavelength.

Energy in the home

Heat energy transfer

A kettle is boiled and then left. The graph shows how its temperature changes with time. The kettle eventually settles to 20°C, the same temperature as the room.

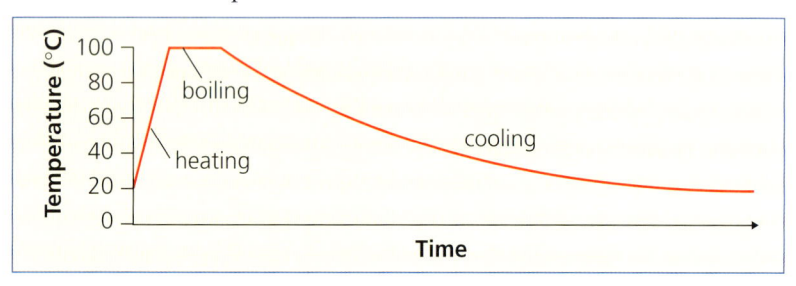

Heat energy flows from the hot kettle to the cold room until they are both at the same temperature.

There are three ways in which the kettle loses its heat energy:
- by **conduction** through the base into the table
- by **convection** as hot air rises from the sides
- by **radiation** as infra-red waves carry energy away.

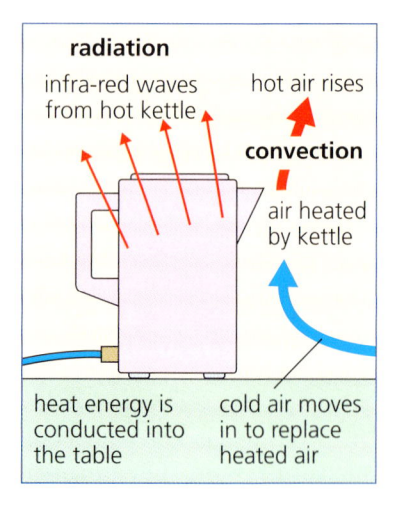

Conduction

The **heat energy** of the kettle is just the **kinetic energy** of its particles. The particles in the solid kettle walls are always moving. They **vibrate**.

When one end of a solid is hotter than the other, the motion of the particles passes kinetic energy from the hot end to the cold end. The heat energy is **conducted**.

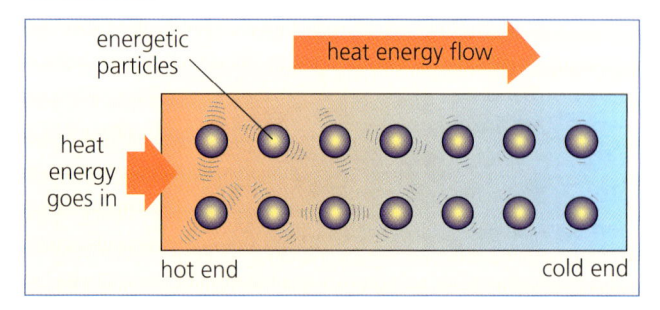

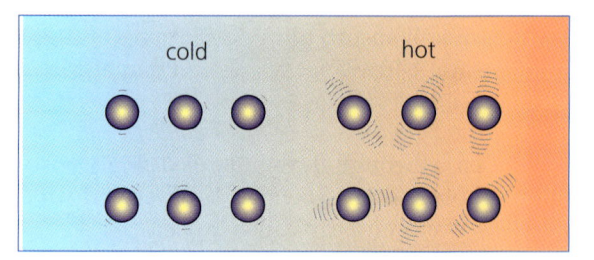

Convection

Air particles which hit the hot surface of the kettle gain extra kinetic energy. So the air around the kettle heats up. This makes the air expand and rise up, carrying the extra heat energy with it. The heat energy is **convected** upwards.

Convection currents are set up around the kettle. There is a flow of cool air towards the kettle to replace the warm air moving upwards.

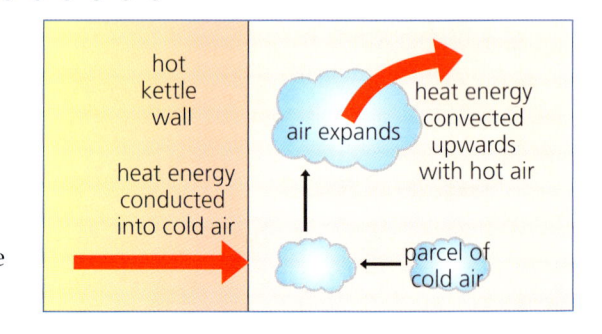

Radiation

Like all hot objects, the surface of the kettle emits infra-red **radiation**. Black surfaces are much better at radiating heat than shiny ones. So a shiny kettle will lose heat energy less rapidly than a coloured one. Infra-red radiation can travel through a vacuum (empty space).

- a microwave oven uses **microwave** radiation to inject energy deep inside food. The heat has to conduct *out* from the centre to cook the outside.
- an electric or gas oven uses infra-red radiation to get energy to the surface of food. The inside is cooked by heat which is conducted *in* from the outside.

- **Shiny** objects reflect infra-red rays, so they heat up slowly.
- **Black** objects absorb infra-red rays, so they heat up quickly.

Insulation

Heat energy lost by conduction from a house can be reduced by trapping air in:

- layers of fluffy material in the roof
- cavities in the outside walls
- double glazing in the windows.

Heat energy lost by radiation from a house can be reduced by:

- painting roofs and walls shiny white
- using window glass which does not transmit infra-red radiation.

Heat energy lost by convection from a house can be reduced by:

- sheltering it from the wind
- keeping the surface area small.

Questions

1. A mug of coffee at 40 °C is placed in a freezer at −20 °C. State the final temperature of the mug. State the three ways in which heat energy leaves the mug.
2. Copy and complete the following sentences.
   Particles in a solid have _____ energy which makes them _____.
   Particles in a hot solid have more _____ than particles in a cold solid.
   The process of heat transfer through a solid is called _____ .
3. The cooling element inside a fridge is always at the top. What happens to the air particles when they hit the element? Describe and explain the convection currents inside the fridge.
4. Copy and complete the following sentences with the words GOOD or BAD.
   Silver objects are _____ radiators and _____ absorbers of heat radiation.
   Black objects are _____ radiators and _____ absorbers of heat radiation.
5. What happens to the energy of the particles in a liquid as it cools?
6. Describe and explain how the rate of heat loss from a house can be reduced.

Energy in the home

Space heating

There are two main ways of heating a home. You can either use electricity or you can burn a fuel, such as wood, coal, oil or gas. The heat from the fuel is usually carried to each room in the home by hot water in pipes or by hot air in ducts.

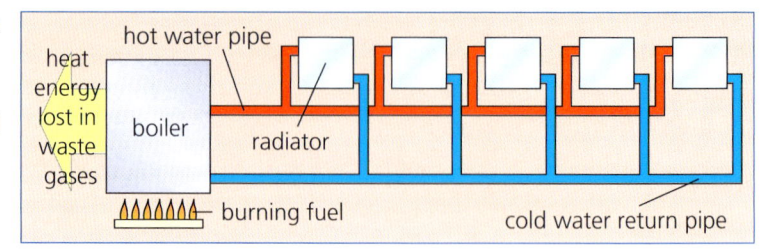

Electricity is dangerous, and the cables needed to get it to your house are expensive to install. You can also get power cuts!

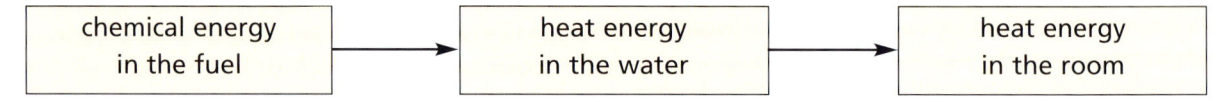

chemical energy in the fuel → heat energy in the water → heat energy in the room

Installing the pipes or ducts is expensive. It is often cheaper to put an electrical heater in each room instead. This also avoids using chimneys to vent the smoke and gases from the burnt fuel. The waste gases from the burnt fuel can **pollute** the environment.

However, making electricity often causes pollution, though it is easier to control this at the power station. Electricity is also expensive.

Sources of electricity

Coal, oil and gas are **fossil fuels**. They are **non-renewable** sources of energy, particularly for making electricity. They will eventually be used up, and people are learning to use **renewable** sources, which use energy from the Sun. Energy is continually arriving from the Sun in the form of heat and light radiation.

Renewable sources of electricity include:

- **solar** energy, using solar cells to make electricity directly
- **wind** energy, caused by the heating of air by the Sun. Winds are convection currents, carrying cool air towards hot places
- **wave** energy, transferred to the oceans from the wind
- **plants**, which use **photosynthesis** to convert light energy into chemical energy
- **hydroelectric** energy, using rainwater which has fallen on mountains. The Sun evaporates the water from the sea and the wind carries the damp air above the mountains. As the air rises, it cools and the water turns to rain. The water is stored behind a dam. The stored water flows through a turbine to generate electricity.

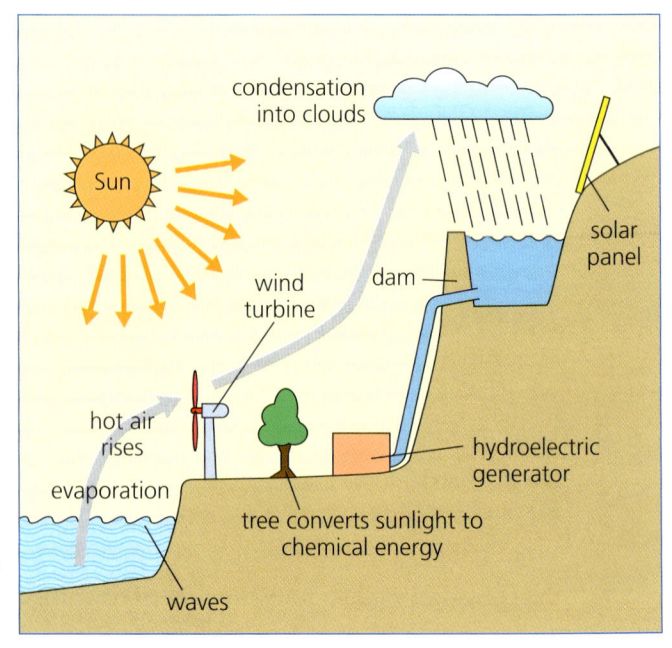

Insulation

It can be expensive to keep a building at a comfortable temperature. The only free energy is that which comes directly from the Sun. It pays to build houses which are **insulated**. Although you have to pay for the insulation, it can usually be paid for out of the saving made on buying energy to keep the house warm.

Insulators and conductors

A material which is used to cut down the flow of heat energy is called an **insulator**. Most insulators contain a lot of air. Air is a poor conductor so it makes a good insulator when it is trapped. Clothes, curtains and double glazing all use trapped air to cut down heat energy loss.

Metals are good **conductors**. Heat energy flows quickly through them. They feel cold to the touch. Insulators feel warm.

Off-peak electricity

Electricity is produced by most power stations all of the time, night and day. The cheapest way of generating electricity is to keep producing it at a constant rate. However, there isn't much demand for electricity at night when most people are asleep. So electricity producers charge less for electricity at these **off-peak** times, to encourage people to use it. (Electricity is impossible to store directly, even for a few seconds.)

Automatic timers are used to switch on electrical devices at off-peak times, saving the consumer a lot of money. Cheap off-peak electricity can be used to:

- run storage heaters which heat bricks up at night and release their heat energy to air passed over them during the day
- operate washing machines and dishwashers overnight
- heat water overnight to be used during the next day.

Worked example

Q It costs £5000 to double glaze all of the windows in a house. This cuts the annual heating bill from £750 to £500. How many years will it take before the double glazing pays for itself?

A Money saved in a year = £750 − £500
= £250
therefore pay-back time
= $\frac{5000}{250}$ = 20 years

Questions

1. Draw an energy flow diagram to show how the energy in gas can become heat energy in a room using hot air ducts.
2. Give **two** good reasons why electrical heaters should be used.
3. Give **one** good reason why fuels are better for heating than electricity.
4. Name **three** non-renewable fuels for heating homes. State **two** reasons why it might be better to use electricity instead.
5. Name **one** renewable source of energy for heating a home.
6. Describe **five** renewable sources of electricity.
7. The annual cost of heating a house drops from £800 to £600 when £1000 is spent on insulating the roof and walls. Calculate the pay-back time.
8. Copy and complete the following sentences.
   Wool is an _____ because it contains trapped _____ . Copper is a _____ because it is a _____ .

Energy in the home

Using electricity

Every electrical appliance should be marked with its **voltage** and **power rating**. The voltage rating is usually 230 V in Europe. The power is measured in **watts** (**W**) or **kilowatts** (**kW**).

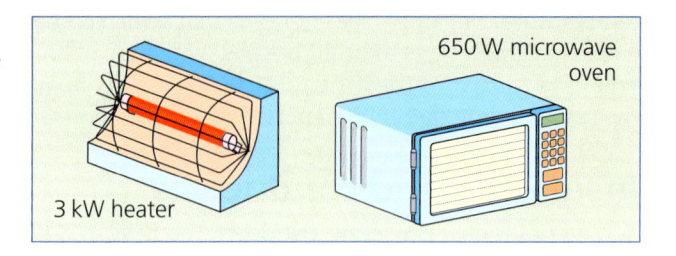

1 kW = 1000 W

650 W microwave oven

3 kW heater

Calculating the cost

The power rating of an appliance can be used to calculate how much electrical energy it will need when it is switched on.

energy (kilowatt-hour) = **power** (kilowatt) × **time** (hour)

One kilowatt-hour (kWh) of energy is called a **unit** of electricity. It costs about 10p. Off-peak electricity at night costs less.

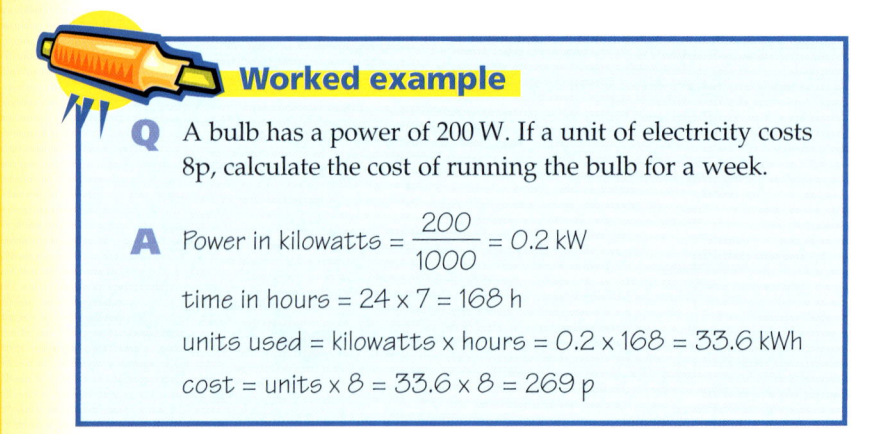

Worked example

Q A bulb has a power of 200 W. If a unit of electricity costs 8p, calculate the cost of running the bulb for a week.

A Power in kilowatts = $\frac{200}{1000}$ = 0.2 kW

time in hours = 24 × 7 = 168 h

units used = kilowatts × hours = 0.2 × 168 = 33.6 kWh

cost = units × 8 = 33.6 × 8 = 269 p

Electrical wiring

Electric currents in metals make them get hot. Thin, high-**resistance** wires get hotter than thick, low-resistance ones. Electrical appliances are connected to the 230 V mains supply by a pair of insulated metal wires. They are called **live** and **neutral**.

If the appliance has a metal exterior, there will be a third **earth** wire as well.

Each wire has a different coloured insulation.

Wire	Insulation colour
live	brown
neutral	blue
earth	green and yellow

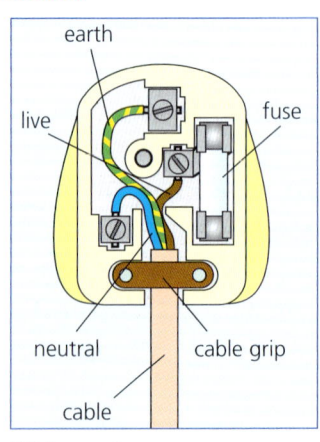

Wiring a plug

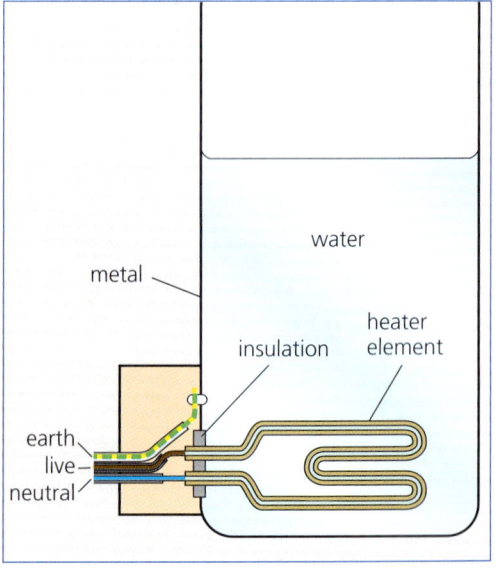

Electrical connections to a kettle

The live wire carries the energy from the supply to the appliance. The live wire is therefore the one which is most dangerous to touch, so it has the **switch**. The neutral wire completes the circuit for the electric current.

Fuses and safety

There should also be a **fuse** or **circuit breaker** in the live wire. This switches off the current automatically if it gets too high.

Large currents in a wire can cause it to get hot and damage its insulation. The fuse is the thinnest wire in the circuit, so it melts (blows) first, before the other wires are damaged.

The earth wire should always be connected to the metal outside of an appliance. This protects anyone using the appliance. If the live wire comes loose and touches the outside, a large current flows in the earth wire and the fuse blows.

Appliances which are **double insulated** do not need an earth wire. Should the live wire come loose, it can't touch any metal which is on the outside of the appliance. Any appliance which has a non-metallic case is definitely double insulated and doesn't need an earth wire.

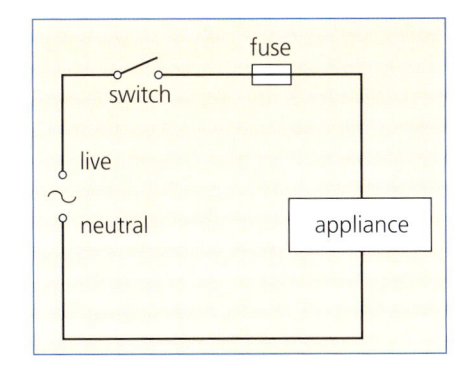

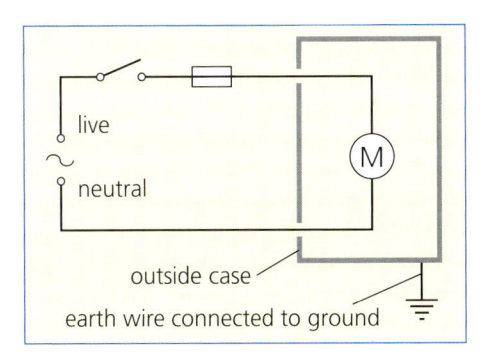

Questions

1. A TV is rated at 230 V, 150 W. If a unit of electricity costs 9p, calculate how much it costs to run the TV for 5 hours.
2. If an off-peak unit of electricity costs 6p, calculate how much it costs to run a 2.5 kW water heater for 4 hours at night.
3. Suppose a unit of electricity costs 8p. How much money do you waste by leaving a 100 W bulb on for 10 minutes?
4. Name the three wires connecting an electrical heater to the mains supply. State the colour of their insulation.
5. Explain why the wire in the heating element of a water heater is much thinner than the wire in the cable connecting the heater to the mains supply.
6. State the function of each of the three wires connecting an appliance to the mains electricity supply.
7. Explain how a fuse or circuit breaker protects the insulation of mains wires.
8. Explain how a fuse can protect people from electric shock.
9. Where should the fuse and switch be connected?
10. What type of appliance does not need an earth wire?
11. Where should the earth wire be connected to an appliance? Why?

Forces and motion

Measuring motion

Joe's car has a top speed of 35 metres per second (m/s). This means that it can move forwards 35 metres in each second, or 70 metres in two seconds.

The following formula can be used to calculate a speed if you know the distance and the time.

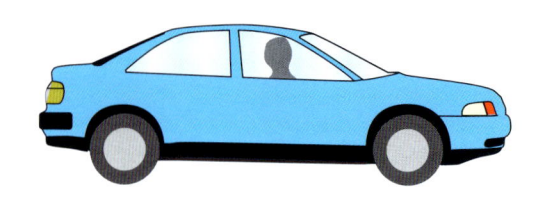

$$\text{speed} = \frac{\text{distance}}{\text{time}}$$

$$v = \frac{s}{t}$$

Symbol	Meaning	Units of measurement
v	speed	metres per second or m/s
s	distance	metres or m
t	time	seconds or s

You must know this one by heart!

(v is for velocity, a word which can mean speed. s is for space, another word for distance. It is easy to get confused – don't!)

Worked example

Q A car at 30 m.p.h. travels 1.2 km in a minute. Calculate its speed in metres per second.

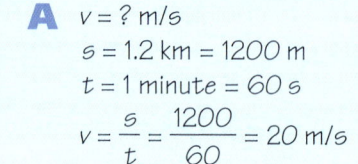

A $v = ?$ m/s
$s = 1.2$ km $= 1200$ m
$t = 1$ minute $= 60$ s
$$v = \frac{s}{t} = \frac{1200}{60} = 20 \text{ m/s}$$

Always make sure that you have the distance and the time in the correct units before you calculate the speed!

Worked example

Q How far will a car with a speed of 15 m/s go in 10 minutes?

A $v = 15$ m/s
$s = ?$ m
$t = 600$ s

$$v = \frac{s}{t}$$

$s = vt$ $? = 15 \times 600 = 9000$ m

List the data ... write the formula ... draw the triangle ... change the formula ... insert the data.

Distance–time graphs

Distance–time graphs are a very good way of describing motion.

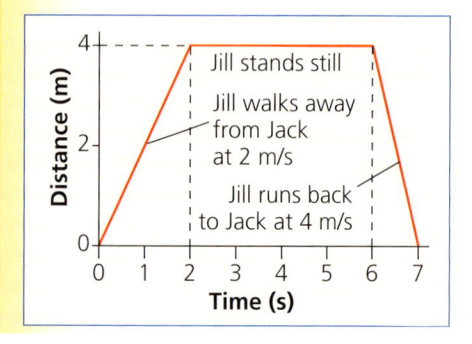

Jill stands still
Jill walks away from Jack at 2 m/s
Jill runs back to Jack at 4 m/s

Speed–time graphs

Here are distance–time and speed–time graphs for Paul. He walks away slowly, stops for a while and then runs away quickly.

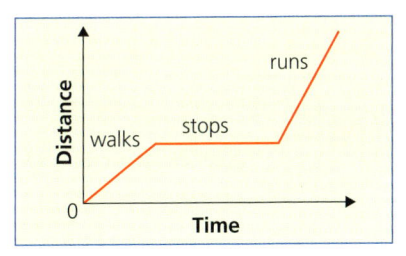

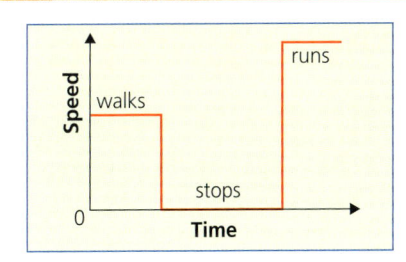

Here is a speed–time graph for Jake as he goes from rest to top speed on his bike.

The distance travelled is equal to the area under the line. The area is triangular in shape, with a base of 10 s and a height of 12 m/s.

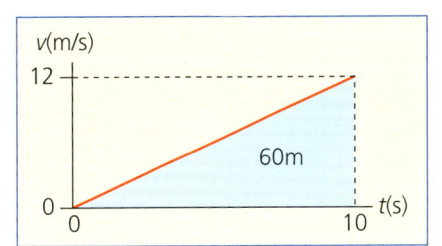

distance = ½ base × height = 0.5 × 10 × 12 = 60 m

Questions

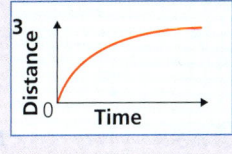

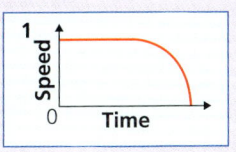

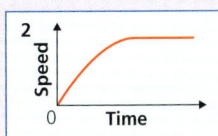

1. Write down the symbols, units and formula for speed, distance and time.
2. A car travels 400 m in 20 s. Calculate its speed.
3. Bill can walk 0.5 km in 5 minutes. How fast can he walk?
4. A plane has a speed of 50 m/s. How far will it go in a minute?
5. A cheetah runs at 20 m/s. How long will it take to run 100 m?
6. Here are three different distance–time graphs. Match each one with a sentence from this list.
   a. Going away then coming back again.
   b. Starting off quickly and slowing to a halt.
   c. Moving at a steady speed.
   d. Moving away faster and faster.
7. Here are three speed–time graphs. Match each one with a sentence from this list.
   a. Speeding up to a steady speed.
   b. Moving at a steady speed.
   c. Moving at a steady speed and then slowing to a halt.
8. Use the speed–time graph to calculate the distance travelled between
   a. 0 s and 5 s
   b. 5 s and 15 s
   c. 15 s and 25 s. 
9. Use the distance–time graph to calculate the speed at
   a. 5 s
   b. 15 s
   c. 25 s.

Forces and motion

Speeding up and slowing down

Here is the speed–time graph for a bike which is **accelerating**.

Its speed increases as time goes on. The speed increases from 4 m/s to 10 m/s, a change of 6 m/s. This takes a time of 3 s. So the speed changes by 2 m/s each second.

The bike accelerates at **2 m/s² (metres per second squared)**.

Here is the formula for calculating acceleration.

$$\text{acceleration} = \frac{\text{change of speed}}{\text{time taken}}$$

You need to know this one by heart!

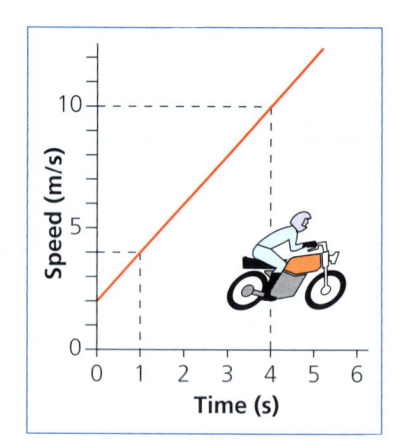

Friction

Jo pedals her bike along a level road. She stops pedalling. The force of **friction** slows her down until she stops. The friction comes from

- the air in front of the bike, which is pushed aside
- the contact between the tyres and the road
- the moving parts of the bike rubbing past each other.

The acceleration of the bike depends on the size of Jo's **thrust** compared with the friction.

Forces on the bike	Motion of the bike
thrust greater than friction	speed increases
thrust and friction the same	speed doesn't change
thrust smaller than friction	speed decreases

Mass and acceleration

The acceleration of any object depends on the overall (**resultant**) force and the mass.

force = mass × acceleration   F = ma

Symbol	Meaning	Units of measurement
F	force	newtons or N
m	mass	kilograms or kg
a	acceleration	metres per second squared or m/s²

You need to know this one by heart!

Worked example

Q A car has a mass of 800 kg. If the thrust is 600 N and the friction is 200 N, what is the acceleration of the car?

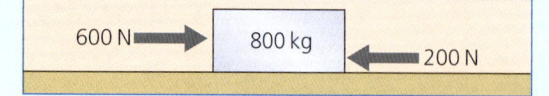

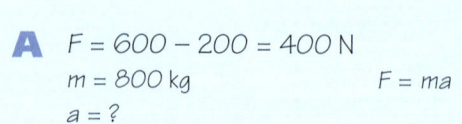

600 N → 800 kg ← 200 N

A F = 600 − 200 = 400 N
m = 800 kg
a = ?
F = ma

$$a = \frac{F}{m} \quad ? = \frac{400}{800} = 0.5 \text{ m/s}^2$$

Road safety

Sam is driving along the road at a steady speed. He notices that there is a tree across the road. He puts on the brakes and stops. Here are speed–time and distance–time graphs for the car as it slows down.

The **thinking distance** is how far the car travels between Sam noticing the tree and the brakes starting to slow down the car.

It will increase if

- Sam is not concentrating, or is tired or ill
- Sam is driving too fast or there is poor visibility
- Sam has been drinking alcohol or using drugs.

The **braking distance** is how far the car travels once the brakes have started to slow it down. It will increase if

- the brakes are not adjusted correctly
- the road surface is wet or loose
- the tyres are inflated incorrectly or don't have enough tread
- the car is travelling too fast.

stopping distance = thinking distance + braking distance

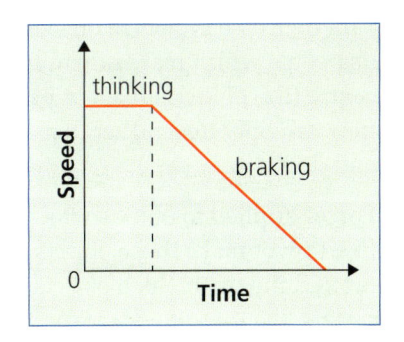

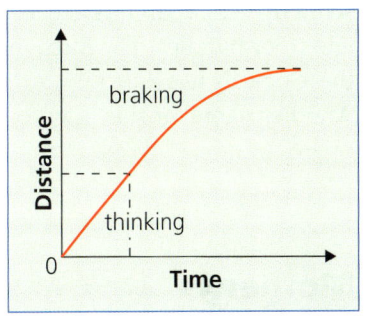

Questions

1. Write down the formula for calculating acceleration. What are the units of acceleration?
2. A plane takes 4 s to get from a speed of 5 m/s to 45 m/s. Calculate its acceleration.
3. A car accelerates at 5 m/s^2. How long will it take to get from rest to a speed of 30 m/s?
4. A car at 20 m/s slows with an acceleration of –2 m/s^2. How fast will it be going after 5 s?
5. State the sources of friction on a moving car.
6. Describe the motion of these objects:

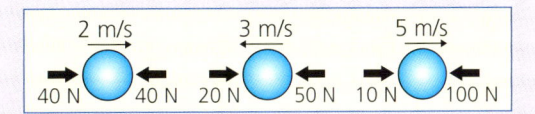

   2 m/s   3 m/s   5 m/s
   40 N 40 N   20 N 50 N   10 N 100 N

7. A 1000 kg car accelerates at –6 m/s^2 when the brakes are on. Calculate the force needed.
8. A rocket has a mass of 5000 kg and a weight of 50 000 N. It accelerates upwards at 3 m/s^2. Calculate the upwards thrust from its engines.
9. The thrust on a 600 kg car is 1500 N. Calculate its acceleration when the friction is 300 N.
10. Explain what the thinking distance is. State what will increase its value.
11. Explain what the braking distance is. State what will increase its value.
12. Thinking time is 0.7 s. Calculate the thinking distance for a car moving at 30 m/s (70 m.p.h.).
13. The acceleration of a car during braking is –6 m/s^2. For a car moving initially at 30 m/s, calculate
    a. the braking time   b. the braking distance.
14. Repeat 12 and 13 for a car moving initially at 15 m/s.

Turning forces

Sam owns a bicycle. He pushes *down* on its pedals which makes them *turn*. Their centre (the **pivot**) is fixed in place, so they can only turn rather than move up and down.

Forces applied to objects which have a fixed pivot make those objects turn around the pivot. Such objects include pedals, the tops of water taps, screwdrivers, spanners, steering wheels and door handles. The force that turns these objects has a **turning effect**. Another name for this is a **moment**.

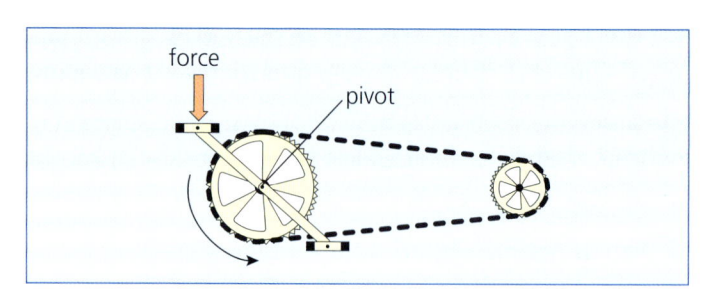

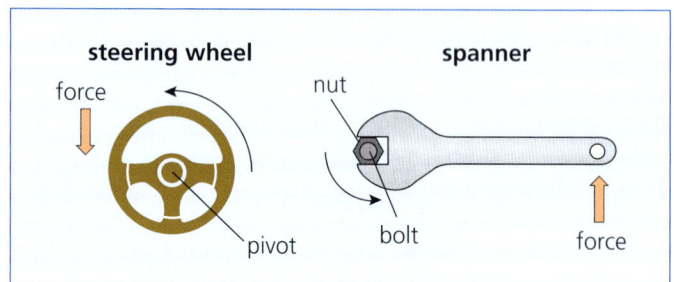

Moments

Sam uses his spanner to undo a nut. He applies a force of 30 N at a point on the handle which is 0.2 m from the pivot. He exerts a **moment** of 30 N × 0.2 m = 6 Nm to the nut.

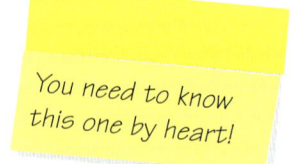

You need to know this one by heart!

> **moment = force × perpendicular distance from point of the force to pivot**

Sam is worried about breaking the thread on the bolt. He can reduce the size of the moment by:

- reducing the force on the handle
- applying the force closer to the pivot, i.e. reducing the distance from the force to the pivot.

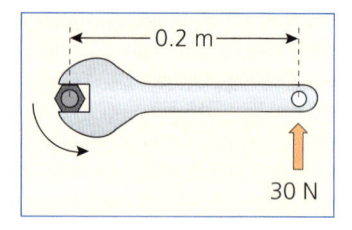

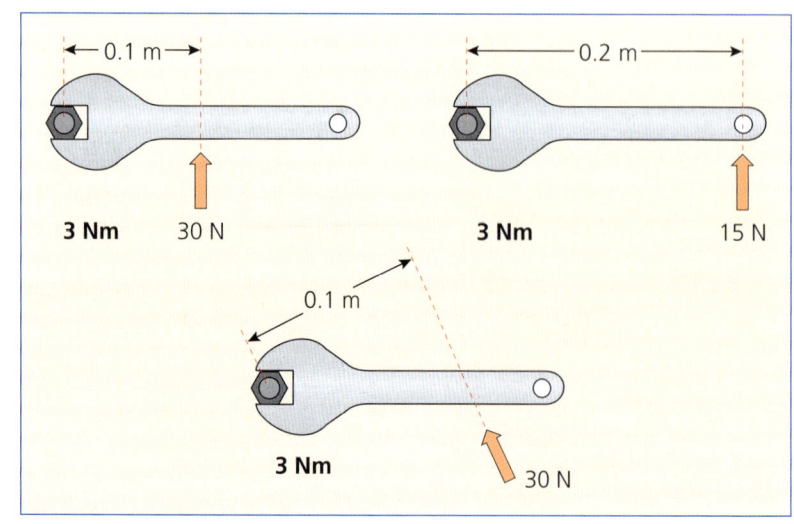

Questions

1. Give **five** examples of forces being used to turn things.
2. State the rule for calculating a moment.
3. A force of 12 N is applied at right angles to a lever, 0.5 m from the pivot. Calculate the moment of this force.
4. State **two** ways of making the moment of question 3 bigger.

Balancing levers

Sam and Jo are sitting on a plank of wood. The centre of the plank is a pivot. Jo weighs less than Sam, so she needs to sit further from the pivot to make the plank balance.

Sam provides a **clockwise moment** of 800 N × 3 m = 2400 Nm.

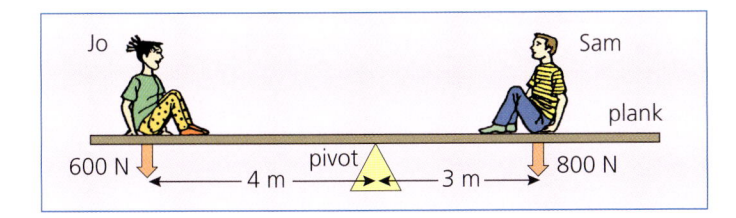

Jo must provide an **anticlockwise moment** of 2400 Nm for the plank to balance. Her weight is 600 N, so she must sit 4 m from the pivot (600 × 4 = 2400).

For a balanced lever:

> **sum of clockwise moments = sum of anticlockwise moments**

Sue pushes up on Sam's end of the plank with a force of 200 N, at a distance of 4 m from the pivot. This adds an extra anticlockwise moment of 200 × 4 = 800 Nm. The **total** clockwise moment must now be 2400 Nm for balance. Sam has to move to 4 m from the pivot (800 N × 4 m = 3200 Nm)!

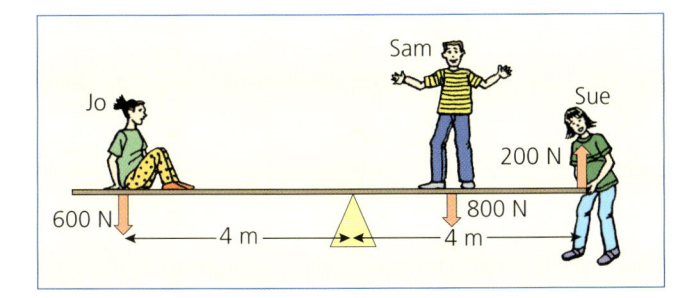

Questions

1 Calculate the values of x required for balance.

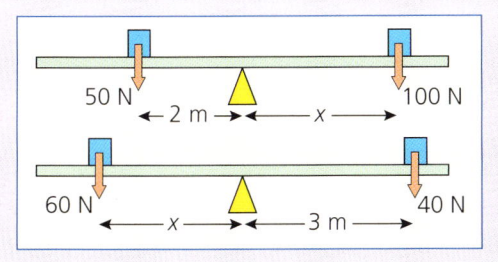

Physical processes

Concept map

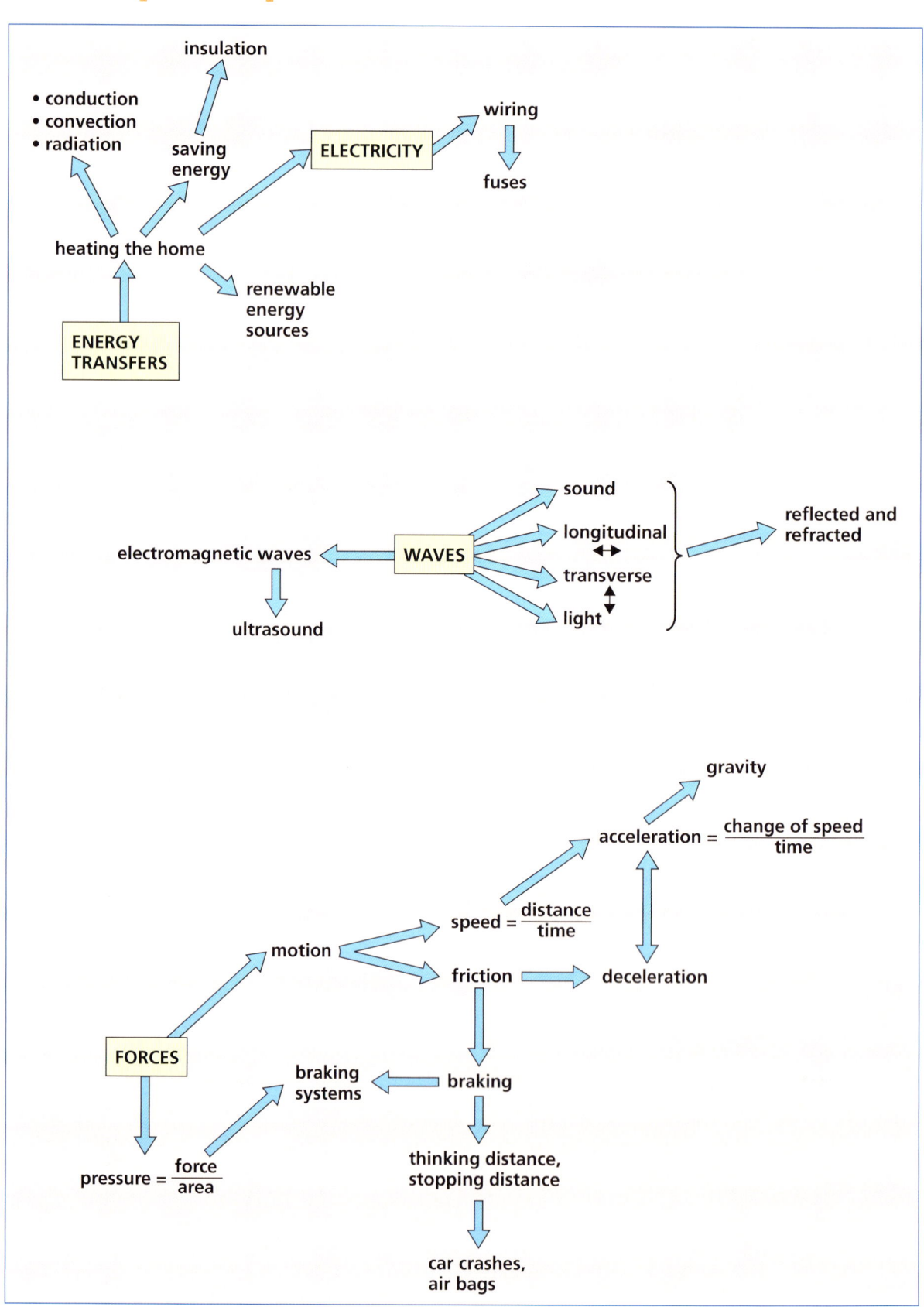

- conduction
- convection
- radiation

insulation

saving energy → **ELECTRICITY** → wiring → fuses

heating the home

renewable energy sources

ENERGY TRANSFERS

WAVES:
- sound
- longitudinal ↔
- transverse ↕
- light

electromagnetic waves → ultrasound

longitudinal, transverse, light → reflected and refracted

FORCES → motion
- speed = distance / time
- acceleration = change of speed / time → gravity
- friction → deceleration
- friction → braking → thinking distance, stopping distance → car crashes, air bags
- braking systems

pressure = force / area

Exam questions

1 Tom sends a wave to Jill along a rope. Look at the diagram.

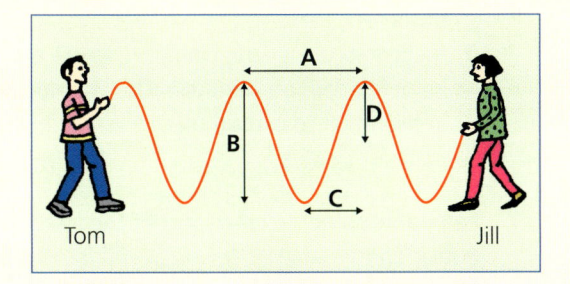

a i State the type of wave. Explain how you can tell. [2]
  ii Which letter shows the wavelength of the wave? [1]
  iii Tom moves his hand up and down six times in two seconds. Calculate the frequency of the wave. [2]
  iv The wavelength is 0.5 m. Calculate the speed of the wave. [2]
b Jill uses two paper cups to send a different wave along the rope. Look at the diagram.

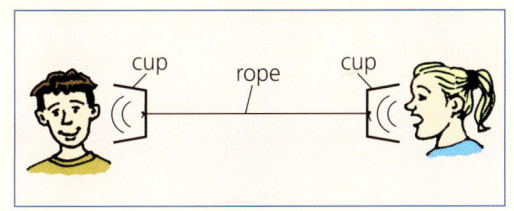

Jill speaks into her cup. Explain why Tom hears a sound from his cup. [3]

[10 marks]

2 Sanjay shines his torch on a mirror. The light reflects off the mirror. Look at the diagram.

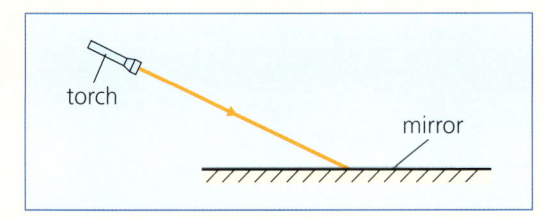

a Draw on the diagram the path taken by the ray. [1]
b Some reflected light reaches Susan. Susan sees an image of Sanjay's torch behind the mirror. Explain why she sees the image there. [2]

[3 marks]

3 a Here are the names of some waves:
   infra-red   microwaves   radio   ultrasound   X-rays
   Answer the following questions, choosing answers from the list.
   i Which wave is longitudinal? [1]
   ii Which wave has the longest wavelength? [1]
   iii Which wave can cause cancer? [1]
   iv Which wave can detect airplanes? [1]
   v Two of the waves can be used to find broken bones. Which two? [2]
b Infra-red can pass down optical fibres.
   i Describe what happens to a ray of infra-red as it passes from air into glass? [2]
   ii Describe what happens to a ray of infra-red when it hits the side of the fibre. [1]

[9 marks]

4 Freddie spends £100 a month to keep her house warm. Look at the table.

How the heat escapes	Value
through the windows	£10
through the floor	£15
through the roof	£25
through the walls	£35
by draughts	£15

a The most heat escapes through the walls. Use your idea of particles to describe how the heat travels through a wall. [2]
b Freddie decides to save money by reducing heat lost through the roof.
   i What is the best insulating material to put in the loft? Choose from:
      brick   wood   fibre wool   steel   tile [1]
   ii Explain why the material you have chosen is a good insulator. [2]
c Freddie draughtproofs her house.
   i What could she could do to stop the draughts? [1]
   ii The cost of heat wasted through draughts is now only £5 a month. The draughtproofing cost £80. How long does it take for the money saved to pay for the draughtproofing? [2]

Exam questions

d Freddie wants to save even more money on her heating bills. Explain **two** ways in which she could do this. [4]

[12 marks]

5 Julie has five electrical appliances in her room. Look at the table.

Appliance	Power in kW
hair dryer	1.2
lamp	0.1
heater	2.0
TV	0.2
computer	0.4

a Julie turns on her computer for 3 hours.
  i Calculate how many units of electricity this uses, in kilowatt-hours. [1]
  ii Each unit of electricity costs 8p. Calculate how much it costs for Julie to run her computer. [1]
b The heater is connected to the mains supply by three wires. Complete the sentences below.
Electrical energy flows to the heater from the mains along the _____ wire. The _____ wire completes the electrical circuit. The _____ wire prevents Julie being electrocuted. [3]

[5 marks]

6 Melissa cycles along the road. Look at the graph below.

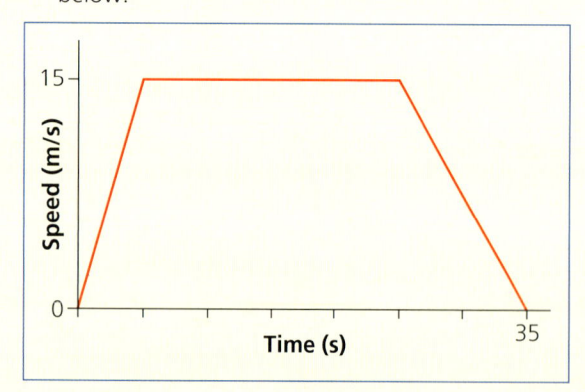

a Melissa starts off by accelerating.
  i Calculate her acceleration. [2]
  ii The overall pushing force on Melissa during acceleration is 180 N. Calculate Melissa's mass. [2]

b Melissa travels at a top speed of 15 m/s. Calculate how far she moves at that speed. [2]
c Melissa stops pedalling after 25 s. Explain why she stops moving at 35 s. Use your idea of forces. [3]
d Melissa wears a cycle helmet. This will protect her if she falls off her cycle. Use your idea of acceleration to explain this. [3]

[12 marks]

7 Pete takes some ice cream out of the freezer. He puts it on the table.
a What will happen to the temperature of the ice cream? [1]
b Energy is transferred by conduction through the ice cream. Use the idea of particles to explain how. [3]
c Pete wraps the ice cream in shiny foil. This keeps it cold for a long time. Explain how. [2]
d Suggest what else Pete could do to keep the ice cream on the table cold for a long time. Explain your answer. [2]
e The cooling unit of Pete's freezer is at the top. Suggest a reason why it is at the top. [1]

[9 marks]

8 The Highway Code states the distance required to stop an average car in good weather on a normal road. Look at the information.
For a typical driver at an initial speed of 30 m/s:
  thinking distance = 20 m
  braking distance = 85 m
  stopping distance = 105 m
a i Explain what is meant by thinking distance. [1]
  ii Use the information to calculate the thinking time of a typical driver. [2]
  iii State two things which could increase the thinking distance. [2]
b A car initially travelling at 30 m/s takes 5.6 s to travel the braking distance.
  i Calculate the acceleration of the car as it is stopped. [3]
  ii The braking force on a typical car is 5000 N. Calculate the mass of a typical car. [3]

[11 marks]

Year 11

Life processes and living things

Variation, inheritance and evolution
The working plant
Health in the balance
Concept map
Exam questions

Materials and their properties

Carbon chemistry
Chemical economics
The Periodic Table
Concept map
Exam questions

Physical processes

Using electricity
Applications of physics
Earth, space and radiation
Concept map
Exam questions

Reproduction

Passing on characteristics

Characteristics are passed on from parents to offspring during reproduction. There are two different forms of reproduction:

- **asexual** – there is only one parent and the offspring are genetically identical to the parent
- **sexual** – there are two parents and the offspring are not genetically identical to either parent.

Chromosomes

Every cell nucleus contains **chromosomes** which carry all the information about our characteristics.

- Chromosomes are made of DNA.
- The DNA is divided into thousands of **genes** and each gene helps to control the way our bodies are formed. For example, one set of genes controls eye colour.
- Some of each parent's genes are passed on to the offspring enabling features to be passed from one generation to the next.
- Most body cells have the same number of chromosomes, although each species of plant or animal has a different number of chromosomes.
- Human body cells have 46 chromosomes, arranged in 23 pairs.
- Although each body cell contains a full set of genes, only some genes are used in each cell. For example, all cells contain the gene coding for the hormone insulin, but this gene is only switched on in the cells of the pancreas where insulin is produced.

Mitosis

In asexual reproduction, growth and repair, exact copies of the chromosomes are passed on. This is done by **mitosis**. The chromosomes in one cell are copied exactly and then one copy moves to each end (pole) of the cell. The cell divides into two, producing two genetically identical cells.

Meiosis

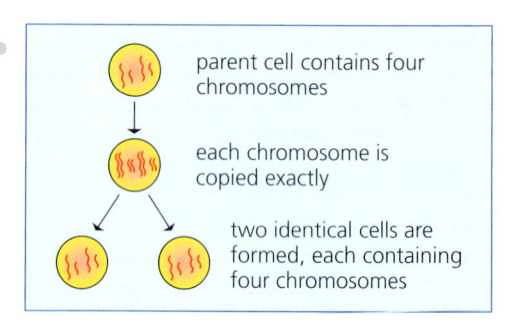

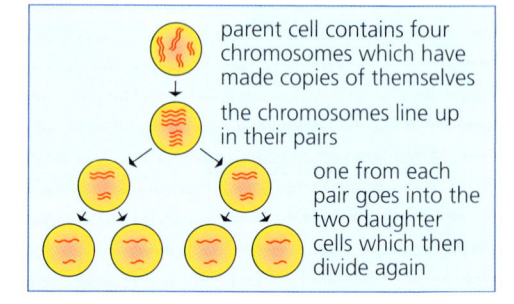

In sexual reproduction, gametes have half the usual number of chromosomes. Gametes are produced in the sex organs of the parents by **meiosis**. During meiosis, the chromosome number is halved. To do this, the chromosomes make exact copies of themselves and line up in their identical pairs. The pairs are then separated in the first stage forming two new cells. In the second stage each of the copies are separated to form two more cells. Therefore four cells are produced in total, each containing half of the original number of chromosomes. When male and female gametes join together at fertilisation the resulting zygote has a full set of chromosomes.

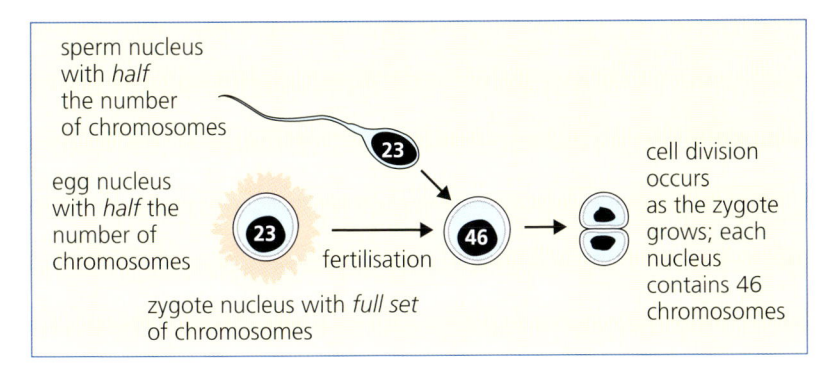

sperm nucleus with half the number of chromosomes

egg nucleus with half the number of chromosomes

fertilisation

zygote nucleus with full set of chromosomes

cell division occurs as the zygote grows; each nucleus contains 46 chromosomes

Variation

Not even identical twins are exactly the same. These differences between parents and their offspring and between people in a population are called **variation**. There are two types:

1. **genetic variation** such as differences in eye or hair colour which are characteristics controlled by the genes people have inherited from their parents
2. **environmental variation** such as differences in height or body mass, which are in part controlled by genetic factors, but are also controlled by environmental factors.

Intelligence, sporting ability and health appear to be a combination of genetic and environmental factors. A lot of discussion has failed to establish the relative importance of each component in determining the end product.

There are two sources of genetic variation.

- **fertilisation** – because the variation depends on which of your parents' genes were carried by the gametes that formed you
- **mutation** – sometimes there are changes (mutations) to the genetic code (genes) or to chromosomes. For example, some human eggs have 24 not 23 chromosomes and this gives rise to Down's syndrome in offspring formed from the egg.

Other mutations are caused by:

- chromosomes not being copied correctly in cells
- exposure to radiation
- exposure to certain chemicals.

> For example, a child's weight at birth is partly determined by genes but partly by its mother's health and age. Very hot sun can make fair skin brown and bleach brown hair. And, you can change your hair colour and shape with chemicals any time you like!

Questions

1. When plants or animals grow, their cells increase in number by mitosis. Why does this cell division use mitosis and not meiosis?
2. Make a table comparing mitosis and meiosis.

Variation, inheritance and evolution

Inheritance

How inheritance works

Many genes have several different versions, called **alleles**. For example, there are blue and brown alleles for eye colour. If you inherit a blue allele from each parent you will have blue eyes. However, if you inherit one blue allele and one brown allele you will not have stripy eyes, you will have brown eyes. This is because some alleles are stronger than others. Strong alleles are called **dominant** and weak alleles **recessive**. We show a dominant allele by a capital letter and a recessive one by a small letter.

The allele for brown eyes is dominant (**B**), the one for blue is recessive (**b**). If you inherit a **B** allele from one parent and a **b** allele from the other parent, you will have brown eyes because the brown allele is dominant.

If both the alleles are the same, **BB** or **bb**, the individual is said to be **homozygous**. If the alleles are different, **Bb**, the individual is called **heterozygous**. Dominant alleles are therefore expressed in a heterozygous individual.

The alleles you inherit are called your **genotype**. How you look because of these alleles is called your **phenotype**. A person with the phenotype of blue eyes can only have one genotype, **bb**. A person with the phenotype of brown eyes could have a genotype of **BB** or **Bb**. If you know the genotype of the parents, you can work out what their offspring are likely to be. For example, if one parent is **BB** for brown eyes and the other **bb** for blue eyes, we can work out the possible combinations of alleles with a diagram like this:

genetic diagram for cross of two parents homozygous for brown and blue eyes

gametes	B	B
b	Bb	Bb
b	Bb	Bb

all offspring have brown eyes

If one of these children has offspring with another **Bb** individual, the combination of offspring would be this:

Some diseases are caused by faulty genes inherited from the parents. Examples are sickle-cell anaemia, cystic fibrosis, muscular dystrophy and haemophilia. Many of these are caused by recessive alleles.

genetic diagram for cross of two parents heterozygous for brown eyes

gametes	B	b
B	BB	bB
b	Bb	bb

three brown-eyed, one blue-eyed offspring

gametes	F	f
F	FF	fF
f	Ff	ff

Both parents are heterozygous Ff.

Cystic fibrosis is controlled by the recessive allele f.

A child with homozygous ff will suffer from cystic fibrosis.

A child with heterozygous Ff will be a carrier like its parents.

A child with homozygous FF will not have the abnormal allele at all.

Working out the probabilities

The way a characteristic is inherited can be studied by breeding two individuals and observing the characteristics in their offspring. This is called a **monohybrid cross** because it only follows the inheritance of one characteristic. We can make predictions about the probable outcome of a monohybrid cross.

The probability of two heterozygous brown-eyed parents producing a blue-eyed child is 1 in 4, or 25%. This means that when they have a child there is a 25% chance that it will have blue eyes.

Inheritance of sex

One pair of chromosomes determines your sex. There are two types of sex chromosome: the **X chromosome** and the **Y chromosome**. Female gametes (eggs) have an X chromosome. Male gametes (sperm) have either an X or a Y chromosome. If two gametes with X chromosomes fuse, the offspring is female (XX). If one gamete carrying an X and one carrying a Y fuse, the offspring is male (XY).

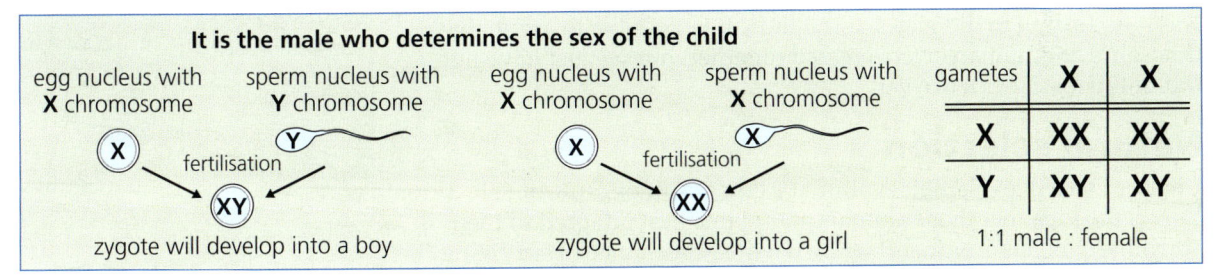

It is the male who determines the sex of the child

gametes	X	X
X	XX	XX
Y	XY	XY

1:1 male : female

Sex linkage

Some inherited human disorders, such as red-green colour blindness and haemophilia, are caused by a recessive allele which appears only on the X chromosome. These are called **sex-linked disorders**.

A female can carry a recessive allele on one of her X chromosomes without being affected. However, if a male has the allele on his X chromosome there is no corresponding allele on the paired Y chromosome, so he will have the disorder. For example, a normal-sighted woman carrying one allele for colour blindness (X^cX) and her unaffected husband (XY) can have a colour-blind son.

gametes	X	X^c
X	XX	X^cX
Y	XY	X^cY

X normal X chromosome
X^c chromosome with allele for colour blindness
Y normal Y chromosome

Questions

1. Explain what ratio of offspring would be expected from a cross between a blue-eyed parent and a heterozygous brown-eyed parent.

2. Tongue rolling is an inherited characteristic. The tongue-rolling allele is dominant (**T**). What ratio of tongue-rolling offspring would you expect from a heterozygous tongue-rolling mother and a non-rolling father?

3. Girls can be born colour blind, although this is rare. Draw a genetic diagram showing how a girl could inherit two recessive alleles for colour blindness.

Variation, inheritance and evolution

Natural selection and evolution

Animals and plants have gradually developed (**evolved**) from much simpler forms over many millions of years. This process is called **evolution**.

We only know about evolution from the fossils that have been found. **Fossils** are the remains of dead organisms which have become preserved in rock.

The fossil record

The fossil record shows that the variety of living things in the world today did not appear all at once many years ago. This happened very gradually over millions of years, with some things dying out while new ones evolved.

Dinosaurs existed until 65 million years ago, but we only know about them from fossils. Human beings are relative newcomers to the world, with our earliest ancestors making an appearance only 6 million years ago.

However, what we know about evolution from fossils is not the whole story. There are reasons for this:
- some body parts may not have fossilised
- fossilisation was a comparatively rare event
- we have not yet discovered all the fossils.

This means that what fossils show can be interpreted in different ways, according to the views at the time. It is possible to argue that dinosaurs and humans were created together, but we just have not found the fossil evidence yet!

Natural selection

Charles Darwin explained evolution as the result of **natural selection**. This is the idea that those animals and plants best adapted to their surroundings (environment) will have the best chance of surviving and reproducing.

The genes of animals and plants determine how well they are adapted to their surroundings. These genes can then be passed on to the next generation. So, over a very long time a population can become better adapted to its surroundings. This happens because some alleles become more common and some (the less desirable ones) become less common.

Charles Darwin's theory was based on:
- the presence of natural variation within a population
- the inheritance of some of the variations, the successful adaptations
- the fact that all organisms potentially over-reproduce and yet population numbers tend to remain fairly constant over long periods of time
- the fact that the best adapted individuals are more likely to survive – this is **survival of the fittest**.
- the extinction of species unable to compete.

At the time, Darwin's theory was greeted with hostility. This was because most people believed in the idea of creation, which was the belief that all living things had been created at the same time. Darwin's theory was difficult to understand because most people knew little or nothing about inheritance.

Natural selection in action!

1 Before the Industrial Revolution trees had pale bark, so the pale speckled peppered moth was camouflaged.

2 Chance mutation produced a black (melanic) version.

3 As the Industrial Revolution progressed, the landscape became coated with smoke and soot and the trees turned black.

4 By the start of the 20th century, 98% of the peppered moths were black. They were more numerous because they were better adapted to the environment and the pale ones were easier for the predators to spot.

Questions

1. Suggest why fossils do not provide a complete record of evolution.
2. Explain what is meant by the term natural selection.
3. Use the peppered moth as an example to explain what is meant by survival of the fittest.
4. Why have some species become extinct?

Artificial selection

We take advantage of variation when we **selectively breed** animals and plants. We pick individuals with the characteristics we want and breed them. Their best offspring are selected and bred. This is repeated over many generations.

We selectively breed for many reasons. In animals we may want better yields of meat or milk, less aggression or a more attractive appearance. In plants we may want better yields of grain or fruit, better flavour or resistance to disease.

Making use of mitosis

We can use mitosis to produce **clones** – individuals which are genetically identical to their parent, and cloning plants is big business. When we take **cuttings** of plants we are producing clones when we grow them. Commercially, very much smaller pieces of plant material are used. This is called **micropropagation** or **tissue culture**.

A plant with the desired characteristics is divided into many small pieces of tissue. These are grown in a suitable growth medium using an **aseptic** technique, which prevents any microbes growing and spoiling the culture. When ready, the small plantlets are transferred to pots and sold.

Genetic engineering

Selective breeding takes a long time. It is unreliable because we cannot control exactly which genes are passed on, and is limited to living things within the same species. So, for example, you cannot breed a cow with a giraffe to produce a long-necked cow able to feed over hedges!

Genetic engineering gets round these problems by transferring genes directly from the cells of one living thing to the cells of another. The desired gene is first identified in an organism and then removed and isolated. It is replicated to make lots of copies and then inserted into the genetic material (the DNA) of the host organism.

For example, inserting the gene for human insulin into microbes has led to microbes capable of producing large amounts of human insulin for use in treating diabetes, which would otherwise be very difficult to produce.

Genetic engineering has a number of possible drawbacks. It is expensive to set up and develop. There are also worries about transferred genes finding their way into other species, and about eating food which has been genetically engineered. Finally, there is a lot of concern about possibly engineering humans in the future for 'desirable' characteristics.

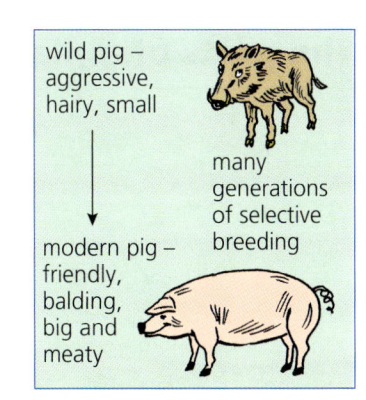

wild pig – aggressive, hairy, small

↓ many generations of selective breeding

modern pig – friendly, balding, big and meaty

Advantages of cloning
all the desirable parental characteristics are transferred to the clones
once the technique is set up, it is a relatively quick and cheap way to obtain large numbers of quality offspring
it is very useful for propagation of plants that are difficult to grow from seed

Disadvantages of cloning
produces a genetically uniform population, therefore no variation is available to overcome environmental change, e.g. a new disease could wipe all the clones out
any genetic weaknesses or defects will be passed on
increasing ethical concerns, especially if cloning of animal species is extended

Questions

1. **a** What characteristic would you want to breed into racehorses?
   b How would you do it?
2. Give **two** similarities and **two** differences between artificial selection and natural selection.
3. What do you understand by the word clone?
4. What sort of cell division produces a clone?
5. Make a table showing the advantages and disadvantages of genetic engineering and selective breeding.

The working plant

The parts of a plant

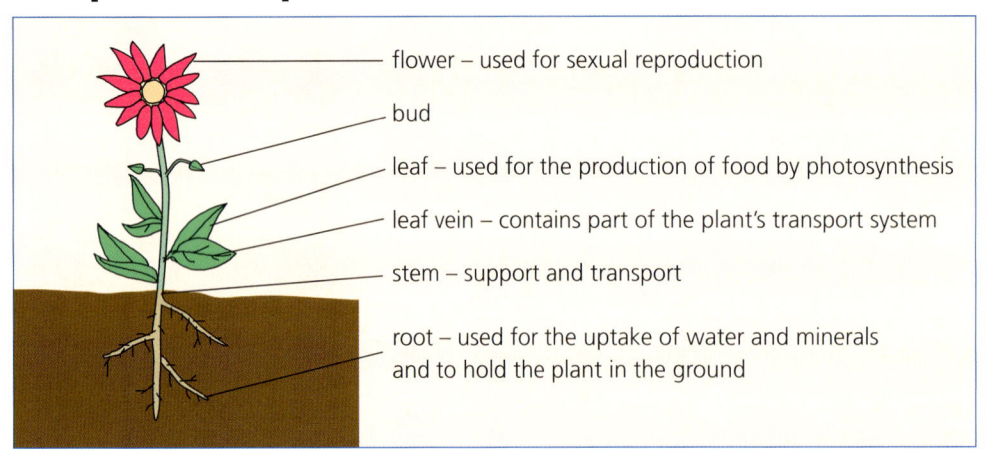

- flower – used for sexual reproduction
- bud
- leaf – used for the production of food by photosynthesis
- leaf vein – contains part of the plant's transport system
- stem – support and transport
- root – used for the uptake of water and minerals and to hold the plant in the ground

How do plants produce their food?

Plants **make** their own food by **photosynthesis**. To do this plants use light energy to join water and carbon dioxide, producing carbohydrates. (Photosynthesis comes from 'photo', meaning light, and 'synthesis', meaning to make.)

> Green plants do not eat, they photosynthesise.

Photosynthesis can be written as an equation:

$$6CO_2 + 6H_2O \xrightarrow{\text{chlorophyll and light energy}} C_6H_{12}O_6 + 6O_2$$

carbon dioxide + water → glucose + oxygen

- Carbon dioxide and water are needed for photosynthesis. They are called the **reactants**.
- Glucose and oxygen are produced by photosynthesis. They are called the **products**.

Labels on leaf diagram:
- sunlight absorbed by chlorophyll in the plant's leaf
- energy in the sunlight used to drive the photosynthesis reaction
- water comes in through root hair cells
- carbon dioxide comes in from the air
- oxygen out

What makes plants photosynthesise faster?

- The more carbon dioxide that is available, the faster the photosynthesis, because carbon dioxide is one of the reactants.
- The more light that is available, the faster the photosynthesis, because the energy of the light is used to drive the reaction. The colour of the light is also important. Most plants appear green because they reflect green light. This means green light is not absorbed to be used to drive photosynthesis. Red and blue light are absorbed, therefore these colours are the most important ones for photosynthesis.
- The higher the temperature, the faster photosynthesis will occur.

What happens if carbon dioxide, light and warmth are in short supply?

If any of these are in short supply they limit the amount of photosynthesis which can occur. Therefore they are called **limiting factors**.

On a hot, sunny day the temperature is usually high enough and there is plenty of light for photosynthesis to take place. In these conditions the rate of photosynthesis will depend on how much carbon dioxide there is. Carbon dioxide is then said to be the limiting factor.

Therefore a hot, sunny day will allow a plant to photosynthesise more quickly than a cold, dull day. Plants grow faster in the summer because they can produce more food by photosynthesis.

one stoma
lots of stomata

Where do plants make their food?

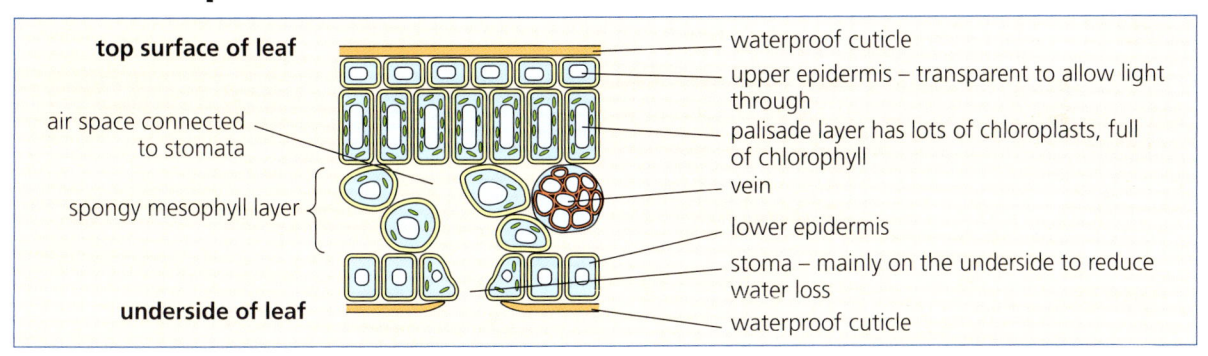

- top surface of leaf
- air space connected to stomata
- spongy mesophyll layer
- underside of leaf
- waterproof cuticle
- upper epidermis – transparent to allow light through
- palisade layer has lots of chloroplasts, full of chlorophyll
- vein
- lower epidermis
- stoma – mainly on the underside to reduce water loss
- waterproof cuticle

Plants make their food in their leaves because they:
- are **broad**, so they can catch as much sunlight as possible
- are **thin**, so that light reaches all the cells easily
- are **full of chlorophyll** to trap light energy
- are supplied by a **good transport system** (**veins**)
- have **stomata** to allow gases (carbon dioxide and oxygen) in and out
- have a large internal surface area to volume ratio.

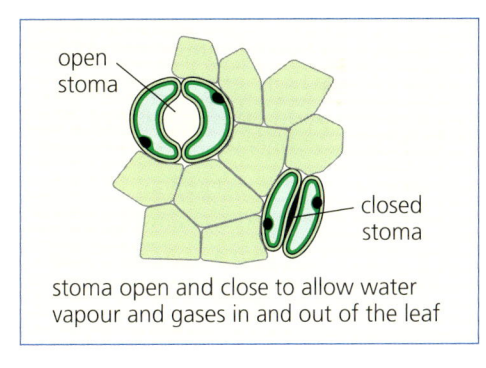

open stoma
closed stoma
stoma open and close to allow water vapour and gases in and out of the leaf

Questions

1. Explain, with the help of an equation, how green plants make their food.
2. Explain where a plant gets the reactants for photosynthesis from.
3. Give **three** ways in which leaves are adapted for photosynthesis.
4. Name **two** substances which pass out through stomata on a sunny day.
5. Do plants photosynthesise at night? Explain your answer.
6. Many offices have lovely pot plants that are illuminated by green lights. The lights make the leaves look attractive and healthy, but the plants do not grow very well. Explain why this happens.

The working plant

Moving materials around the plant

Plants use glucose produced during photosynthesis to make all the materials they need to live and grow.

Glucose is soluble and may be:

- moved around the plant
- changed into sucrose to be transported to the growing areas in the roots, shoots, flowers, fruits and buds
- changed into cellulose for new cell walls
- changed into proteins
- changed into large insoluble storage substances such as starch.
- used to release energy (respiration).

Sucrose on the move

The **phloem** is part of the transport system of plants. It carries dissolved sucrose to other parts of the plant and is made of living cells. The movement of materials through the phloem is called **translocation**.

Moving materials in and out of cells

There are three ways of moving materials in and out of cells.

- **Diffusion**
  This is the movement of particles from an area where there are lots of particles (high concentration) to an area where there are very few particles (a low concentration). Substances with small particles, e.g. water, minerals, oxygen and carbon dioxide, pass across cell membranes by diffusion down a **concentration gradient**. It does not require energy and is therefore a **passive** process. It is a consequence of the random motion of the particles.

- **Active transport**
  This is the movement of particles from an area with low concentration to an area with high concentration. It uses energy because it is against the concentration gradient.

- **Osmosis**
  This is a special case of diffusion for water. Osmosis is the movement of water particles from an area of a high water concentration to an area of lower water concentration through a **partially permeable membrane**. Cell membranes are partially permeable because they allow some things to pass through, but not others.

Water on the move

Plants need water in their leaves for photosynthesis. Water enters the plant by osmosis through the root hairs, and travels up to the leaves in the second plant transport system, the **xylem**. The xylem forms long tubes throughout the plant. It is made up of dead cells with no cytoplasm (they look a bit like drinking straws).

Root hair cells are good at taking up water because they:

- are long and thin, and therefore have a large surface area
- have thin walls to help water to pass through.

Root hair cells also take up minerals, e.g. nitrates, dissolved in the water. Depending on the concentration gradient, minerals are taken up by diffusion or active transport.

Once in the root hair cell the water and dissolved minerals move by diffusion across the root to the xylem.

Plant minerals

Nitrogen, phosphorus and potassium are the main minerals a plant requires, together with small amounts of magnesium, which is needed to make chlorophyll.

Plants will not grow so well, or as much, if there is not enough of any of these minerals. Fertilisers contain these important minerals.

Nitrogen is used to make amino acids, proteins and DNA. Phosphorus is used to make DNA and cell membranes.

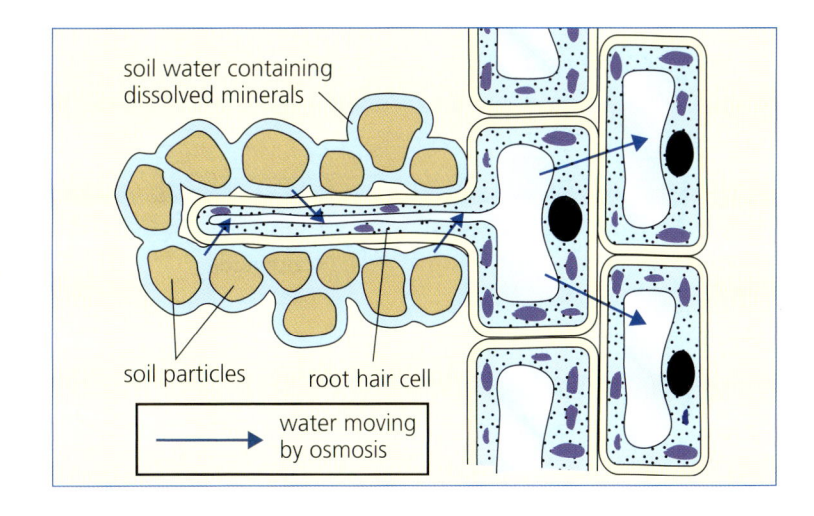

Questions

1. Describe **three** uses of glucose in a plant.
2. Why is a cell membrane considered to be partially permeable?
3. Explain why raw potato chips become shorter when left in concentrated sugar solutions, but become longer when left in dilute sugar solutions.
4. Name the **two** transport systems in plants, and state what each one is used for.
5. Suggest why plants which do not get enough magnesium look yellow and small.
6. Explain why farmers need to use fertilisers if they are going to grow the same crop, in the same field, every year.
7. Explain **two** functions of root hair cells.

84 The working plant

Tracking the xylem and phloem

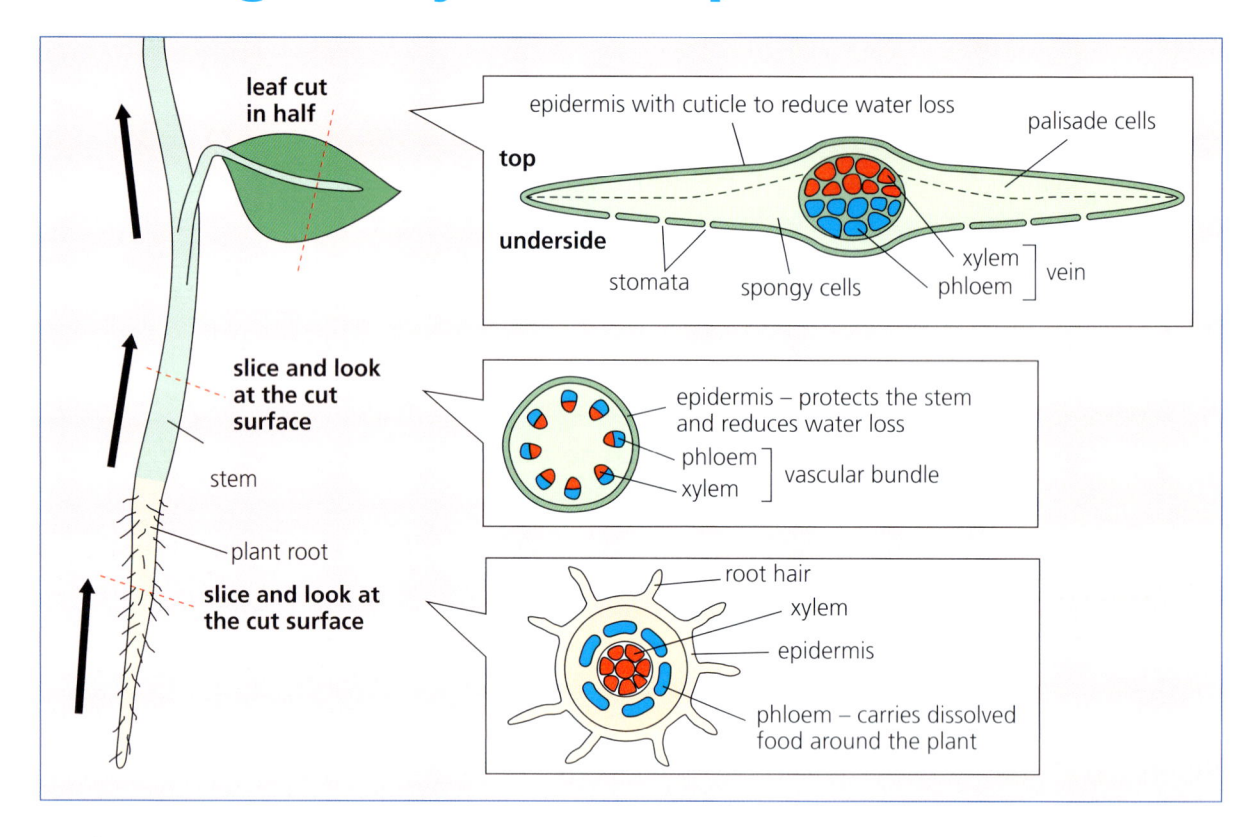

[Diagram showing a plant with leaf, stem, and root. Cross-sections labelled:]

- **Leaf cross-section (leaf cut in half):** epidermis with cuticle to reduce water loss, palisade cells, top, underside, stomata, spongy cells, xylem, phloem, vein
- **Stem cross-section (slice and look at the cut surface):** epidermis – protects the stem and reduces water loss, phloem, xylem, vascular bundle
- **Root cross-section (slice and look at the cut surface):** root hair, xylem, epidermis, phloem – carries dissolved food around the plant

Going up!

The xylem transports water and dissolved minerals from the roots to the leaves. They are 'sucked' up the xylem by a process called **transpiration**.

Transpiration is the evaporation of water from inside the leaves to the surrounding air. The water vapour passes out of the leaves by diffusion.

This is what happens in transpiration:

- water molecules diffuse from the xylem into the spongy mesophyll cells through cell membranes

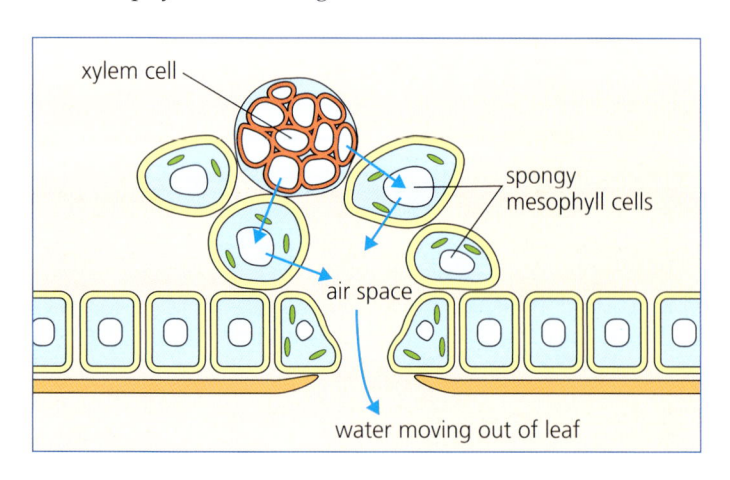

[Diagram showing xylem cell, spongy mesophyll cells, air space, water moving out of leaf]

Transpiration provides water for:
- photosynthesis
- cooling the plant (it is the plant version of sweating)
- movement of minerals
- support.

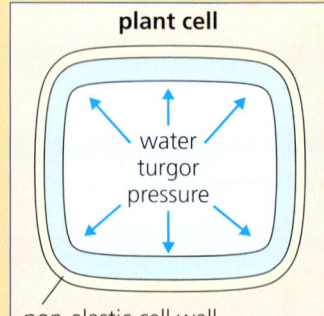

[Diagram of plant cell showing water, turgor pressure, non-elastic cell wall]

If the vacuole contains a lot of water it pushes against the cell wall forming a firm structure that is ideal to build a plant from.

- water evaporates into the air space
- water vapour diffuses out of the stomata
- water lost from the spongy mesophyll cells is replaced by more water from the xylem.

What affects the speed of transpiration?

Transpiration is increased by:
- more light, because water is used up as the plant photosynthesises more
- increased temperatures, because photosynthesis and evaporation increase with temperature
- increased air movement, which increases evaporation
- decreased humidity, because water evaporates more easily into dry air
- the state of the stomata, their number, distribution, position and size.

Stomata

Stomata can open or close by changing the shape of their guard cells.

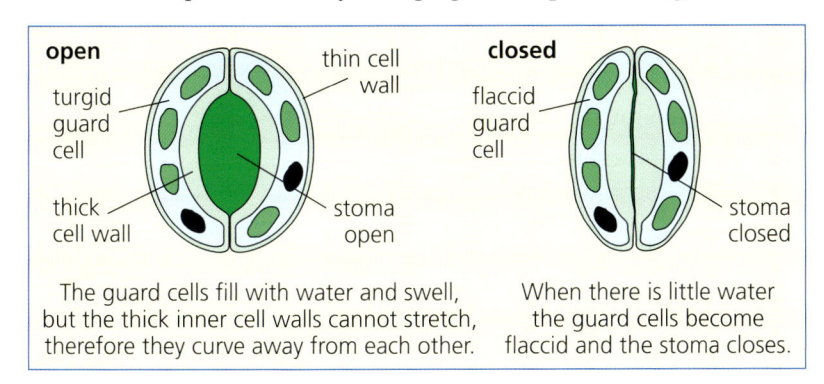

open
- turgid guard cell
- thin cell wall
- thick cell wall
- stoma open

The guard cells fill with water and swell, but the thick inner cell walls cannot stretch, therefore they curve away from each other.

closed
- flaccid guard cell
- stoma closed

When there is little water the guard cells become flaccid and the stoma closes.

cell appears flaccid and limp
- cell wall
- cytoplasm
- cell membrane
- vacuole with little water

cell appears turgid and swollen
- cell wall resisting water pushing against it
- full vacuole
- cell membrane

Stomata can open or close in response to what is going on outside the plant. They may close to prevent excessive water loss, but if they do, carbon dioxide cannot get in for photosynthesis. Stomata tend to be found mainly on the underside of leaves away from direct sunlight. Plant cells are able to survive some water loss by wilting, because the cell wall is too stiff to shrink too much.

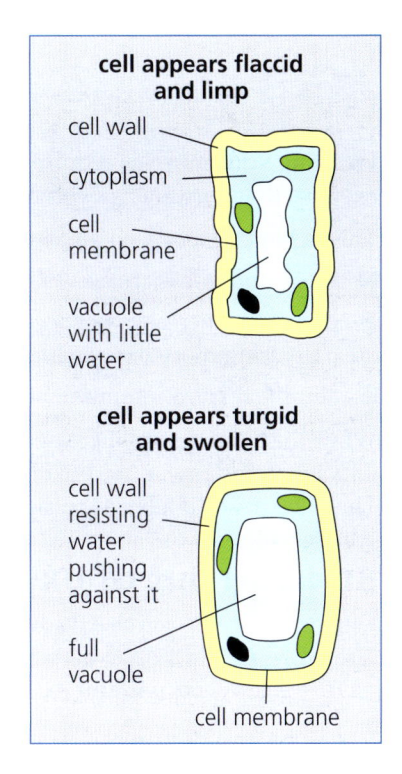

Questions

1. What is a vascular bundle?
2. Stomata are mainly on the underside of a leaf. Suggest why this is advantageous to the plant.
3. Explain what is meant by transpiration.
4. Give **three** reasons why transpiration is so important for plants.
5. Suggest how:
   a. the carbon dioxide needed for photosynthesis can get into a leaf
   b. the oxygen produced during photosynthesis can leave the plant.

Health in the balance

Respiration – releasing energy

Your body needs energy just to stay alive!

You use energy to:
- keep the heart pumping
- work your muscles for movement
- keep your body temperature constant
- grow and repair cells
- actively transport materials

and many, many other activities in the body.

Energy is released from glucose, when it reacts with oxygen in our cells. This is called **aerobic respiration**.

> Plant cells also respire all the time to produce energy.

It happens in *all* of our cells *all* of the time.

Aerobic respiration can be written as an equation.

$$C_6H_{12}O_6 + 6O_2 \rightarrow 6CO_2 + 6H_2O + \text{ENERGY}$$
$$\text{glucose} + \text{oxygen} \rightarrow \text{carbon dioxide} + \text{water} + \text{ENERGY}$$

Working your muscles requires energy. Therefore, the more you exercise the more energy you need.

This is how the body copes with the need for more energy:
- breathing rate increases to bring more oxygen into the body
- pulse rate increases to speed up blood flow around the body, delivering more oxygen and glucose to the respiring cells
- aerobic respiration in the muscle cells increases.

When the brain detects increased carbon dioxide levels in the blood it initiates an increase in the breathing rate to remove the carbon dioxide. This is because high levels of carbon dioxide in the blood are toxic.

Running out of oxygen

During vigorous exercise the body cannot get enough oxygen. Therefore, in addition to aerobic respiration the cells respire **anaerobically**, i.e. without oxygen.

Anaerobic respiration can be written as a word equation:

$$\text{glucose} \rightarrow \text{lactic acid} + \text{some ENERGY}$$

Anaerobic respiration releases energy, but much less than aerobic respiration. This is because a lot of the energy remains locked up in the lactic acid.

The lactic acid produced is a mild poison and builds up to cause **muscle fatigue** and **cramp**.

To get rid of the lactic acid the body needs oxygen. Therefore the build up of lactic acid causes an **oxygen debt**. The more lactic acid there is, the more oxygen is needed to get rid of it. This is why we puff and pant after vigorous exercise – we are trying to pay back our oxygen debt!

Sample examination question

Look at the diagrams. They show how an experiment was set up. Each tube contains red hydrogencarbonate indicator. It turns yellow with carbon dioxide.

(a) After 30 minutes the indicator in some of the tubes has changed colour. What colour does the indicator turn if carbon dioxide is present?

It turns yellow

(b) The indicator in tubes A and B was yellow. Explain what had happened.

Yellow indicates there was carbon dioxide present in tubes A and B. This was produced by the snails respiring.

(c) The indicator in tube C was reddish-orange. Explain what had happened.

The reddish-orange colour indicates there was some carbon dioxide in tube C but not as much as in A and B. This is from the pond weed respiring though not producing as much carbon dioxide as the snails. The pond weed is also photosynthesising and using up carbon dioxide.

(d) The indicator in tube D stayed red. Why was this?

There was no carbon dioxide in tube D.

(e) Why was tube D included in the experiment?

D is the control and it shows the pond water and indicator will not change colour on their own.

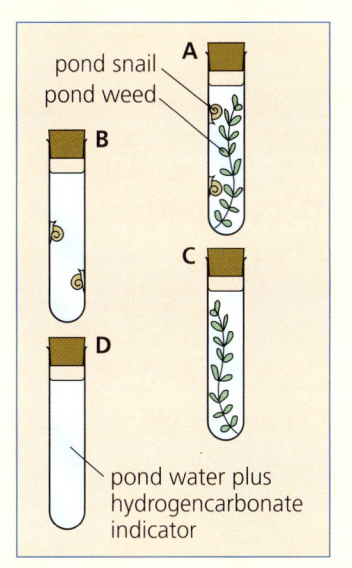

> Link colour changes to the behaviour of the indicator. Explain where the carbon dioxide has come from. Plants are living things and they respire. Any part of an experiment which shows no change is likely to be a control.

Questions

1. What is respiration?
2. Write word equations for
   a aerobic respiration
   b anaerobic respiration.
3. Give **two** differences between aerobic and anaerobic respiration.
4. Where does respiration occur?
5. Give **two** ways in which the body changes to cope with increased exercise.
6. Explain how **one** of these changes helps the body when it is exercising actively.
7. Explain what is meant by oxygen debt.

Homeostasis

Homeostasis literally means keeping conditions inside your body more or less constant, to enable your cells to work most efficiently.

What conditions need controlling?

In the human body the following conditions need controlling:

- blood glucose concentration
- blood water and salt concentration
- blood carbon dioxide level
- blood temperature
- waste products in the blood, such as urea
- the composition of body tissue fluid.

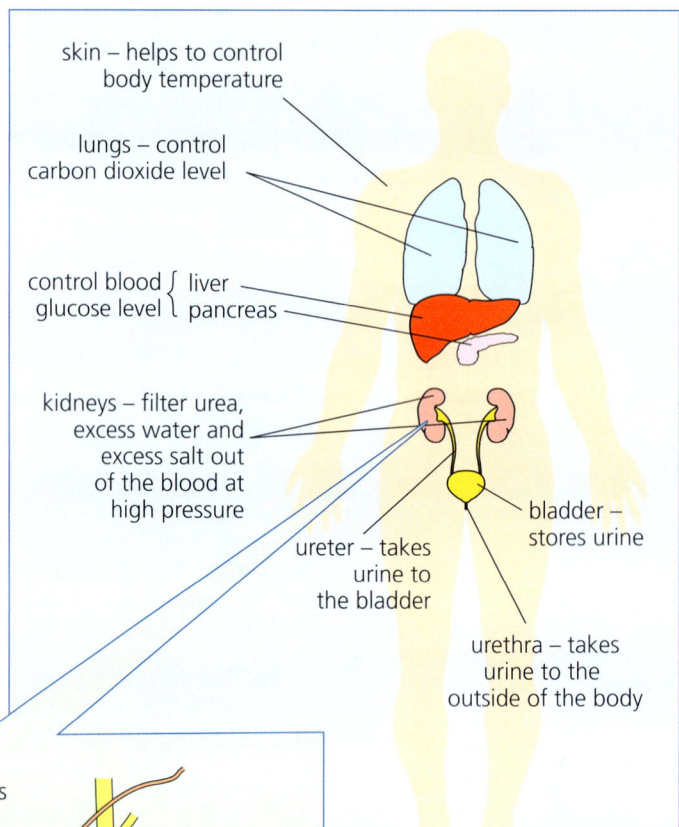

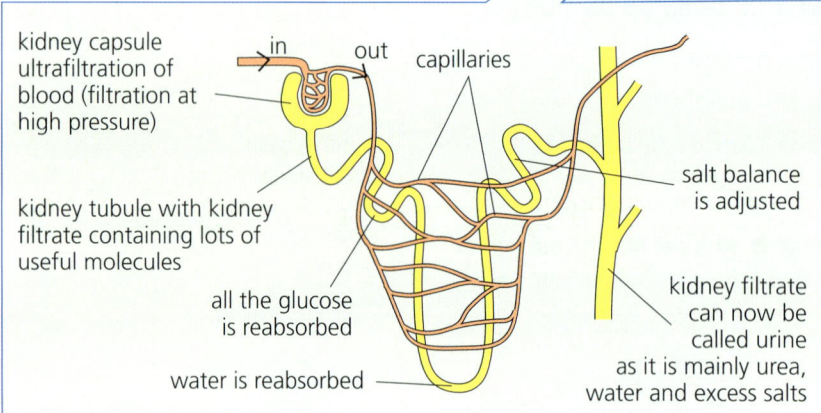

skin – helps to control body temperature

lungs – control carbon dioxide level

control blood glucose level { liver, pancreas

kidneys – filter urea, excess water and excess salt out of the blood at high pressure

bladder – stores urine

ureter – takes urine to the bladder

urethra – takes urine to the outside of the body

kidney capsule ultrafiltration of blood (filtration at high pressure)

in out capillaries

kidney tubule with kidney filtrate containing lots of useful molecules

all the glucose is reabsorbed

water is reabsorbed

salt balance is adjusted

kidney filtrate can now be called urine as it is mainly urea, water and excess salts

The water balance

If the balance of water in the body is upset we either dehydrate (dry out) or swell up with excess fluid.

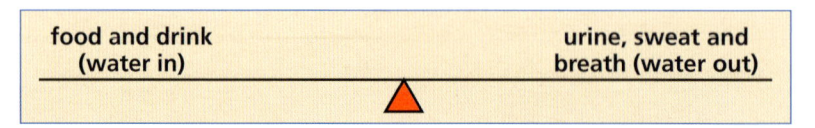

food and drink (water in)	urine, sweat and breath (water out)

We cannot survive either extreme for long. The water content of the blood is monitored by the brain. If the water content of the blood is low, the brain causes the kidney to reabsorb more water. If the water content of the blood is high the brain causes the kidney to reabsorb less water, therefore more watery urine is produced and the water content of the body begins to return to normal.

Controlling body temperature

When our cells respire, some of the energy released is heat energy. We use this to keep us warm.

Think about what you do when you feel cold. You might stamp your feet or rub your hands together, or even shiver. All of these actions involve respiration, which releases energy, therefore heat energy is also released to warm you up. The liver has a lot of reactions going on all the time, therefore it releases a lot of heat energy. It is like the boiler in your central heating system.

If the core body temperature increases, it causes the blood temperature to increase. If the core body temperature goes above 37 °C cells in the brain notice and switch on **cooling mechanisms** (e.g. sweating) to reduce the temperature. If the blood temperature goes below 37 °C the brain switches on **warming mechanisms** (e.g. shivering).

Negative feedback

Homeostasis is achieved by **negative feedback**. This means that:
1 a change is detected by the body, e.g. the blood carbon dioxide concentration increases
2 the body responds to the change, e.g. the brain brings about an increase in the breathing rate
3 the situation returns to normal, e.g. blood carbon dioxide concentration decreases back to normal
4 the body response stops, e.g. the breathing rate returns to normal.

The mechanisms

Cooling mechanisms	Warming mechanisms
• Sweating – heat from the body is used to evaporate sweat from the skin surface. • Vasodilation – blood vessels near the skin surface open to allow blood to flow near to the surface of the body and lose heat by radiation to the air. • Behavioural – take some clothes off.	• Shivering – muscles make heat by respiration to warm us up. • Vasoconstriction – blood vessels running near the skin surface close, diverting the blood back to the warmer parts of the body. • Behavioural – put some extra clothes on.

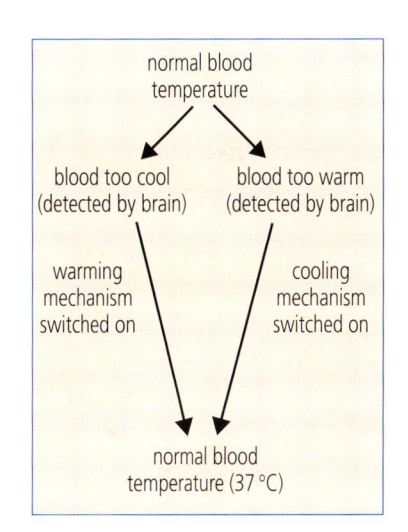

Questions
1 What does homeostasis mean?
2 Which **two** body organs are used to control blood glucose level?
3 What is passed out of the bladder down the urethra?
4 Suggest why high levels of carbon dioxide in the blood are harmful to the body.
5 Explain why you produce less urine on a hot sunny day than on a cold day.
6 Which part of the body checks the temperature of the blood?
7 Explain how sweating helps to cool us down.

Health in the balance

Defence against disease

Your body has to defend itself against microbes which are able to attack it and cause disease. The body has a number of ways of stopping microbes getting in.

- The eyes: tears contain a substance that destroys microbes.
- The nose and breathing passages are protected by mucus and cilia.
- The mouth leading to the digestive system: relies on the stomach acid to destroy microbes.
- The skin: provides a barrier to entry.

Fighting back

If the skin is damaged, blood forms a second line of defence by:

- forming a clot and scab to block entry to microbes
- allowing white blood cells to escape from blood vessels to attack any invading microbes.

Another word for microbes and other foreign materials in your body is **antigens**.

There are two types of white blood cell.

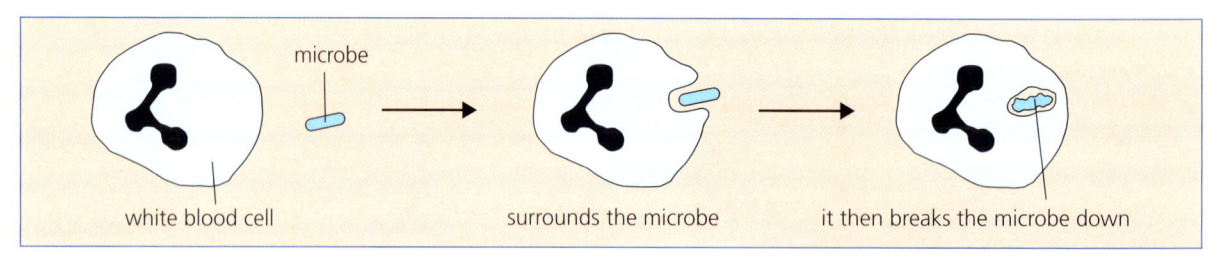

white blood cell → surrounds the microbe → it then breaks the microbe down

One type engulfs (eats) the microbes. The other type produces chemicals called **antibodies**, which attack the microbes and destroy them. The white blood cell makes contact with the microbe and identifies it. It then divides to produce a lot more white blood cells, all capable of releasing the right antibody. Each disease has its own antigens, therefore each one can be attacked by its own **specific antibodies**.

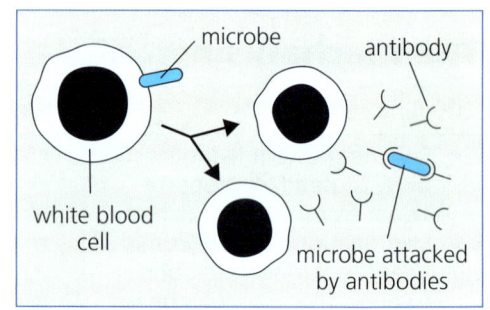

Immunity

Once your body has met a microbe and made antibodies against it, it does not forget. When you meet the same type of microbe again, your body is waiting. It quickly produces lots of antibodies, so you are unlikely to get the disease again. This is called **immunity**.

Immunisation is a means of giving the antigen without the disease. For example, a vaccine contains dead or inactive microbes which will enable your body to make antibodies against them without the risk of developing the disease. This is a way of protecting the population from serious diseases such as polio or smallpox.

Unfortunately it does not work very well with colds and flu, because there are so many different strains of them. Antibodies to cold strain A will not give you immunity to any of the other cold strains!

If you do become ill, you may need medicine to make you feel better. Medicines contain drugs. A **drug** is a substance that changes the way in which your body works.

Problems with drugs

Many drugs work either by speeding up brain activity or by slowing it down.

- **Stimulant** – speeds up brain activity by increasing the activity of brain synapses.
- **Depressant** – slows down brain activity by blocking some of the brain synapses.

The drug, nicotine, is inhaled as part of cigarette smoke. Normally your lungs are kept free from bacterial infection by the action of cells in the trachea. These cells have tiny hairs called cilia which beat rhythmically. Other cells produce mucus to stick bacteria together. The cilia then beat to move the bacteria and mucus back up the trachea to the back of the throat, where they can be swallowed and destroyed by the stomach acid. Nicotine stops the cilia beating, thereby leading to smokers cough, caused by an accumulation of mucus and bacteria in the lungs. If the cilia do not beat to remove mucus and trapped microbes, the only other way to try and shift the material is through coughing.

Drug	Action	Negative effects
caffeine	stimulant	can cause sleeplessness
nicotine	stimulant	increases brain activity
alcohol	depressant	may slow down brain activity to the point of passing out; reduces ability to make judgements; prolonged use may result in damage to the brain; it poisons the liver leading to liver damage when the liver removes the toxic alcohol
solvents	depressants	may slow down brain so much that the brain stops

Some drugs are **addictive**, meaning that they produce a dependence in the person taking the drug. The person then has to keep taking the drug.

Some drugs produce **withdrawal symptoms** if the user stops, or is prevented from, taking the drug. These vary in severity from a headache if you are deprived of coffee for the day, to sickness, blinding headaches and an inability to sleep, eat or do anything.

The body gets used to some drugs, which means that the drug user needs larger and larger doses to get the same effect. This is called **drug tolerance**.

Questions

1. How are the eyes protected from microbe invasion?
2. If the skin is damaged, how does the body continue to protect itself?
3. What is an antibody?
4. Why is it important that white blood cells can escape from blood vessels?
5. What is a drug?
6. Explain why smoking may make someone more likely to get lung infections.
7. What is the difference between a depressant and a stimulant? Give an example of each.

Concept map

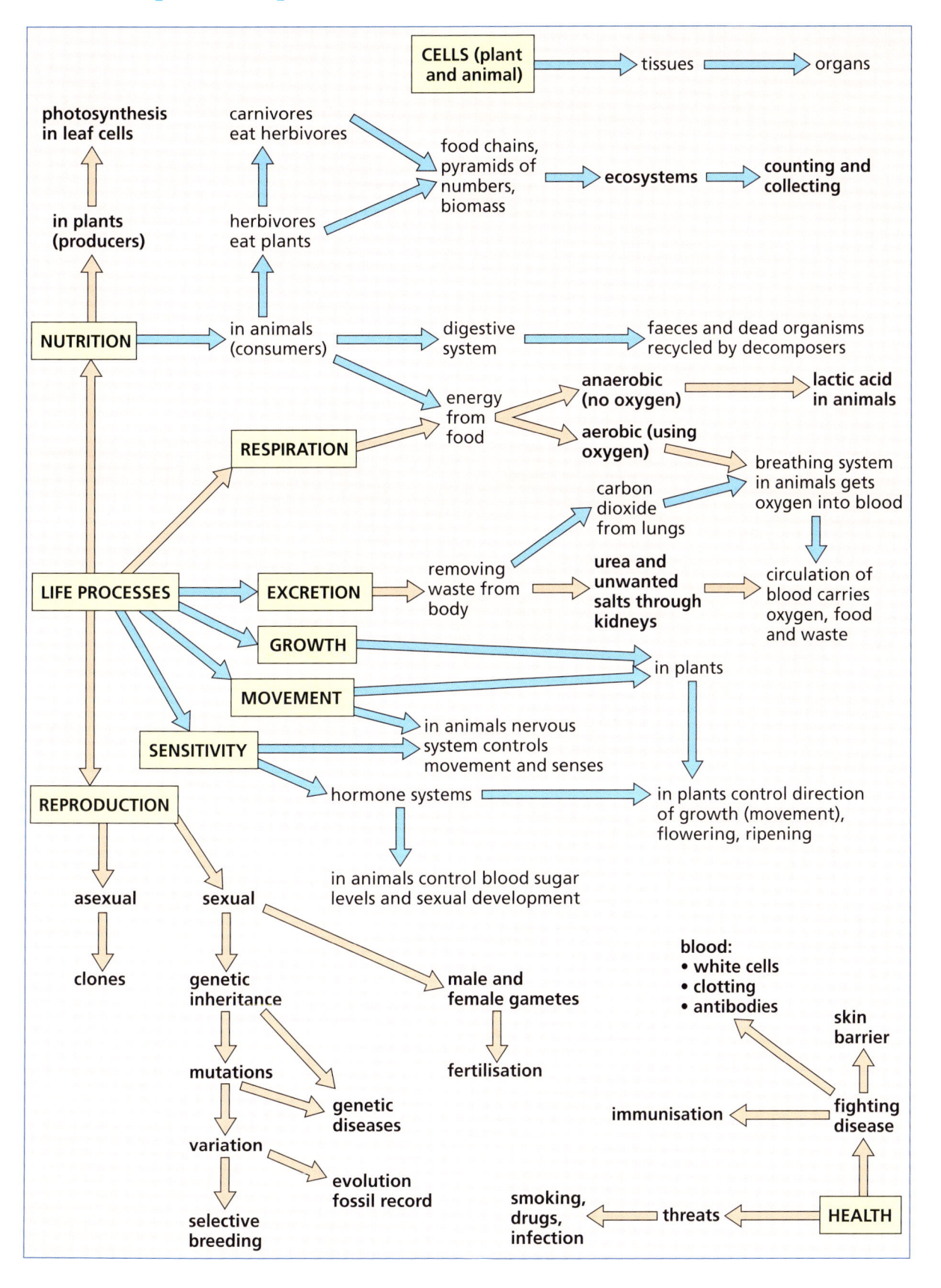

CELLS (plant and animal) → tissues → organs

NUTRITION
- photosynthesis in leaf cells ← in plants (producers)
- in animals (consumers)
  - carnivores eat herbivores
  - herbivores eat plants
  → food chains, pyramids of numbers, biomass → ecosystems → counting and collecting
  → digestive system → faeces and dead organisms recycled by decomposers
  → energy from food

LIFE PROCESSES

RESPIRATION — energy from food
- anaerobic (no oxygen) → lactic acid in animals
- aerobic (using oxygen) → breathing system in animals gets oxygen into blood → circulation of blood carries oxygen, food and waste

EXCRETION → removing waste from body
- carbon dioxide from lungs
- urea and unwanted salts through kidneys

GROWTH → in plants

MOVEMENT

SENSITIVITY
- in animals nervous system controls movement and senses
- hormone systems
  - in plants control direction of growth (movement), flowering, ripening
  - in animals control blood sugar levels and sexual development

REPRODUCTION
- asexual → clones
- sexual
  - genetic inheritance
    - mutations → genetic diseases
    - variation → evolution fossil record
    - selective breeding
  - male and female gametes → fertilisation

blood:
- white cells
- clotting
- antibodies

skin barrier

immunisation ← fighting disease

HEALTH → threats → smoking, drugs, infection

Life processes and living things

Exam questions

1. Chromosomes are made of DNA. DNA carries the genetic code (genes) for cells to control our characteristics.
   a. Write down where in the cell chromosomes are found. [1]
   b. How many chromosomes would you expect one of your liver cells to contain? [1]
   c. Sometimes the genetic code is changed by a process called mutation. What are the causes and effects of mutation? Explain as fully as you can. [4]
   d. Sarah and Gemma are sisters with the same mother and father. However, they do not have the same DNA as each other. Suggest **two** reasons why their DNA is not the same. [2]

   [8 marks]

2. Look at the diagrams. They show stages in mitosis.

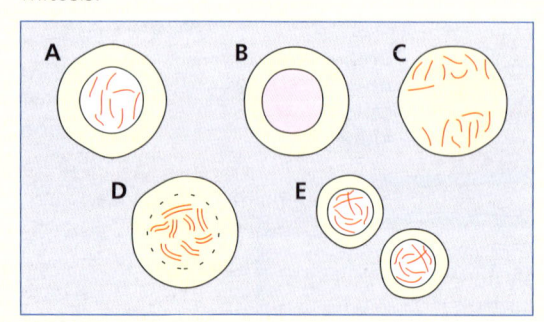

   a. Write down the stages in the correct order. [4]
   b. How many chromosomes does the cell normally contain? [1]
   c. Write down **two** uses of mitosis in living organisms. [2]
   d. There is another form of cell division called meiosis. Write down **two** ways in which meiosis is different from mitosis. [2]

   [9 marks]

3. This question is about cloning. A clone is genetically identical to its parent. Cloning is widely used commercially to produce large numbers of plants.
   a. Explain fully how a plant is cloned using tissue culture. [4]
   b. Suggest **two** advantages and **two** disadvantages of cloning plants. [4]

   [8 marks]

4. Petal shape in poppies is controlled by a single gene with two alleles. One allele produces smooth regular-shaped petals, and the other allele produces smaller petals with jagged edges. When a plant breeder crossed the two poppies, all the offspring had smooth regular petals.
   a. Which of the poppy alleles is dominant? [1]
   b. Write down what you understand by the term recessive allele. [1]
   c. Draw a genetic diagram to show the cross the breeder carried out. [4]
   d. Explain what would be produced if the breeder crossed two of these smooth regular petal poppies. Use a genetic diagram to help you. [4]
   e. The poppies with the jagged edged petals are very attractive. Explain as fully as you can how the breeder could be sure of producing more jagged poppies. [3]

   [13 marks]

5. Until the early twentieth century there were only red squirrels living in Britain. They were small, non-aggressive animals which lived in pine forests and ate pine cones. They produced two or three babies each year. About the turn of the century, the grey squirrel was introduced from the USA. They are larger, produce lots of babies each year and eat a variety of different types of food.
   Explain, as fully as you can, why red squirrels have died out in most of the British Isles. [5]

   [5 marks]

6. Plants make their food by the process of photosynthesis. Photosynthesis mainly occurs in the leaves. Therefore the structure of a leaf is well adapted for efficient photosynthesis.
   a. Explain **three** ways in which the leaf is adapted for photosynthesis. [3]
   b. On a warm, sunny day, what is most likely to be the factor limiting the rate of photosynthesis? [1]

   [4 marks]

7 Look at the drawing of Max swimming.

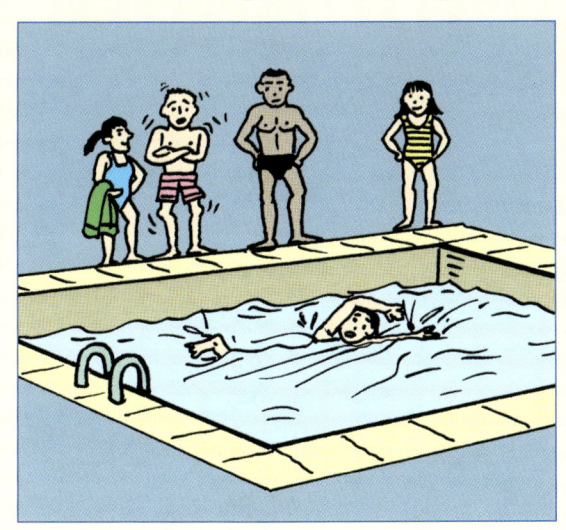

He needs lots of energy to swim. The energy is released by the process of respiration.
  a Where does respiration occur? [1]
  b Write down the symbol equation for aerobic respiration. [3]
  When Max gets out of the water, he sits by the side of the pool talking to his friends. Although it is a hot, sunny day, Max is surprised to feel cold.
  c Explain why the wet Max is feeling cold, but his friends are not. [2]

[6 marks]

8 Caffeine is a stimulant and is present in coffee and chocolate.
  a Explain what is meant by the term stimulant. [1]
  b Some people claim to be addicted to chocolate and if they try to give it up, they can suffer from headaches, bad temper and loss of concentration.
    i Write down what is meant by the terms addiction and withdrawal symptoms. [2]
    ii Explain what is meant by drug tolerance, and suggest how it can lead drug addicts into deeper and deeper troubles. [2]

[5 marks]

9 Max cut 50 cylinders of beetroot each 50 mm long. He then put 10 in each flask of sugar solution and after 30 min he remeasured the length of each cylinder. This is a table of his results.

Sugar concentration (mol/dm^3)	Mean length after 30 min (mm)	Change in length (mm)
0.0	54	+4
1.0	51	
2.0	48	
3.0	46	
4.0	45	

  a Calculate the change in length and complete the end column of the table. [4]
  b Use your calculated values to draw a graph on the grid below. The first point has been plotted for you. [3]

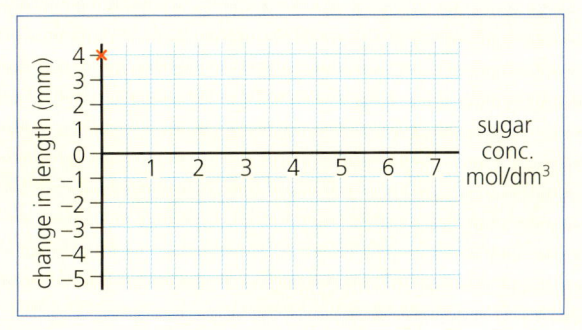

  c Use the graph to determine the concentration of cell sap in beetroot cells. [2]
  d Explain fully why the beetroot gets smaller in the high-concentration sugar solutions. [4]

[13 marks]

10 The kidneys help the body to maintain conditions at a favourable level for cells to work efficiently.
  a What is the name given to this type of control process? [1]
  b List three conditions which the body needs to control. [3]
  c Briefly explain how the kidney produces urine. [4]
  d Explain the difference between the urine you would produce after a game of tennis on a hot summer's day, and that which you would produce watching a rugby match on a cold winter day. [3]

[11 marks]

Carbon chemistry

Bonding

Ionic bonding

Ions with opposite charges will hold each other together. This is **ionic bonding**.

We can use 'dot and cross' diagrams to show how these ions are made – this one is for sodium chloride, salt.

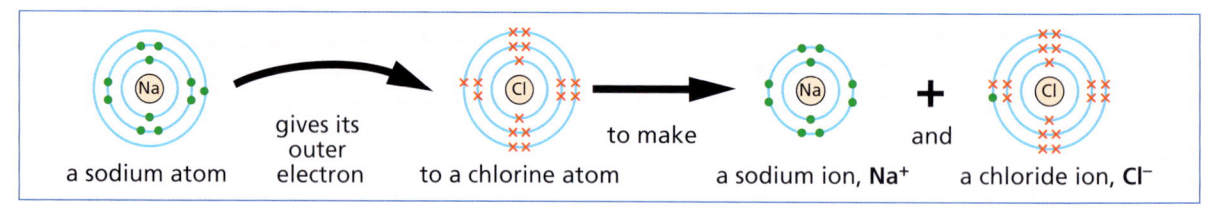

a sodium atom **gives its outer electron** to a chlorine atom **to make** a sodium ion, **Na⁺** **and** a chloride ion, **Cl⁻**

Elements form ions to gain a stable outer shell – a noble gas configuration.

Ionic bonds are very strong forces. Substances with ionic bonds form enormous groups called **ionic giant structures**. Giant structures have high melting and boiling points because all the strong forces holding the particles together are difficult to overcome. Sodium chloride and magnesium oxide have ionic giant structures. Solid ionic compounds don't conduct electricity because their ions can't move. If the compound is melted or dissolved in water, the ions can move so it will then conduct.

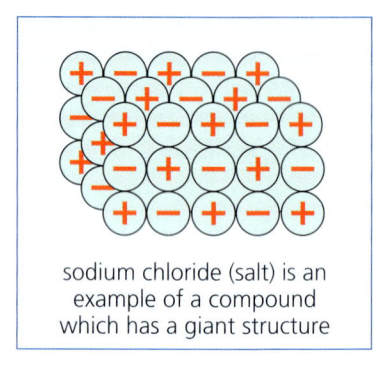

sodium chloride (salt) is an example of a compound which has a giant structure

Covalent bonding

When non-metals react with each other they don't form ions, they share electrons instead. This is **covalent bonding**, and it is just as strong as ionic bonding. Both carbon dioxide and water are small molecules.

The hydrogen molecule, H_2, has a single covalent bond. The outer shell of each hydrogen atom needs two electrons to make it stable.

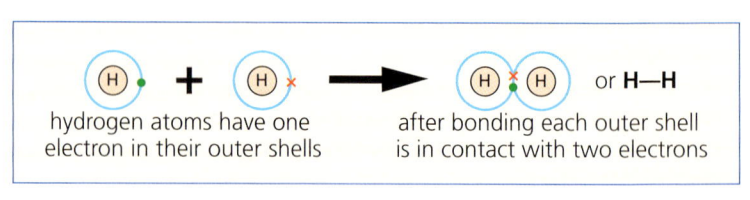

hydrogen atoms have one electron in their outer shells — after bonding each outer shell is in contact with two electrons — or H—H

The chlorine molecule, Cl_2, also has a single covalent bond. The outer shell of each chlorine atom needs eight electrons to make it stable.

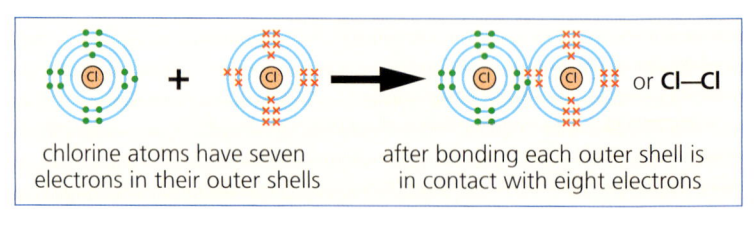

chlorine atoms have seven electrons in their outer shells — after bonding each outer shell is in contact with eight electrons — or Cl—Cl

The oxygen molecule, O_2, has a double covalent bond. The outer shell of each oxygen atom needs eight electrons to make it stable.

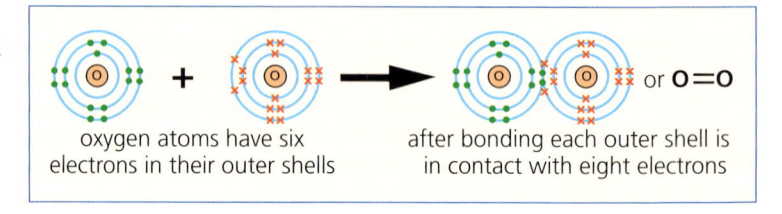

oxygen atoms have six electrons in their outer shells — after bonding each outer shell is in contact with eight electrons — or O=O

Molecules and giants

Covalent compounds can form giant structures or they can form small molecules.

Covalent molecules

Molecules have strong covalent bonds inside them, but only very weak forces holding one molecule to another. The weak forces between molecules make it easy to separate molecules from each other; in other words they have low melting and boiling points. Molecules do not have free electrons so they don't conduct electricity.

weak forces between each molecule

strong covalent bonds inside each molecule

Covalent giant structures

Sometimes all the atoms inside a structure are held together with covalent bonds, there are no weak forces. This makes a covalent **giant structure**. As the covalent bond is just as strong as the ionic bond, the structure will have very high melting and boiling points.

Carbon is special because it is an element that has three different forms; diamond, graphite and Buckminster Fullerene. Diamond and graphite are both covalent giant structures.

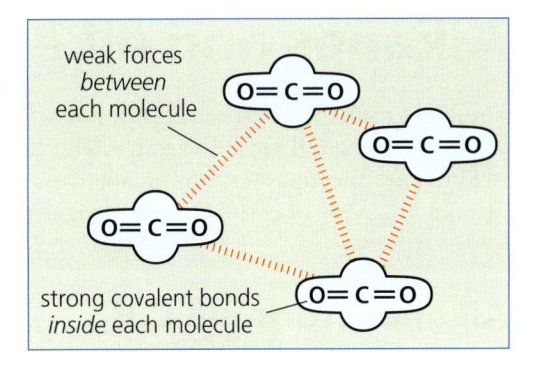

Covalent giant structure
- strong forces between molecules
- high melting/ boiling points

Ionic giant structure
- strong forces between molecules
- high melting/ boiling points
- solid won't conduct electricity, liquid will

Molecular structure
- weak forces between molecules
- low melting/boiling points
- doesn't conduct electricity

diamond
covalent giant structure: hard, no free electrons, so does not conduct electricity

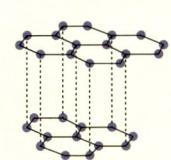

graphite
covalent giant structure: soft, weak forces *between* the layers allow them to slide, so used as a lubricant. Free 'delocalised' electrons, so conducts electricity

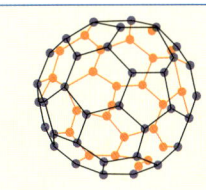

Buckminster Fullerene
carbon atoms joined together to make a microscopic football! This was only discovered in 1983.

Questions

1. Draw 'dot and cross' diagrams for the bonds in the following molecules: water, H_2O; methane, CH_4; carbon dioxide, CO_2; ethene, C_2H_4

2. Sodium has one electron in its outer shell and forms Na^+.
   Magnesium has two electrons in its outer shell and forms Mg^{++}.
   Chlorine has seven electrons in its outer shell and forms Cl^-.
   Oxygen has six electrons in its outer shell and forms O^{--}.
   Draw dot and cross diagrams to show how bonding takes place in NaCl, MgO, Na_2O and $MgCl_2$.

3. Solid **A** melts at 100 °C. Solid **B** melts at 1000 °C. What type of structure does each have?

Carbon chemistry

Alkanes and alkenes

There are millions of carbon compounds. Some of them are very similar so we put them into groups. The two groups that you need to know are the **alkanes** and the **alkenes**. The compounds in both groups are made of carbon and hydrogen only, so they are both hydrocarbons.

You should be able to use a molecular formula to draw the displayed formula. Practise doing this!

Alkanes (formula C_nH_{2n+2})

The displayed and the molecular formulae for the first three alkanes are:

Name	methane	ethane	propane
Molecular formula	CH_4	C_2H_6	C_3H_8
Displayed formula	H–C–H with H above and below	H–C–C–H with H's above and below	H–C–C–C–H with H's above and below

The carbon atoms in the alkane molecules are linked by single covalent bonds only, so we say that they are **saturated**. As the alkane molecule gets bigger, the weak forces between the molecules increase, so their melting points and boiling points increase.

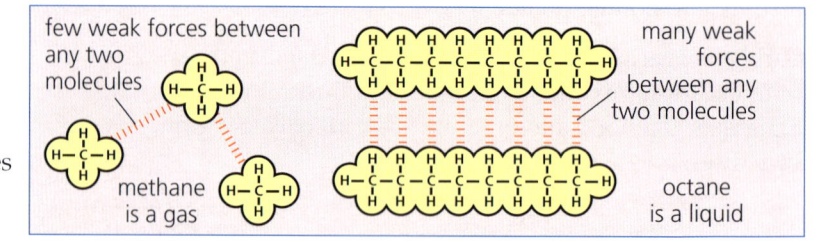

few weak forces between any two molecules — methane is a gas

many weak forces between any two molecules — octane is a liquid

See page 39 for what happens when alkanes burn.

Alkanes are obtained from crude oil by fractional distillation. Crude oil never has the 'right' amounts of the different alkanes that we need – there are too many of the large molecules which make up fuel oil, naphtha and bitumen. At the same time, there aren't enough small alkanes to make the amounts of petrol and diesel that we need, so we 'crack' the large alkanes such as naphtha into the smaller molecules. To do this we use a catalyst, high temperatures and high pressure.

Cracking breaks a covalent bond between carbon atoms inside the large alkane. Any of the carbon bonds might break, so cracking produces a mixture of different molecules, all smaller than the original. The new molecules are all hydrocarbons, they are a mixture of alkanes and **alkenes**.

a large alkane molecule → a smaller alkane, used in petrol + an alkene, used in plastics

Alkenes (formula C_nH_{2n})

Alkenes are also hydrocarbons, but they all contain one double covalent bond between carbon atoms. Molecules with a C=C bond are **unsaturated**.

The displayed and the molecular formulae for the first two alkenes are:

Name	ethene	propene
Molecular formula	C_2H_4	C_3H_6
Displayed formula	H H | | C=C | | H H	H H | | C=C−C−H | | | H H H

It is always easy to see if a hydrocarbon is unsaturated by looking at its formula. If the number of hydrogen atoms is just twice the number of carbons, it is unsaturated. If there are more hydrogens than this, it is saturated.

Alkenes are very important because other chemicals can easily attach to the double bond of the alkene molecule. This is called an **addition reaction**. During the addition reaction the double bond turns back to a single bond, so the **unsaturated** alkene becomes **saturated**. Addition reactions are used to make **plastics** – see page 100.

> You should be able to use a molecular formula to draw the displayed formula. Practise doing this!

Alkenes and bromine water

Bromine forms an addition compound with alkenes. The orange colour of the bromine disappears as the bromine reacts with the alkene.

We use this reaction to see if a hydrocarbon is an alkane or an alkene.

H   H   H   H
\| \| \| \|
C=C + Br_2 → Br−C−C−Br
\| \| \| \|
H   H   H   H

$C_2H_4 + Br_2 \rightarrow C_2H_4Br_2$

This reaction produces a saturated dibromo compound.

- Unsaturated hydrocarbons have a C=C bond. They turn orange/brown bromine water colourless.
- Saturated hydrocarbons have no C=C bond. They do not affect bromine water.

Alkenes and hydrogen

Alkenes turn back into alkanes when they react with hydrogen. The hydrogen has to be at high pressure and a nickel catalyst must be used.

H   H   H   H
\| \| \| \|
C=C + H_2 → H−C−C−H
\| \| \| \|
H   H   H   H

$C_2H_4 + H_2 \rightarrow C_2H_6$

This reaction needs a nickel catalyst and hydrogen under high pressure.

Questions

1. How many C—C bonds are present in ethane?
2. How many C—H bonds are present in ethane?
3. Draw a dot and cross diagram to show the covalent bonds inside an ethane molecule.
4. Why is octane a liquid at room temperature?
5. Which of the compounds shown here: CH_4, C_2H_4, C_2H_6, C_3H_6, C_3H_8
   a. are saturated?
   b. are unsaturated?
6. Write a balanced equation for the reaction between
   a. propene and bromine.
   b. propene and hydrogen.

Carbon chemistry

Plastics

Monomers and polymers

Plastics are made of small molecules which are joined together into long chains. The small molecules are called **monomers**; the large chain molecule is a **polymer**.

monomer	+	monomer	+	monomer	+	monomer	→	polymer
(M)	+	(M)	+	(M)	+	(M)	→	–(M)–(M)–(M)–(M)–

Alkenes make excellent monomers. The double bond allows the alkene molecules to join to each other to make the chains – this is called **addition polymerisation**. The double bond in the alkene monomer turns back to a single bond when it reacts, so the polymer that it forms is **saturated**. The reaction needs high pressure and a catalyst to work.

Different alkene monomers make different types of plastic which have different uses.

Monomer	Polymer
ethene	poly(ethene)
propene	poly(propene)
chloroethene	poly(chloroethene)
styrene	polystyrene

Ethene is the monomer used to make poly(ethene), or polythene.

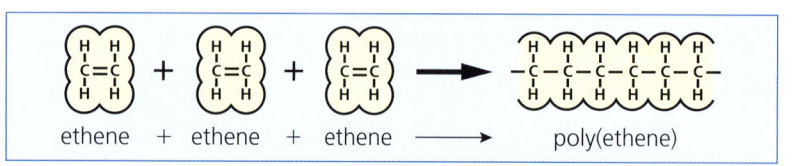

ethene + ethene + ethene ⟶ poly(ethene)

Cloroethene is the monomer used to make poly(chloroethene), PVC.

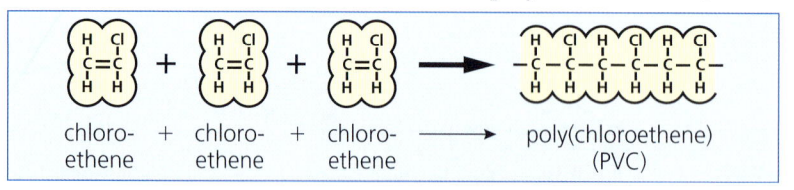

chloro-ethene + chloro-ethene + chloro-ethene ⟶ poly(chloroethene) (PVC)

Here are some uses for various types of plastics.

Polythene is cheap and flexible, so it is used to make polythene bags.

Propene is the monomer used to make poly(propene). Poly(propene) is stiffer than poly(ethene) so it is used to make plastic chairs.

Styrene is the monomer used to make polystyrene. It is not strong, but makes a good insulator so is used in plastic cups. It is also used for packaging.

Chloroethene is also called vinyl chloride. Poly(chloroethene) is also called polyvinylchloride (PVC). PVC is not as cheap as polythene but it lasts better outdoors, so it is used for drainpipes and window frames, as well as records.

Why do some plastics stretch?

Some plastics can be stretched easily, and have low melting points. The polymer molecules inside the plastic are held together by strong covalent bonds. Forces inside the molecules – the covalent bonds – are **intramolecular** forces.

The forces connecting each molecule to the next molecule are **intermolecular** forces. These forces are weak. When the plastic is stretched, the molecules slide past each other. The intermolecular forces aren't strong enough to hold each molecule in place.

Other plastics are rigid, with high melting points. These plastics have strong intermolecular forces connecting one molecule to another and so they cannot be stretched. These intermolecular forces are usually covalent bonds or cross links between molecules, which hold the molecules together.

flexible plastic
long chain molecules

strong forces within the molecules   weak forces between the molecules

rigid plastic
long chain molecules

strong covalent bonds between chains

Problems with plastic

Millions of tonnes of plastic products are made every year and are thrown away after they have been used. This is a problem because:

- it is a waste of a valuable resource – the crude oil that plastics are made from.
- plastics don't **biodegrade** (rot) – bacteria can't break them down.
- if plastics are put into landfill sites they last a long time.
- if plastics are burnt they often give off toxic fumes.

Addition polymers are increasingly being recycled, but it is expensive to sort plastics into groups of the same type. It is even expensive just to collect the plastics – plastic bottles are difficult to squash, so the containers for used plastic bottles fill up very quickly. This means that the containers have to be emptied more often, which costs money.

Questions

1. Why do we use poly(propene) instead of polythene to make plastic chairs?
2. Why do we use PVC instead of polythene to make drainpipes?
3. The displayed formula for propene is:

   $$\begin{array}{c} H \quad CH_3 \\ | \quad\; | \\ C = C \\ | \quad\; | \\ H \quad H \end{array}$$

   Show three links for a poly(propene) molecule.

4. 'Orlon' is a plastic used to make clothes. Part of an Orlon molecule looks like this:

   $$\begin{array}{c} H \;\; CN \; H \;\; CN \; H \;\; CN \; H \;\; CN \; H \;\; CN \; H \;\; CN \; H \;\; CN \\ | \;\; | \;\; | \;\; | \;\; | \;\; | \;\; | \;\; | \;\; | \;\; | \;\; | \;\; | \;\; | \;\; | \\ -C-C-C-C-C-C-C-C-C-C-C-C-C-C- \\ | \;\; | \;\; | \;\; | \;\; | \;\; | \;\; | \;\; | \;\; | \;\; | \;\; | \;\; | \;\; | \;\; | \\ H \;\; H \;\; H \;\; H \;\; H \;\; H \;\; H \;\; H \;\; H \;\; H \;\; H \;\; H \;\; H \;\; H \end{array}$$

   Draw a monomer of Orlon.

Chemical economics

Acids and fertilisers

Acidity is caused by the presence of hydrogen ions, H⁺.

How acidic is it?

The pH scale tells us how strongly acidic something is. The lower the number, the greater the hydrogen ion concentration.

very acidic	slightly acidic	NEUTRAL ↓	slightly alkaline	very alkaline
0 1 2 3	4 5 6	7	8 9 10	11 12 13 14

Bases, alkalis and neutralisation

Anything that reacts with an acid is called a **base**. A base which will dissolve in water (such as sodium hydroxide) is an **alkali**. Metal oxides and hydroxides are usually bases and alkalis. Non-metal oxides are usually acidic.

Acids contain hydrogen ions, H⁺; alkalis contain hydroxide ions, OH⁻.

When an acid and a base react they **neutralise** each other. The hydrogen ions react with hydroxide ions to form water.

$$H^+(aq) + OH^-(aq) \rightarrow H_2O(l)$$

If you add acid to a beaker of alkali the pH of the liquid in the beaker will start at a high number and drop to pH 7 once the acid and alkali have neutralised each other. If you add too much acid you will go too far. The pH will go below 7.

When acids react with alkalis they produce a **salt** and water. The salt is the substance left over after the hydrogen ions have reacted with the hydroxide ions.

acid	+	alkali	→	salt	+	water
HCl	+	NaOH	→	NaCl	+	H₂O
hydrochloric acid	+	sodium hydroxide	→	sodium chloride	+	water

Acids always form salts when they react.

Names of salts

- hydrochloric acid forms **chlorides**
- nitric acid forms **nitrates**
- sulphuric acid forms **sulphates**.

What acid/base neutralisations do we need to know?

There are really only four different equations for all these reactions:

H_2SO_4 with NH_4OH, KOH, $NaOH$	$H_2SO_4 + 2NaOH \rightarrow Na_2SO_4 + 2H_2O$
H_2SO_4 with CuO	$H_2SO_4 + CuO \rightarrow CuSO_4 + H_2O$
HNO_3 and HCl with NH_4OH, KOH, $NaOH$	$HNO_3 + KOH \rightarrow KNO_3 + H_2O$
HNO_3 and HCl with CuO	$2HCl + CuO \rightarrow CuCl_2 + H_2O$

You should be able to write balanced equations for the reactions between sulphuric acid, H_2SO_4, nitric acid, HNO_3, hydrochloric acid HCl and ammonium hydroxide, NH_4OH, potassium hydroxide, KOH, sodium hydroxide, $NaOH$, copper oxide, CuO.

Using neutralisation reactions to make fertilisers

Fertilisers increase crop yields. They either replace essential elements used by a previous crop or they provide extra essential elements. The three most important essential elements are nitrogen, phosphorus and potassium (N,P,K). Nitrogen is essential to plants for growth – they use it to make protein.

Fertilisers must dissolve in water so that the plant can take them in through its roots. Ammonium salts make good fertilisers because they dissolve and they contain nitrogen. They are made by neutralising ammonia solution with sulphuric and nitric acids.

Nitrogenous fertilisers that can be made from ammonia are:
- ammonium nitrate
- ammonium sulphate
- ammonium phosphate
- urea.

sulphuric acid	+	ammonium hydroxide	→	ammonium sulphate	+	water
H_2SO_4	+	$2NH_4OH$	→	$(NH_4)_2SO_4$	+	$2H_2O$

nitric acid	+	ammonium hydroxide	→	ammonium nitrate	+	water
HNO_3	+	NH_4OH	→	NH_4NO_3	+	H_2O

Eutrophication

If too much fertiliser is added to fields, rain sometimes washes the excess fertiliser into ponds or rivers, increasing nitrate or phosphate levels. As a result the algae grow better, covering the water surface – **algal bloom**. The bloom stops sunlight reaching plants lower down in the pond. Photosynthesis stops so the plants die. Bacteria which rot the dead plants use up oxygen from the water. Most other living things then die through lack of oxygen – **eutrophication**.

Questions

1. If the acidity of something increases, does the pH rise, fall or stay constant?
2. Name the salt formed when:
   a. hydrochloric acid reacts with sodium hydroxide
   b. nitric acid reacts with potassium hydroxide
   c. sulphuric acid reacts with ammonium hydroxide
   d. sulphuric acid reacts with copper oxide.
3. Name the salt produced when sulphuric acid reacts with iron.
4. Copper oxide reacts with nitric acid.
   a. Name the **two** products.
   b. Write a balanced equation for the reaction.

Chemical economics

Reversible reactions and ammonia

Some chemical reactions will go in both directions. If you put acid with pH indicator, the indicator will turn red. If you now add alkali the indicator changes to blue. Add acid again, and it goes back to red.

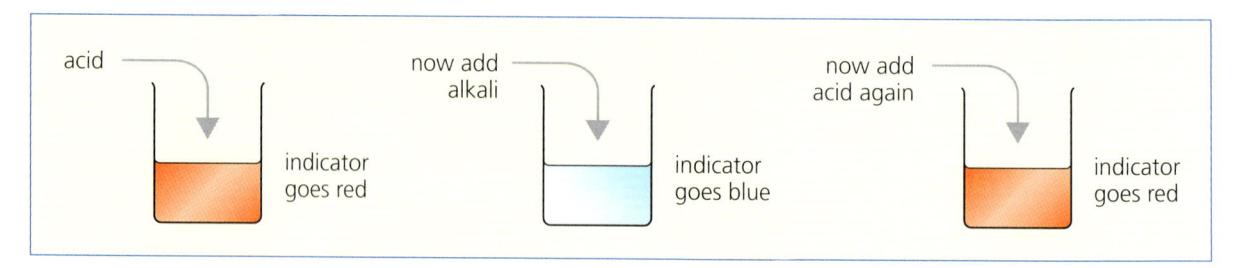

acid	now add alkali	now add acid again
indicator goes red	indicator goes blue	indicator goes red

You can do this as many times as you want. The reaction will go in either direction just as easily.

Usually it is very difficult to make a reaction go backwards, but in this case it is very easy. We call this type of reaction a **reversible reaction**.

Ammonia is made by a reversible reaction

Millions of tonnes of ammonia are produced every year so that we can make fertiliser. The method of making ammonia is called the **Haber Process** after the man who discovered it. Ammonia is made by the reversible reaction between nitrogen and hydrogen.

When nitrogen and hydrogen meet they start to react to form ammonia. The ammonia immediately starts to turn back to nitrogen and hydrogen. The reaction goes in both directions at the same time. We adjust the conditions to give the most suitable yield at the most suitable speed.

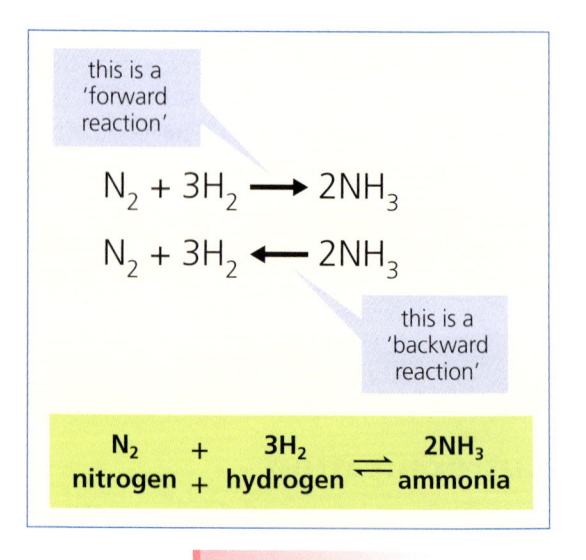

this is a 'forward reaction'

$$N_2 + 3H_2 \longrightarrow 2NH_3$$
$$N_2 + 3H_2 \longleftarrow 2NH_3$$

this is a 'backward reaction'

$$N_2 + 3H_2 \rightleftharpoons 2NH_3$$
nitrogen + hydrogen ⇌ ammonia

⇌ tells us that it is a reversible reaction

The Haber Process

Hydrogen is made by cracking hydrocarbons from crude oil and nitrogen is taken from the air. *High pressure* increases the percentage yield of ammonia. *Low temperature* also increases the percentage yield, but a *high temperature* makes the reaction go faster, so we use an in-between temperature of 450 °C as a compromise, an optimum temperature.

Ammonia is removed as fast as it is made to stop it reacting back into nitrogen and hydrogen. A catalyst of iron, a transition metal, speeds up the reaction. Catalysts do not change the yield for a given amount of nitrogen and hydrogen, because they only increase the rate of the reaction.

Keeping the costs down

Making new substances can often be expensive. The total cost depends on:
- the cost of the equipment needed
- the cost of the energy needed
- the cost of the starting materials
- operators' wages
- how fast it can be made – the quicker you make it, the cheaper it is.

Keeping costs down for the Haber Process

The optimum conditions are those which make the right amount of ammonia every day for the cheapest cost.

We can keep costs down by getting the nitrogen for the Haber Process from the air. The air is an important natural resource. However, the process is still not cheap to run. It needs:

- **high temperature**
  At about 450 °C the reaction is fast enough to be useful. However, this means high energy costs for the fuel.
- **high pressure**
  High pressure increases the yields. However, this means money has to be spent on compressors and also on extra-thick reaction vessels and pipes, which won't explode under the pressure.

Three ways of saving money are to:
- make the ammonia as quickly as possible. We use the catalyst to do this
- recycle any unused nitrogen and hydrogen back through the reaction vessel so that none of it is wasted
- make the process automatic, so that fewer people need to be paid to run it.

Questions

1. What is a reversible reaction?
2. What is produced if you put an iron catalyst with ammonia?
3. Use the list at the top of the page to decide on one way of saving money in the industrial production of alcohol.
4. a Give **two** ways to keep the cost of ammonia down.
   b Give **two** things that push costs up.
5. The table shows how the percentage yield for the reversible reaction that makes ammonia changes with pressure.
   a What happens to the yield as the pressure increases?
   b Suggest why we don't use a pressure of 1000 atmospheres.
   c Plot a graph to find the % yield at 300 atmospheres.

Pressure in atmospheres	% yield of ammonia at 400 °C
10	4
25	9
50	15
100	25
200	39
400	55
1000	80

Chemical economics

Chemical calculations

How much do we need?

If you want to carry out a chemical reaction without wasting any of the chemicals you need to know precisely how much of each reactant to use. To measure out chemical reactions we weigh them. We weigh out atoms in 'pre-packed' quantities called moles. Moles of different elements weigh different amounts. The mass of a mole of atoms of an element is its **relative atomic mass** in grams.

hydrogen ram = 1   carbon ram = 12   oxygen ram = 16

1 mole of hydrogen atoms weighs 1 gram   1 mole of carbon atoms weighs 12 grams   1 mole of oxygen atoms weighs 16 grams

ram = relative atomic mass

For example, the equation for iron reacting with sulphur is

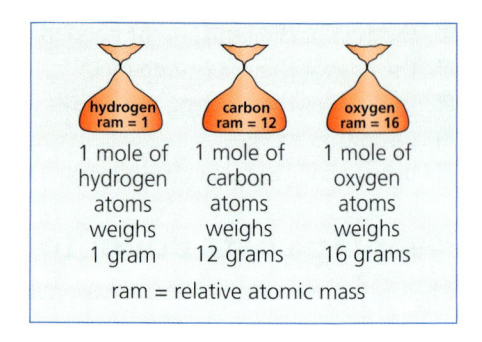

Fe	+	S	→	FeS
1 atom	reacts with	1 atom		
56 grams	reacts with	32 grams		(using relative atomic masses)

Formula masses

When we weigh out substances made of more than one atom, we have to add up the masses of all the atoms inside the formula. This is called the **formula mass**. It is the mass of one mole of the molecule.

A hydrogen molecule is H_2	The formula mass for H_2 is	1 + 1	= 2
An oxygen molecule is O_2	The formula mass for O_2 is	16 + 16	= 32
A methane molecule is CH_4	The formula mass for CH_4 is	12 + 1 + 1 + 1 + 1	= 16
Sodium chloride is NaCl	The formula mass for NaCl is	23 + 35.5	= 58.5
Calcium hydroxide is $Ca(OH)_2$	The formula mass for $Ca(OH)_2$ is	40 + 16 + 16 + 1 + 1	= 74

Copper sulphate crystals look more complicated. Their formula is $CuSO_4 \cdot 5H_2O$, so the formula mass is

$$64 + 32 + (4 \times 16) + 5 \times (2 + 16)$$
$$= 64 + 32 + 64 + 90 = 250$$

Moles and formula masses

You can work out how many moles there are of a chemical if you know its formula mass and how many grams of the chemical you have.

$$\text{Number of moles} = \frac{\text{mass}}{\text{formula mass}}$$

Calculating amounts used in chemical reactions

When chemicals react, their atoms join together in different ways. All the atoms at the start of the reaction are still there at the end. In a reaction the atoms never disappear, new atoms never appear. For example,

$$H_2 + Cl_2 \rightarrow 2HCl$$

This means that the mass of the chemicals is the same at the end of the reaction.

The mass of H_2 and Cl_2 at the start = H + H + Cl + Cl
= 1 + 1 + 35.5 + 35.5 = 73

The mass of 2HCl at the end = H + Cl + H + Cl
= 1 + 35.5 + 1 + 35.5 = 73

The total mass of all the reactants equals the total mass of all the products.

Calculating yields and formulae

Sometimes the amount of product is less than expected. The starting chemicals don't always react completely, and it is hard to get all the product out of the reaction mixture. Small amounts always 'get lost' somewhere.

Here are some reasons for 'missing' product:
- loss in filtration
- loss in evaporation – for something that can evaporate
- loss in heating – for something that can evaporate
- loss in transferring liquids.

Percentage yields

The **percentage yield** is the amount of product actually collected compared to the amount that was expected.

$$\% \text{ yield} = \frac{\text{actual yield of product}}{\text{predicted yield of product}} \times 100$$

If a reaction produced 46 g of product, but we expected to have 80 g, the % yield

$$= \frac{46 \times 100}{80} = \frac{4600}{80} = 57.5\%$$

How to find a formula from reacting masses

To work out a formula you must know the mass of each element inside the substance. The sort of question you might have to answer is:
3.5 g of lithium reacts with 4 g of oxygen to make lithium oxide. What is the formula of lithium oxide?
(Relative atomic masses: Li = 7, O = 16)
These are the stages to go through.

Stage 1
Find out how many moles of each element you used.

3.5 g of lithium is made of $\frac{3.5}{7} = 0.5$ moles of lithium

4 g of oxygen is made of $\frac{4}{16} = 0.25$ moles of oxygen.

Stage 2
Find the ratio of the numbers of moles of the different elements – this is the formula.

0.5 moles of lithium atoms react with 0.25 moles of oxygen atoms.
2 mole of lithium atoms react with 1 mole of oxygen atoms.
The formula of lithium oxide is Li_2O.

Relative atomic masses
hydrogen	H	= 1
lithium	Li	= 7
carbon	C	= 12
nitrogen	N	= 14
oxygen	O	= 16
sodium	Na	= 23
sulphur	S	= 32
chlorine	Cl	= 35.5
calcium	Ca	= 40
iron	Fe	= 56
copper	Cu	= 64

Questions

1 You have 2 g of hydrogen.
 a You want the same number of atoms of carbon. How much do you weigh out?
 b You want twice as many atoms of oxygen. How much do you weigh out?

2 A reaction produced 32 g of chemical. You expected it to produce 50 g of chemical. What is the percentage yield?

3 8 g of copper combine with 1 g of oxygen. What is the formula of the copper oxide?

What if you only have percentage masses?
It works just the same way:
- Lithium oxide is 46.7% lithium and 53.3% oxygen.
- This means that 46.7 g lithium reacts with 53.3 g of oxygen.

The Periodic Table

Atoms, isotopes and electron shells

An atom is made of a tiny positive nucleus surrounded by shells of electrons.

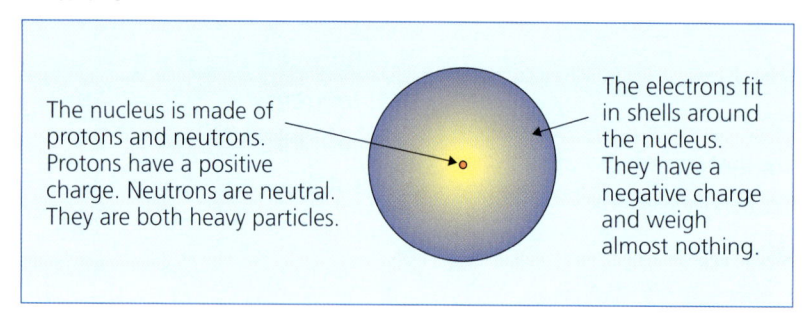

The nucleus is made of protons and neutrons. Protons have a positive charge. Neutrons are neutral. They are both heavy particles.

The electrons fit in shells around the nucleus. They have a negative charge and weigh almost nothing.

Atoms are neutral. Their negative and positive charges cancel out. This means that the number of electrons must be the same as the number of protons.

Name	Charge	Mass	Where found
proton	+1	1	inside the nucleus
neutron	0	1	inside the nucleus
electron	−1	0	outside the nucleus, in shells

The number of protons in an atom is called the **atomic number** or the **proton number**. It tells you what element you have. If an atom has one proton, the element is hydrogen, two protons means helium and so on.

The mass of an atom is made up of all the protons and neutrons, because both are heavy particles. Add the two numbers together to make the **mass number**. The electrons don't weigh enough to matter.

We write all this information in a standard way.

The number of neutrons is the mass number minus the proton number.

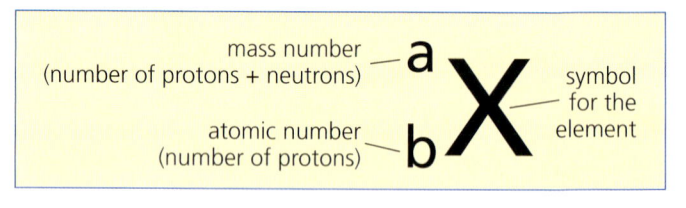

$$_b^a X$$

mass number (number of protons + neutrons) — a
atomic number (number of protons) — b
symbol for the element

Isotopes

Many elements have more than one mass number. These different forms of the same element are called **isotopes**.

$^{35}_{17}Cl$ has 17 protons, so it is chlorine. Work out how many neutrons it must have (mass number – proton number). You should have the answer 18 neutrons.

$^{37}_{17}Cl$ has 17 protons, so it is chlorine. Work out how many neutrons it must have (mass number – proton number). You should have the answer 20 neutrons.

The only difference between them is the number of neutrons in the nucleus. This makes one isotope heavier than the other, but otherwise it doesn't have much effect.

How are the electrons arranged in an atom?

In a neutral atom the number of electrons outside the nucleus is the same as the number of protons inside the nucleus. Electrons are negative, protons are positive, and so the two sets of charges cancel out and the atom is neutral. Remember that the number of protons is the atomic number.

Electrons fit into shells around the nucleus. Two electrons fit into the first shell, then up to eight electrons fit into the next shell. Eight electrons is a stable number for all shells after the innermost shell.

Sodium has 11 electrons, so its electron arrangement is 2,8,1. This means that there are two electrons in the first shell, eight in the next and one in the outer shell.

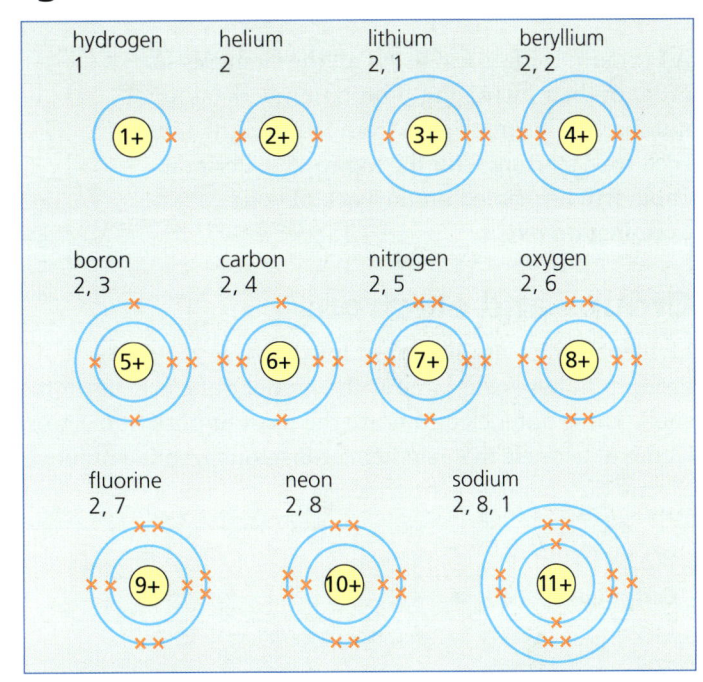

hydrogen 1	helium 2	lithium 2, 1	beryllium 2, 2
boron 2, 3	carbon 2, 4	nitrogen 2, 5	oxygen 2, 6
fluorine 2, 7	neon 2, 8	sodium 2, 8, 1	

Ions

If the outer shell of an element is only a few electrons away from the eight, the element will form an ion. Electrons are gained or lost to end up with the eight. If more than two electrons have to move, the element usually won't form an ion. It shares electrons instead.

Elements whose atoms gain electrons to form ions

If there are 7 electrons in the outer shell, they gain one electron → X^- ion.

If there are 6 electrons in the outer shell, they gain two electrons → X^{2-} ion.

Elements whose atoms give away electrons to form ions

If there is 1 electron in the outer shell, they give away one electron → X^+ ion.

If there are 2 electrons in the outer shell, they give away two electrons → X^{2+} ion.

Questions

1. What is the difference between $^{16}_{8}O$ and $^{18}_{8}O$?
2. How many protons are in $^{56}_{26}Fe$?
3. How many neutrons are in $^{56}_{26}Fe$?
4. The atomic number of nitrogen is 7.
   a. How many protons has it got?
   b. How many electrons has it got?
   c. How are the electrons arranged?
5. The atomic number of sodium is 11. What is its electron arrangement?
6. The atomic number of potassium is 19. What is its electron arrangement?

Formulae of ionic compounds

Overall amounts of charge on the ions must balance. If the ions have different amounts of charge, we need different numbers of each ion for charges to balance.

Ions present in compound	Formula (balanced charges)
Na^+ and Cl^-	NaCl
Mg^{2+} and O^{2-}	MgO
Mg^{2+} and Cl^-	$MgCl_2$
Na^+ and SO_4^{2-}	Na_2SO_4

The Periodic Table

A Periodic Table is is a list of all the elements in order of their increasing proton numbers (atomic numbers). The order goes from left to right along each row, starting with the top row. A Periodic Table will be printed on the back of your examination paper.

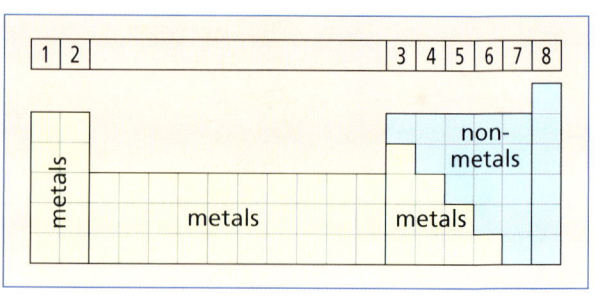

Groups and electrons

Elements which are similar fit into vertical **groups** or **families**. The group number is the same as the number of electrons in the outer shell. These outer electrons are the most important electrons of an element, because that is where atoms touch, so the outer electrons dictate the chemical properties.

Group number	1	2	3	4	5	6	7	8
Outer electrons	1	2	3	4	5	6	7	8

Sometimes the last group on the right is called Group 0.

All the elements in a group are similar, although there is a regular change in their properties as you go down the group. The properties of an element are in between those of elements above and below it in the group.

Eight electrons make a stable shell. Elements in groups which have only one or two electrons in the outer shell lose those electrons and form positive ions. Elements in groups which have six or seven electrons in the outer shell gain electrons and form negative ions.

Periods

A horizontal row of elements is called a **period**. Elements in the same period have the same number of electron shells.

Look at the complete Periodic Table. H and He are in the first period. They have one shell of electrons. Li to Ne are in the second period. They all have two shells of electrons. Na to Ar are in the third period. They all have three shells of electrons.

Worked example

Q An element has an electronic structure 2.8.5. Deduce its group number, period number and identity.

A There are five electrons in the outer shell, **so group 5**. There are 3 electron shells, **so period 3**. The element in period 3, Group 5 is **phosphorus**.

Questions

1. Explain why elements in Group 2 form double positive ions.
2. Why don't Group 8 elements form ions?
3. Here is some information about three elements in Group 7.
   a. Estimate the relative atomic mass and the melting point of bromine.
   b. How did you decide?

Element	Cl	Br	I
Atomic number	17	35	53
Relative atomic mass	35.5		127
Melting point	−101 °C		+113 °C

Group 1: the alkali metals

The Group 1 elements are called the **alkali metals**. You need to know about the first three: lithium, sodium and potassium.

Element	Symbol
lithium	Li
sodium	Na
potassium	K
rubidium	Rb
caesium	Cs

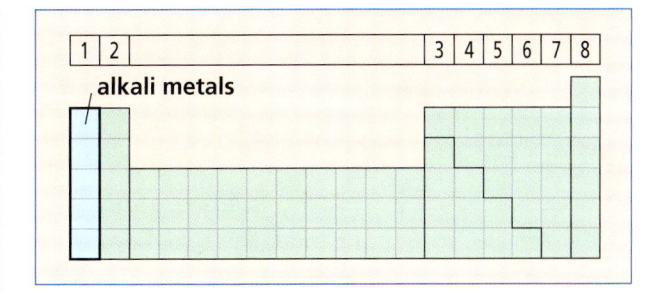

As these elements are in Group 1 they all have only one electron in the outer shell, and they lose that electron to form single positive ions. They are all very reactive, and get more reactive going *down* the group. The easier it is to lose the outer electron, the more reactive the alkali metal. Loss of an electron is **oxidation**.

The alkali metals are all very similar. Like all metals they are shiny and conduct electricity. Unlike most metals they have such low density that they will float on water. They are soft, and get softer as you go down the group.

Alkali metals all tarnish rapidly because they react with the oxygen in the air, so they are stored under oil to stop them reacting.

Reactions with water

All alkali metals float on water and react strongly to make alkaline solutions. They force hydrogen gas out of the water and make the metal hydroxide.

$$\text{lithium} + \text{water} \rightarrow \text{lithium hydroxide} + \text{hydrogen}$$
$$2Li + 2H_2O \rightarrow 2LiOH + H_2$$

The reaction with water gets more violent down the group.
- Lithium reacts but does not melt because it is the least reactive.
- Sodium melts and moves about the surface of the water as it reacts.
- Potassium melts, moves about the surface and bursts into flame.

Testing for alkali metals

The metals and their compounds give coloured flames. You can use this to find out which metal is in a compound.
- Lithium burns with a red flame.
- Sodium burns with a yellow flame.
- Potassium burns with a lilac flame.

---

use safety screens and goggles!

Sodium and potassium melt as soon as they are dropped in water. Lithium does not melt because it is the least reactive metal. Caesium is so reactive that it explodes when it touches water.

If asked to predict the properties of alkali metals you don't know of, remember they are all similar. Rb is more reactive than K, Cs is more reactive than Rb.

Questions

1. Write a word equation for the reaction of sodium with water.
2. Write a balanced chemical equation for the reaction of sodium with water.

Group 7: the halogens

The Group 7 elements are called the **halogens**. You need to know about chlorine, bromine and iodine.

Element	Symbol	Normal state	Colour
fluorine	F	gas	
chlorine	Cl	gas	green
bromine	Br	liquid	orange
iodine	I	solid	grey

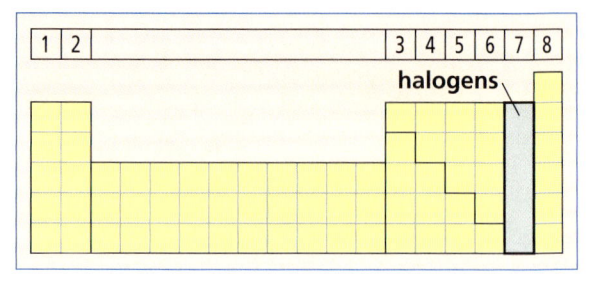

Halogens all have seven electrons in the outer shell, so they are very reactive and they all gain one electron to form a single negative ion. They get more reactive going *up* the group. The easier it is to gain an electron, the more reactive the halogen. Gain of an electron is **reduction**.

The halogens are all very similar non-metals. They are poisonous (bromine and chlorine should be handled only in a fume cupboard). They are acidic, they react vigorously with alkali metals forming ionic compounds.

Reactions with metals

The halogens react with lots of different metals. In each case they form a salt called a **halide**. Even less reactive metals, such as iron, will react vigorously with a halogen.

metal + halogen → metal halide
$2Na + Cl_2 → 2NaCl$
sodium + chlorine → sodium chloride

Displacement reactions

Once a halogen has reacted with a metal, it can be pushed back out again by a more reactive halogen. This is called **displacement**.

Bromine is more reactive that iodine. Bromine will displace iodine from iodine compounds (iodides).

Bromine + sodium iodide → iodine + sodium bromide
$Br_2 + 2NaI → I_2 + 2NaBr$

Chlorine is more reactive than both bromine and iodine, so it will displace either of them.

$Cl_2 + 2NaBr → Br_2 + 2NaCl$
$Cl_2 + 2NaI → I_2 + 2NaCl$

What are the halogens used for?

Chlorine is used
- as a bleach to get rid of stains
- for killing bacteria in drinking water and in swimming pools
- for making plastics and insecticides.

Iodine is an antiseptic. It is used to sterilise wounds.

If asked to predict the properties of halogens you don't know of, remember they are similar. At is less reactive than I; F is more reactive than Cl.

Questions

1. Write a word equation for the reaction between hydrogen and chlorine.
2. Sodium chloride has the formula NaCl. Write a balanced equation for the reaction between sodium and chlorine.

Group 8: the noble gases

The noble gases are helium, neon, argon, krypton, xenon and radon. They are colourless gases and have almost no reactions. This is because they all have a stable outer shell (usually eight electrons, except helium, which has two), so they don't form any bonds. Their densities increase down the group.

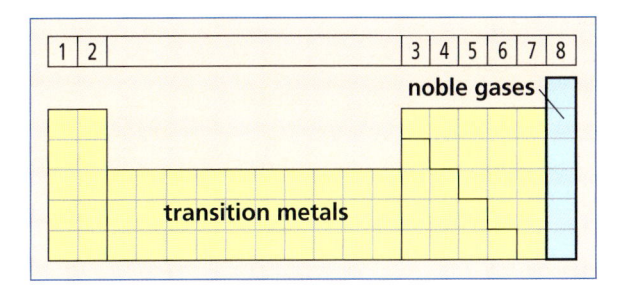

Uses of the noble gases

Helium is used to fill balloons because it is less dense than air and it will not burn. Neon, argon and krypton are used in different sorts of lights, especially coloured 'neon' lights, because they are unreactive.

The transition metals

The **transition metals** contain common metals, such as iron and copper, and also silver and gold. They are all what we normally think of as metals – they conduct electricity and heat, are shiny, hard, strong, dense and have high melting points.

Transition metals and their compounds can make good catalysts. For example iron is the catalyst in the Haber Process for making ammonia, nickel is the catalyst for the reaction between alkenes and hydrogen (hydrogenation).

- Copper compounds are blue.
- Iron(II) compounds are light green.
- Iron(III) compounds are orange-brown.

Compounds of the transition metals

Most transition metal compounds are coloured. The colour is due to the metal ion inside the compound. The colour tells you which transition element is present.

Heating the transition metal carbonates

If you heat transition metal carbonates they break apart into carbon dioxide and the metal oxide. This is called **thermal decomposition**. The metal oxide is often a different colour from the carbonate. You can show that carbon dioxide is formed because it turns limewater milky.

Remember that sodium carbonate does not break down when heated.

copper carbonate → copper oxide + carbon dioxide
$CuCO_3 \rightarrow CuO + CO_2$

Other examples that you should know are:
- iron carbonate, $FeCO_3$
- manganese carbonate, $MnCO_3$
- zinc carbonate, $ZnCO_3$.

Their equations follow the same pattern as $CuCO_3$.

Testing with sodium hydroxide solution

Sodium hydroxide forms a green precipitate with Fe^{2+} ions.
$Fe^{2+} + 2OH^- \rightarrow Fe(OH)_2$

Sodium hydroxide forms a red-brown precipitate with Fe^{3+} ions.
$Fe^{3+} + 2OH^- \rightarrow Fe(OH)_2$

Sodium hydroxide forms a blue precipitate with Cu^{2+} ions.
$Cu^{2+} + 2OH^- \rightarrow Fe(OH)_2$

Materials and their properties

Concept map

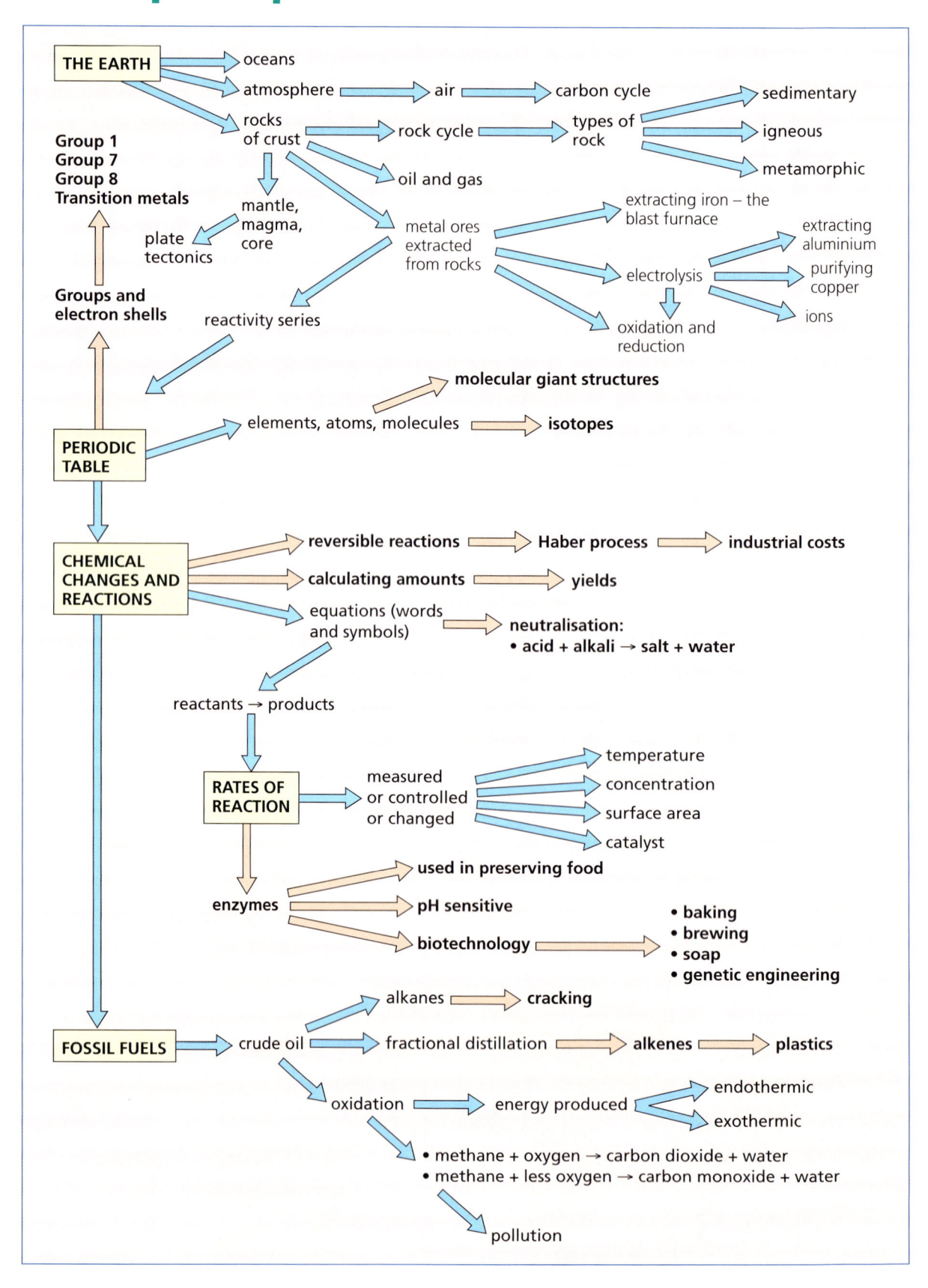

THE EARTH
- oceans
- atmosphere → air → carbon cycle
- rocks of crust → rock cycle → types of rock → sedimentary / igneous / metamorphic
- rocks of crust → oil and gas
- rocks of crust → mantle, magma, core
- rocks of crust → metal ores extracted from rocks → extracting iron – the blast furnace
- metal ores extracted from rocks → electrolysis → extracting aluminium / purifying copper / ions
- metal ores extracted from rocks → oxidation and reduction
- plate tectonics
- reactivity series

Group 1
Group 7
Group 8
Transition metals

Groups and electron shells

PERIODIC TABLE
- elements, atoms, molecules → molecular giant structures
- elements, atoms, molecules → isotopes

CHEMICAL CHANGES AND REACTIONS
- reversible reactions → Haber process → industrial costs
- calculating amounts → yields
- equations (words and symbols) → neutralisation:
  - acid + alkali → salt + water
- reactants → products

RATES OF REACTION
- measured or controlled or changed → temperature / concentration / surface area / catalyst
- enzymes → used in preserving food
- enzymes → pH sensitive
- enzymes → biotechnology →
  - baking
  - brewing
  - soap
  - genetic engineering

FOSSIL FUELS
- crude oil → alkanes → cracking
- crude oil → fractional distillation → alkenes → plastics
- crude oil → oxidation → energy produced → endothermic / exothermic
  - methane + oxygen → carbon dioxide + water
  - methane + less oxygen → carbon monoxide + water
  - pollution

Exam questions

1 The flow chart shows how ammonia is made.

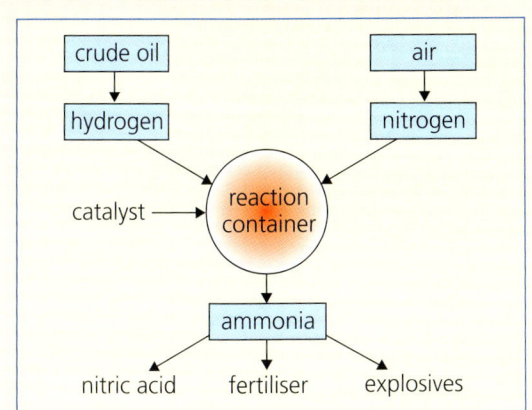

```
crude oil          air
    ↓               ↓
hydrogen       nitrogen
        ↘     ↙
catalyst → reaction
           container
              ↓
           ammonia
          ↙  ↓   ↘
  nitric acid fertiliser explosives
```

a i Air is a raw material used to make ammonia. Write down the name of the other raw material. [1]
  ii Write down **two** uses of ammonia. [2]
  iii What are **three** of the costs in making ammonia? [3]
b A catalyst is used in this reaction.
  i What is a catalyst? [2]
  ii Which catalyst is used in this process? [1]
c The Haber Process is a reversible reaction. What is meant by the term 'reversible reaction'? [1]
d The graph shows what percentage of ammonia is produced by the Haber Process at different pressures.

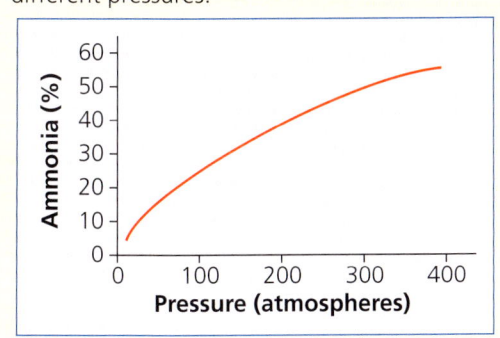

  i The plant is usually operated at about 250 atmospheres pressure. What percentage of ammonia should this produce? [1]
  ii It is too expensive to build a factory which works at a higher pressure, even though a higher percentage of ammonia would be produced. Suggest **one** reason why it is more expensive to use a higher pressure. [1]

[12 marks]

2 When the nuclear power station at Chernobyl released radioactive dust into the air, some of the dust fell on the Lake District in Britain. Sheep ate the dust that settled on the grass and produced radioactive milk. Sheep normally use calcium from the grass to make milk, but this time they were using strontium-90 from the dust as well.
a i Find strontium in the Periodic Table and decide how many protons are in the nucleus of a strontium atom. [1]
  ii Strontium-90 is an isotope of strontium. What is the difference between two isotopes of the same element? [1]
b i Use the Periodic Table to decide how many electrons are in the outer shell of a strontium atom. [1]
  ii Explain why sheep are likely to take in strontium as well as calcium. [2]
c An element has an atomic number of 13 and an atomic mass of 27.
  i How many neutrons are in its nucleus? [1]
  ii Write down the number of electrons in each shell, starting with the innermost shell. [1]

[7 marks]

3 Use this diagram of the Periodic Table to help you answer this question.

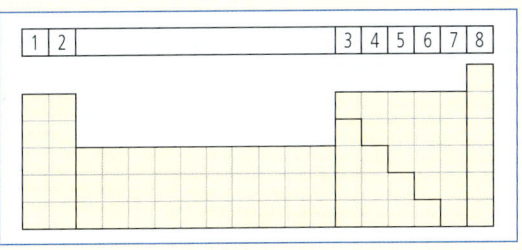

a Use ideas about electron shells to explain why the Noble Gases (Group 8) are not reactive. [1]
b Oxygen has eight electrons and is in Group 6.
  i How many electrons are in the inner shell of an oxygen atom? [1]
  ii How many electrons are in the outer shell of an oxygen atom? [1]
c Magnesium has two electrons in its outer shell. What is the charge on a magnesium ion? [2]

[5 marks]

Exam questions

4 Ammonia solution is an alkali. You can make fertiliser by neutralising ammonia solution with an acid. A student investigated neutralisation reactions by adding acid from a burette to alkali in a flask. She measured the pH during the investigation.

   a Complete the equation
   acid + alkali → _____ + water [1]

   b The fertiliser that she made was ammonium nitrate, $(NH_4)_2NO_3$.

   i How many atoms of nitrogen are in the formula of ammonium nitrate? [1]

   ii How many different elements are in ammonium nitrate? [1]

   iii The relative atomic mass of hydrogen (H) is 1. The relative atomic mass of nitrogen (N) is 14. The relative atomic mass of oxygen (O) is 16.
   What is the relative formula mass of ammonium nitrate? [1]

   c If fertilisers contaminate ponds or lakes, wildlife will be harmed.

   i What do we call this effect? [1]

   ii Briefly describe how the damage is done [3]

   [8 marks]

5 Ethane, C_2H_6, and ethene, C_2H_4, are hydrocarbons with slightly different formulae.

   a How many atoms of carbon are in a molecule of ethane? [1]

   b Hydrogen and carbon are both non-metals.

   i What happens to the electrons on the two atoms when they form a bond? [1]

   ii A carbon atom has a total of six electrons around its nucleus. How are they arranged in their shells? [2]

   c Ethane is part of the alkane group.

   i What group is ethene part of? [1]

   ii What chemical test could you use to tell the difference between ethane and ethene? [1]

   iii What would you see if you tried this test on ethene? [1]

   iv State what you would see if you tried this test on ethane. [1]

   d Ethene is used to make polythene, a polymer.

   i Use the symbol –E– for ethene to draw part of a polythene molecule. [1]

   ii Ethene does not form polythene without help. Give **two** things that you must do so that the ethene will react. [2]

   e Use this table about different plastics to answer the questions below.

Plastic	Information
Acrylic	flexible, will take up dyes
Polycarbonate	rigid, tough and transparent
Polythene	flexible, easily formed into thin sheets, very cheap
PVC	can be rigid, tough, fairly cheap

   Which plastic would be best for making:
   i plastic drainpipes
   ii different coloured clothes
   iii plastic bags to put shopping in
   iv safety spectacles? [4]

   [15 marks]

6 We think that wine was first produced by accident when wild yeasts landed on some crushed grapes and made them ferment.

   a i What are the three important conditions for fermentation to go well? [3]

   ii What are the sugars in the grapes converted to during fermentation? [1]

   b Yeast contains biological catalysts called enzymes.

   i What does a catalyst do to a reaction? [1]

   ii What can you say about a catalyst at the end of a reaction? [1]

   c Yeast is also used in breadmaking. What does yeast produce to make the bread rise? [1]

   d If bread is left in a cold place the yeast will only work very slowly. What will happen to the speed that the yeast works at as the temperature increases? Explain your answer. [4]

   [11 marks]

7 Sodium and chlorine will react to form sodium chloride. Find sodium and chlorine in the Periodic Table.

   a i How many electrons are in the outer shell of a sodium atom? [1]

ii How many electrons are in the outer shell of a chlorine atom? [1]
iii What sort of bond is formed when sodium reacts with chlorine? [1]
iv Explain what happens to the electrons as this bond is formed. [2]
b What sort of boiling point will sodium chloride have? [1]
c i Will solid sodium chloride be an electrical conductor or an insulator? [1]
ii Will molten sodium chloride be an electrical conductor or an insulator? [1]
[8 marks]

8 The energy of combustion of a fuel was found out by using it to heat 500 g of water in a beaker. The water temperature went from 20 °C to 46 °C.
a What do we call reactions that give out heat? [1]
b In what units do we measure heat? [1]
c Calculate the energy transferred by the fuel to the water. (It takes 4.18 J to heat 1 g of water by 1 °C.) [2]
[4 marks]

9 A student wanted to see how fast magnesium reacts with hydrochloric acid. She used the same amount of acid and the same mass of magnesium for each experiment.
a Use the idea of particles to explain why the reaction in beaker **B** was faster than **A**. [2]

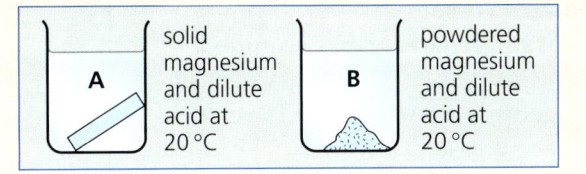

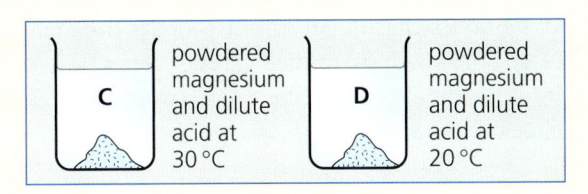

A: solid magnesium and dilute acid at 20 °C
B: powdered magnesium and dilute acid at 20 °C
C: powdered magnesium and dilute acid at 30 °C
D: powdered magnesium and dilute acid at 20 °C

b Use the idea of particles to suggest and explain two reasons why the reaction in beaker **C** was faster than **D**. [4]
c Suggest **two** other ways of speeding reactions up. [2]
[8 marks]

Using electricity

Static electricity

Jo walks across the room. Her feet rub against the carpet, pulling tiny particles (**electrons**) off it. As the number of electrons on her builds up, Jo becomes **charged** with **static electricity**. She acquires a **negative charge** because she has gained some electrons. The carpet acquires a **positive charge** because it has lost electrons.

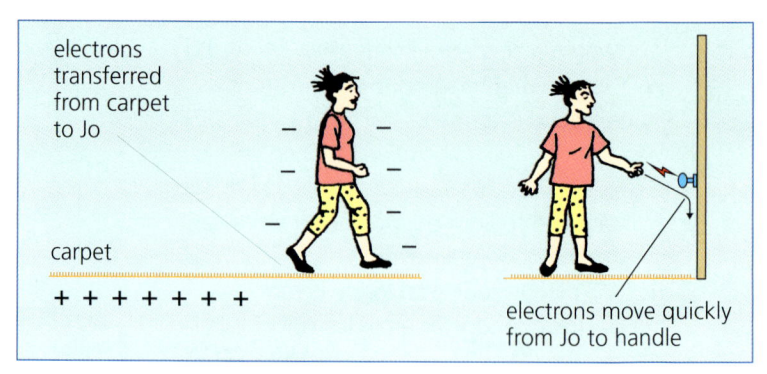

When Jo reaches the door, she touches the metal handle. All the electrons which she pulled off the carpet flow rapidly through her into the metal handle. She **discharges** herself, but gets an electric shock at the same time.

Conductors and insulators

Materials which allow electrons to move through them are **conductors**. Things which electrons can't move through are **insulators**. Metals and water are conductors. Most other materials (such as glass, wood and plastic) are insulators.

Types of charge

There are two sorts of charge, called **positive** and **negative**. The sort of charge picked up by objects when they are rubbed against each other depends on the two materials involved.

In this example, acetate becomes positive when rubbed with wool. This is because the electrons transferred from the acetate to the wool have a negative charge. The acetate becomes positive because it has lost some negative charge.

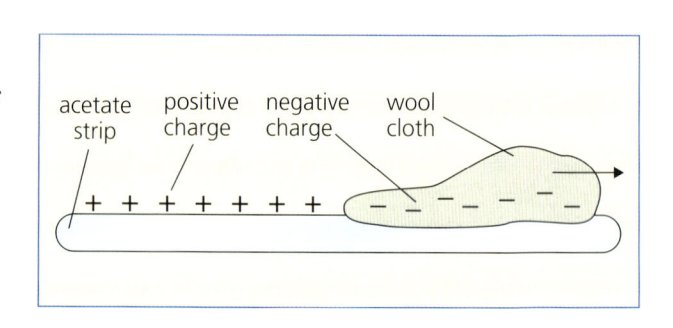

Polythene becomes negative when it is rubbed with wool. The wool becomes positive.

Attraction and repulsion

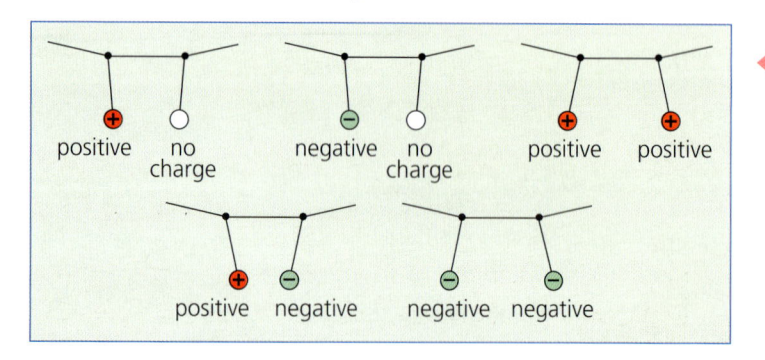

- Objects with any charge attract objects with no charge.
- Objects with the same charge always repel each other.
- Objects with different charges always attract each other.

Using static electricity

Electrostatic forces are very useful.

Droplets of paint spray can be charged. They then repel each other, to give a fine mist which is strongly attracted to any uncharged metal objects nearby. The result is a very even coat of paint on the object, even round the back.

Photocopiers and laser printers use static electricity. Reflected light from a document is used to coat an insulating surface with a pattern of positive charge. This attracts tiny particles of negatively charged toner. The pattern of toner is then transferred to paper which has been strongly positively charged. The toner is fixed to the paper by heating to create a copy.

Electrostatic discharge can be dangerous.

Airplanes in flight become charged as they move rapidly through the air. The charge must be removed safely when the aircraft lands. Otherwise, there may be a spark between the airplane and the metal nozzle of the refuelling pipe. The spark (which is a rapid flow of electrons through the air) could ignite the fuel.

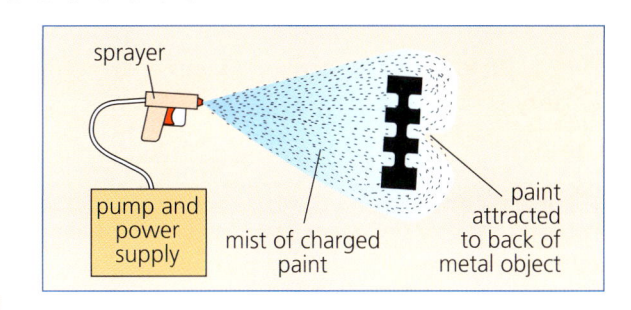

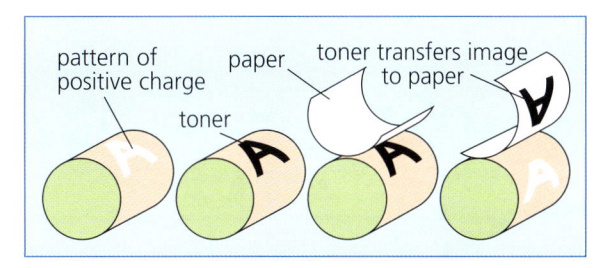

Questions

1. What can move through conductors but not through insulators?
2. Name **two** materials which are insulators.
3. Name **two** materials which are conductors.
4. Copy and complete the following sentences.
   A nylon comb is an _____. When it passes through hair, _____ are pulled off the hair and carried away by the _____. This leaves the comb _____.
5. Copy and complete the following sentences.
   Fur becomes positive when rubbed on glass. This is because electrons are transferred from the _____ to the _____ during the rubbing. Electrons have a _____ charge. Objects which have lost electrons have a _____ charge.
6. When glass is rubbed with silk, electrons are transferred from glass to silk. What are the charges of the glass and the silk after rubbing?
7. The table shows the effect of bringing object L close to object R.
   Complete the table with the words attract and repel.

Charge on L	Charge on R	Effect
positive	negative	
positive	none	
negative	negative	

8. Name **two** devices which use static electricity.
9. Explain why static charge can be dangerous when flammable substances are present.
10. Suggest why you can get an electric shock when you touch the body of a car after a journey.

Using electricity

Electrical circuits

Here is the **circuit diagram** for a **lamp** connected to a **battery** by a pair of **wires**.

Chemical energy in a cell makes electrons in the metal parts of the circuit flow from the negative terminal ⊖ to the positive one ⊕. A flow of electrons or charge is called a **current**. There is only a current if there is a complete conducting circuit between the terminals of the cell. Several cells make a **battery**. The current is the rate of flow of charge.

$$\text{current} = \frac{\text{charge}}{\text{time}} \qquad I = \frac{Q}{t}$$

You must know this one by heart!

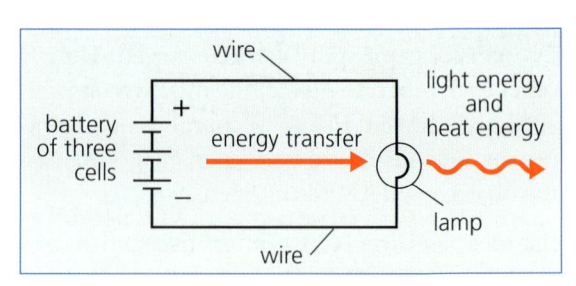

Symbol	Meaning	Units of measurement
I	current	ampere or A
Q	charge	coulomb or C
t	time	seconds or s

Component	Circuit symbol	Energy output
lamp		light and heat
resistor		heat
buzzer		sound
motor	(M)	kinetic
LED		light

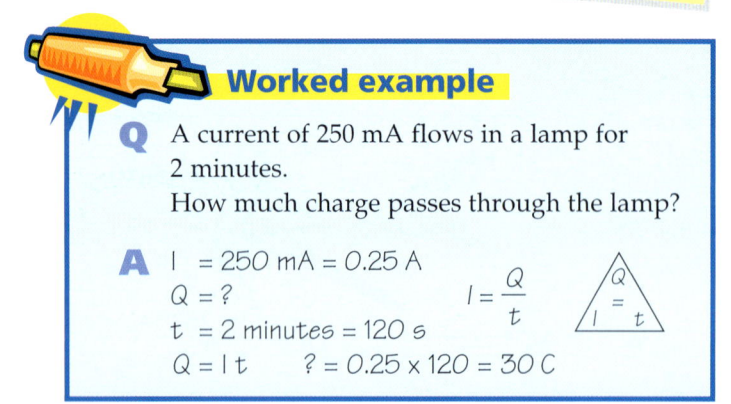

Worked example

Q A current of 250 mA flows in a lamp for 2 minutes.
How much charge passes through the lamp?

A I = 250 mA = 0.25 A
Q = ?
t = 2 minutes = 120 s
Q = I t   ? = 0.25 × 120 = 30 C

$I = \frac{Q}{t}$

Voltage

All electrical components have a **voltage rating**. This should be the same as the voltage of the electricity supply. You can run more than one component from one supply by connecting them in **parallel** with each other. If you put components in **series** with each other, low voltage components can be run off a high voltage supply.

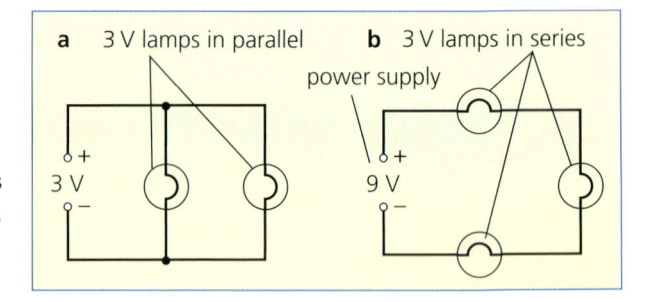

a 3 V lamps in parallel — power supply 3 V

b 3 V lamps in series — 9 V

Current

The amount of current in a component is measured with an **ammeter**. The meter is connected in **series** with the component. Current is measured in **amps (A)**. It has the same value all the way round a series circuit. When components are connected in parallel, the current drawn from the electricity supply is the sum of the currents in the components.

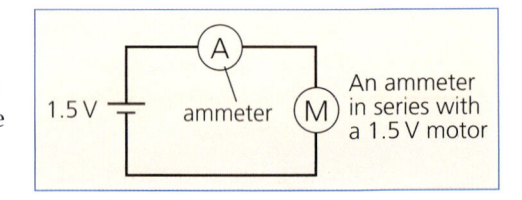

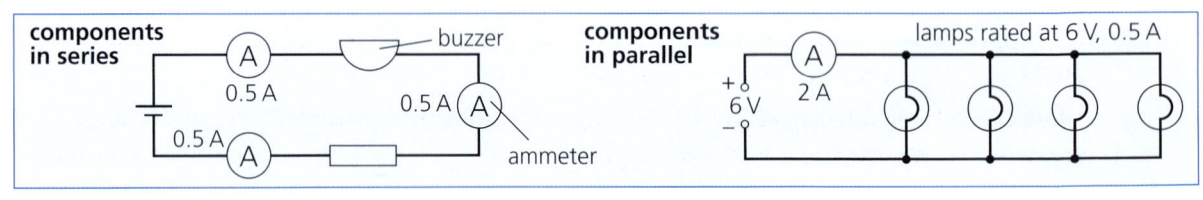

An ammeter in series with a 1.5 V motor

components in series — 0.5 A, 0.5 A, 0.5 A — buzzer, ammeter

components in parallel — 6 V, 2 A — lamps rated at 6 V, 0.5 A

Measuring voltage

The voltage drop across a component is measured by connecting a **voltmeter** in **parallel** with it. Voltage (or **potential difference**) is measured in **volts** (**V**). The voltage at a point in a circuit is the energy of each coulomb of charge at that point.

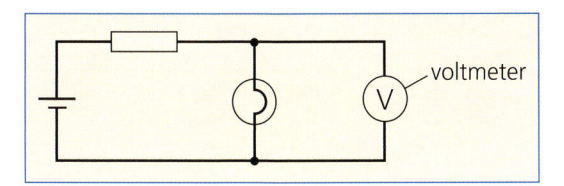

A **cathode ray oscilloscope** (or CRO) can be used to show the difference between a.c. and d.c. supplies.

Types of electricity

There are two **sources** of electrical energy: **direct current** (or **d.c.**) and **alternating current** (or **a.c.**). Batteries supply d.c., dynamos and generators supply a.c.

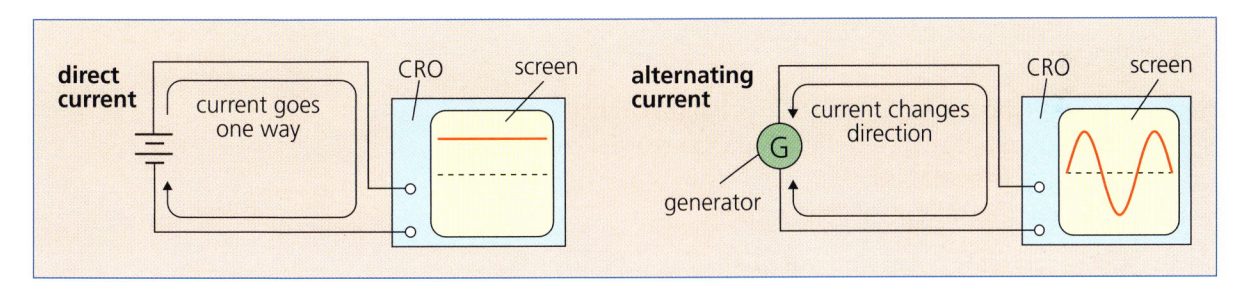

Questions

1. Calculate the charge which flows through a 500 mA lamp in 30 s.
2. If 1200 C of charge passes through a motor in a minute, what is the current in it?
3. Name **five** different electrical components. Draw their circuit symbols and state what type of energy they produce.
4. Draw the circuit diagram for a motor run off a battery.
5. Draw a diagram to show how to measure the current in a lamp being run off a 6 V battery.
6. Fill in the readings of the ammeters in this circuit. 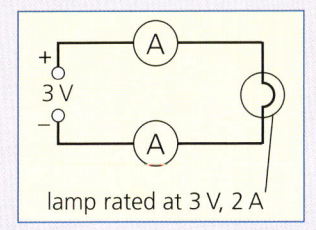
   (3 V, lamp rated at 3 V, 2 A)
7. A single 60 W lamp draws a current of 0.25 A when connected to a 240 V supply. How much current will be drawn by 8 lamps connected in parallel to 240 V?
8. A resistor and a motor are connected in series with a 12 V battery. Draw a circuit diagram to show how the voltage across the motor can be measured.
9. There is a voltage drop of 12 V across a lamp. How much energy is delivered to the lamp when 8 C of charge flow through it?

Using electricity

Power

The **power** of an electrical component is given with this formula:

power = current × voltage   P = I V

You must know this one by heart!

Worked example

Q There is a current of 2 A in an electric drill connected to 230 V. Calculate the power of the drill.

A P = ?   V = 230 V   I = 2 A
P = I × V
? = 2 × 230 = 460 W

Symbol	Meaning	Units of measurement
P	power	joules/s or watts (W)
V	voltage	volts or V
I	current	amperes or A

Resistance

Resistors control the current in a circuit. A big **resistance** means a small current. Two bulbs in series have a larger resistance than just one on its own. A **rheostat** is a variable resistor which controls the current in a circuit by altering its resistance.

As the voltage across a resistor increases, so does the current.

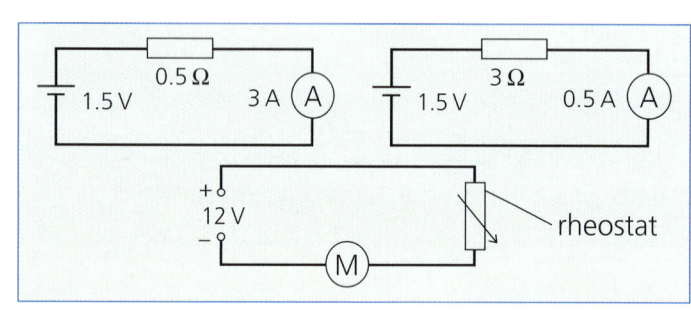

[Circuit diagrams: 1.5 V battery with 0.5 Ω resistor and ammeter reading 3 A; 1.5 V battery with 3 Ω resistor and ammeter reading 0.5 A; 12 V supply with motor M and rheostat]

The **resistance** of an electrical component is calculated with this formula:

resistance = voltage / current   R = V / I

You must know this one by heart!

Symbol	Meaning	Units of measurement
R	resistance	ohms or Ω
V	voltage	volts or V
I	current	amperes or A

Worked example

Q There is a current of 0.2 A in a resistor connected to a 3.0 V battery. Calculate the resistance.

A R = ?
V = 3.0 V   R = V/I   ? = 3.0/0.2 = 15 Ω
I = 0.2 A

Temperature and light-sensitive components

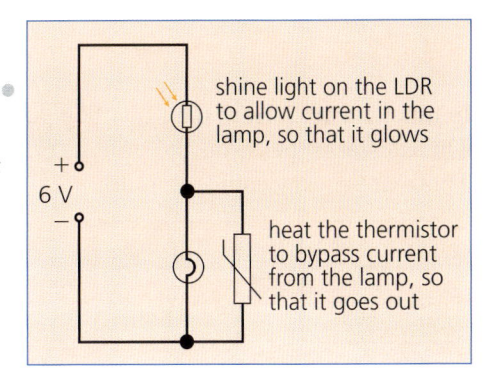

Things which contain a lot of free electrons have a low resistance. The number of free electrons in a metal is fixed, but can be changed in a **semiconductor**. The electrons in thermistors and LDRs can be freed by giving them extra energy. Increased light reduces the resistance of a light-dependent resistor (LDR). Similarly, increased temperature reduces the resistance of a thermistor.

shine light on the LDR to allow current in the lamp, so that it glows

heat the thermistor to bypass current from the lamp, so that it goes out

Voltage–current curves

These graphs show how the current in a wire resistor and a lamp depend on the voltage across them. Neither of these components have a polarity, so the graphs look exactly the same if the voltage is reversed.

The resistance of a **diode** depends on the voltage across it. The current rises steeply when the **anode** voltage rises above the **cathode** voltage.

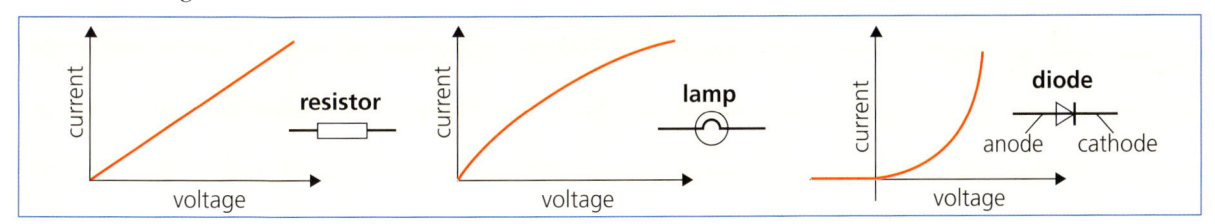

Questions

1. Write down the symbols and units for power, voltage and current. State the formula relating them.
2. There is a current of 5 A in a lamp connected to a 12 V battery. Calculate the power of the lamp.
3. Draw a circuit diagram to show how an ammeter and a voltmeter should be connected to measure the power of a motor.
4. A 100 W lamp is connected to a 250 V supply. Calculate the current in the lamp.
5. Which of these circuits has the highest resistance? 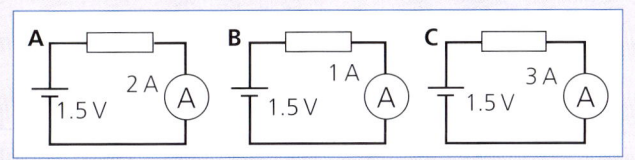
6. Write down the formula for electrical resistance. Explain the symbols and give their units.
7. A resistor has a current of 0.5 A when the voltage across it is 24 V. Calculate its resistance.
8. Show how a rheostat can be used to adjust the brightness of a lamp connected to a battery.
9. What is the current in a 3 Ω resistor when the voltage across it is 12 V?
10. What is the voltage across a 25 Ω resistor when there is a current of 4 A in it?
11. Describe the behaviour of thermistors and LDRs.

Applications of physics

Work, energy and power

Jo lifts up a brick from the floor. She puts it on the table. This increases the **potential energy** (**PE**) of the brick. This extra energy comes from Jo.

Chemical energy in Jo's muscles = Potential energy in the brick + Heat energy in Jo

Calculating work

The work done by Jo equals the PE gained by the brick.

work = force × distance   W = F × s

You must know this one by heart!

Worked example

Q Sam moves a table across the floor, pushing with a force of 20 N. How much work does he do if the table moves 4 m?

A W = ?   F = 20 N   s = 4 m
W = F × s   ? = 20 × 4 = 80 J

Symbol	Meaning	Units of measurement
W	work	joules or J
F	force	newtons or N
s	distance	metres or m

PE and KE

Moving objects have **kinetic energy** (**KE**). The faster they go, the more KE they have. Like all forms of energy, both PE and KE are measured in joules.

Sam does work on Jo

Jo gains kinetic energy

30 J KE + 70 J PE

50 J KE + 50 J PE

100 J heat energy

Sam throws ball of clay into the air. As it rises, it transfers its KE into PE. The clay has maximum PE at the top of its flight. On the way down again, the PE is transferred back into KE. When the clay lands on the ground, all of the KE that Sam gave it becomes heat energy.

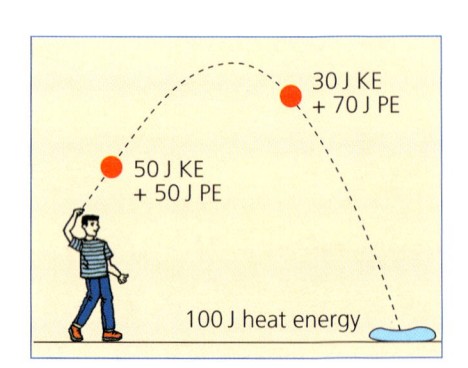

Calculating KE and PE

KE and PE can be calculated with the help of these formulae.

$KE = \frac{1}{2} mv^2$ $PE = mgh$

Worked examples

Q Calculate the KE of a 500 kg car at 15 m/s.

A KE = ? m = 500 kg v = 15 m/s
KE = $\frac{1}{2}mv^2$? = 0.5 × 500 × (15^2) = 56 250 J

Q A ball has a mass of 0.5 kg. Calculate the increase in PE when it is thrown 20 m into the air. Assume that the acceleration of free fall is 10 m/s².

A PE = ? PE = mgh m = 0.5 kg g = 10 m/s² h = 20 m
? = 0.5 × 10 × 20 = 100 J

Symbol	Meaning	Units
KE	kinetic energy	J
PE	potential energy	J
m	mass	kg
v	speed	m/s
g	acceleration of free fall	m/s²
h	height raised	m

Machines (such as motors) are often labelled with their **power**. This tells you how much work they can do in a second. A motor with a high power can deliver energy more quickly than one with a low power. So cars with high-power engines can accelerate and climb up hills faster than cars with low-power engines.

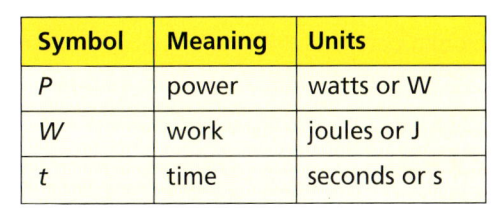

Symbol	Meaning	Units
P	power	watts or W
W	work	joules or J
t	time	seconds or s

power = $\frac{\text{work}}{\text{time}}$ P = $\frac{W}{t}$

Worked example

Q Joe does 2000 J of work lifting bricks up a building. This takes him 50 s. Calculate his power.

A P = ?
W = 2000 J P = $\frac{W}{t}$ P = $\frac{2000}{50}$ = 40 W
t = 50 s

Questions

1. Write down the formula for work. Explain the symbols and their units.
2. A brick weighs 25 N. Calculate the work needed to raise a brick by 3 m. How much PE does the brick gain in the process?
3. If 1000 J of work is done lifting a block of weight 50 N, through what height is it raised?
4. 50 000 J of work must be done to stop a car going at 10 m/s. If the car stops in a distance of 20 m, how big a force is required?
5. Jo applies a force of 50 N to her bike. It moves forwards on level ground. How much KE has it gained after moving 10 m?
6. Which of these situations involve doing work:
   a lifting up a weight from the floor
   b stretching an elastic band
   c holding a weight still above your head
   d thinking out these answers?
7. Copy and complete the following sentences.
   Sally climbs up the ladder of a slide, transferring _____ energy into _____ energy. As she moves down the slide, she transfers _____ energy into _____ energy. As she slides to a halt at the end, all of the KE has become _____ energy.
8. Calculate the KE of a 70 kg man running at 10 m/s.
9. Calculate the increase in PE of a 50 kg girl who climbs a vertical distance of 5 m up a ladder.
10. A crane does 1600 J of work in 8 s. Calculate its power.

Applications of physics

Electromagnetism

Forces on currents in magnetic fields

There is a force on a conductor which carries a current in a magnetic field. The force is at right angles to both the current and the field. The direction of the force can be reversed by reversing the direction of either the current or the field.

Motors

An electric motor contains a coil of copper wire inside a magnet. The coil is free to rotate on its axis. It sits in a magnetic field from a permanent magnet or an electromagnet.

Electric current in the coil interacts with the magnetic field to create a pair of forces. These act in opposite directions, forcing the coil to turn round.

The current enters and leaves the coil via the commutator and brushes. These act as a switch which ensures that the forces on the coil always turn it in the same direction.

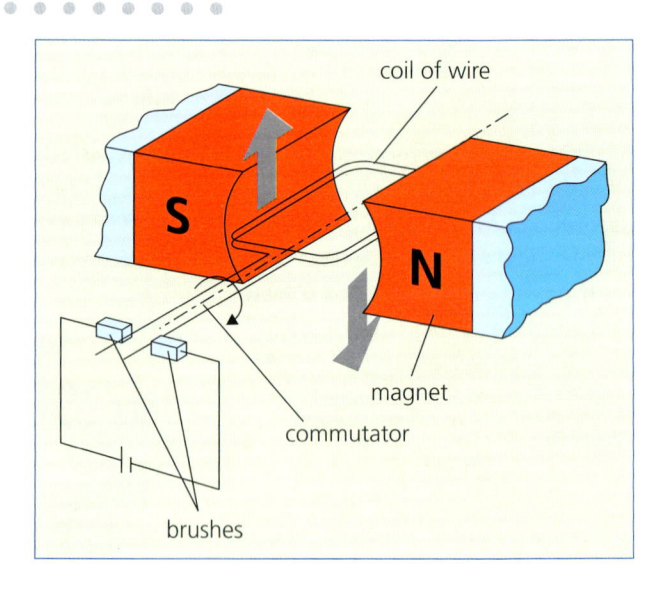

Generators

Electricity is **generated** whenever a wire is moved through a magnetic field. The voltage changes sign if the wire is moved the other way.

The size of the voltage can be increased by speeding up the motion and increasing the strength of the field.

A voltage is **induced** across the ends of a coil of wire whenever the magnetic field inside it changes. The sign of the induced voltage changes when the change of magnetic field is reversed.

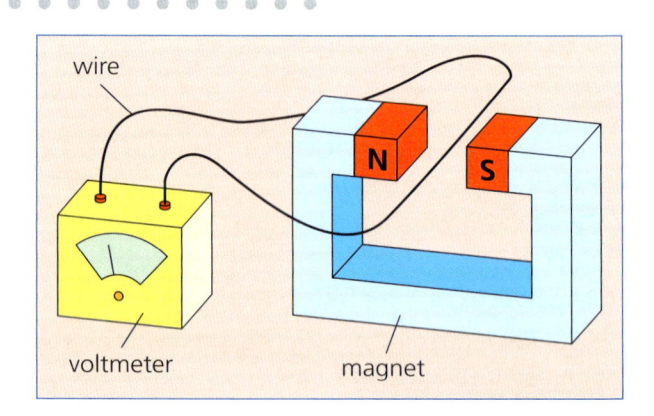

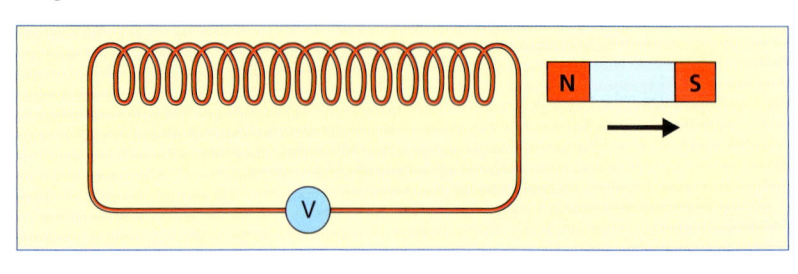

The size of the voltage can be increased by:
- speeding up the change of magnetic field
- increasing the number of coils of wire
- increasing the area of the coil
- winding the coil around soft iron.

Electricity can be generated by spinning large coils of copper wire inside the fields of large magnets. The alternating current in the coil is brought out of the **generator** by **brushes** pressing on **slip rings**.

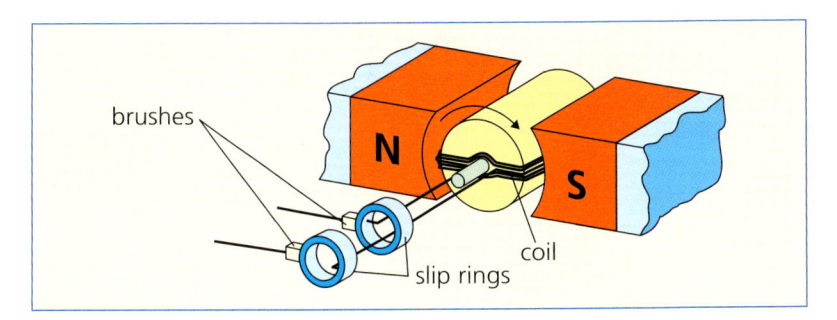

Questions

1. The wire in diagram (a) is pushed to the left. Which way does the wire get pushed in diagrams (b), (c) and (d)?

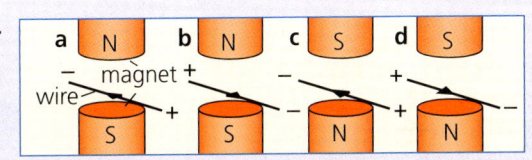

2. Electric motors contain copper and steel. Explain what each material is used for.

3. Draw a diagram to show the forces on the coil of an electric motor.

4. Explain the function of the commutator in an electric motor.

5. Suggest **three** alterations to an electric motor which will increase its speed.

6. The voltmeter reads +0.1 V as the wire is pulled up through the poles of the magnet. What will it read when the wire is
   a pushed down
   b held still between the poles of the magnet?

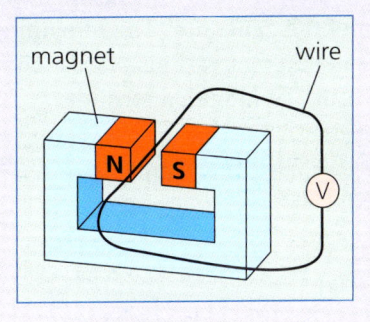

7. State **two** things you could do to increase the reading of the voltmeter in question 6.

8. Copy and complete the following sentences.
   There is a positive voltage across a coil when a magnet is placed in it. The voltage is _____ when the magnet is left in the coil and becomes _____ as the magnet is removed from the coil.

9. State **four** ways of increasing the voltage induced in a coil when a magnet is brought close.

10. A generator always contains lots of steel, soft iron and copper. Suggest what each material is used for in the generator.

11. Here is the voltage–time graph for a coil spinning in a magnetic field. How would the graph change if the coil spun round twice as fast?

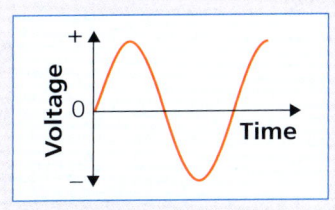

Applications of physics

Generating electricity

Electricity is made on a large scale by boiling water to make high-pressure **steam**. The steam passes through a **turbine**, making it spin round. The turbine is connected to the shaft of a **generator**. Electromagnets are attached to the shaft. As it spins round, the magnetic field inside the coils of wire changes, generating electricity.

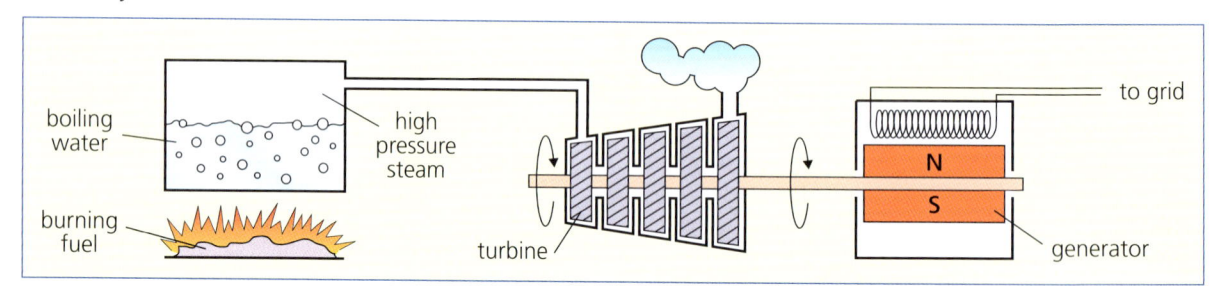

The water can be boiled by burning a fuel (such as coal, oil or gas) or by a nuclear reaction. Here is an energy flow diagram for a typical gas-fired electricity power station.

Efficiency

Each time the energy is **transferred**, some heat energy is lost. Overall, 1000 J of chemical energy in the gas becomes 400 J of electrical energy in the wires coming out of the generator. The remaining 600 J becomes heat energy at various places. The **efficiency** can be calculated with a formula.

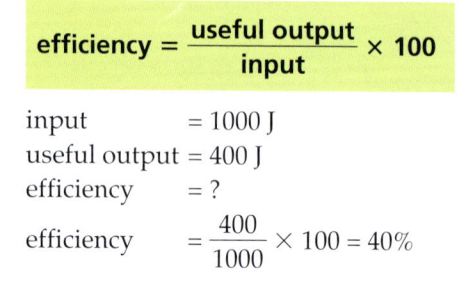

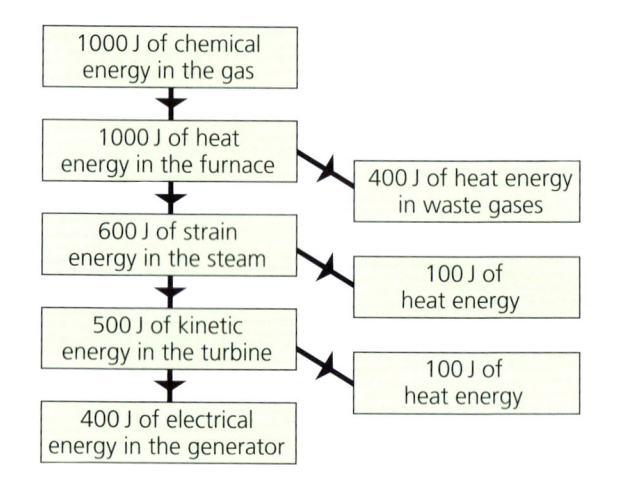

$$\text{efficiency} = \frac{\text{useful output}}{\text{input}} \times 100$$

input = 1000 J
useful output = 400 J
efficiency = ?
efficiency = $\frac{400}{1000} \times 100 = 40\%$

The final value for the efficiency is quoted as a percentage. This is why it is sometimes called **percentage efficiency** (% efficiency).

Transporting electricity

Electricity is carried from power stations around the country by the **National Grid**. The electric current in this network of wires generates some heat energy. This is a waste of energy and it reduces the efficiency of the network.

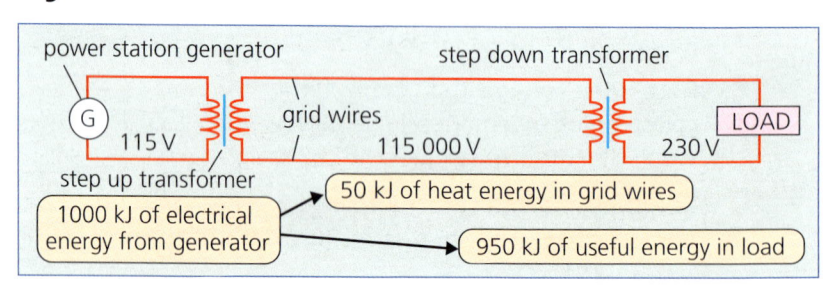

The efficiency is improved by keeping the wires in the grid at a very **high voltage**. This reduces the current in the wires, resulting in less wasteful heat energy.

Transformers are used to raise and lower the voltage of the alternating current as it enters and leaves the grid.

A transformer is a loop of **soft iron**. Alternating current (a.c.) in the **primary coil** (made of **insulated copper**) continually changes the magnetism of the iron. This change of magnetism generates a voltage across the ends of the **secondary coil**.

Transformers have a very high efficiency. Very little electricity gets converted to heat energy on the way through them.

$$\frac{\text{primary voltage}}{\text{secondary voltage}} = \frac{\text{primary turns}}{\text{secondary turns}}$$

$$\frac{V_p}{V_s} = \frac{n_p}{n_s}$$

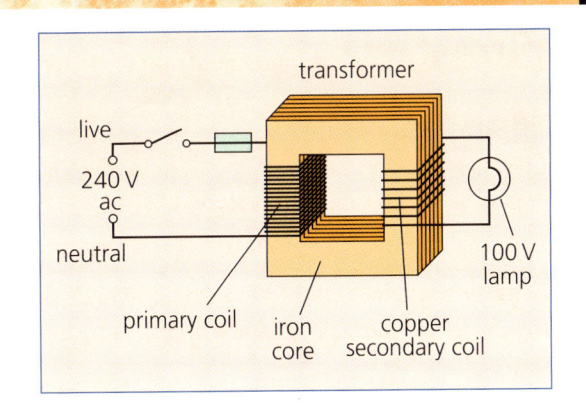

Worked example

Q A transformer steps down 230 V to 12 V. If it has 60 turns of wire in its secondary coil, how many turns does it need in the primary coil?

A $\frac{V_p}{V_s} = \frac{n_p}{n_s}$ so $\frac{230}{12} = \frac{?}{60}$

$? = 60 \times \frac{230}{12} = 1150$

Questions

1. Describe how electricity is generated from oil.
2. Draw an energy flow diagram for a power station.
3. State the places where heat energy is lost in a power station.
4. Write down the formula for calculating efficiency.
5. 200 J of chemical energy in coal becomes 50 J of electrical energy in a power station. Calculate the efficiency of the power station. What happens to the 150 J which doesn't become electricity?
6. What is the National Grid? What does it do?
7. For every 1000 kJ of electricity fed into a grid, only 950 kJ can be extracted from it. What happens to the missing energy? Calculate the efficiency of the grid.
8. Explain why running the grid at a high voltage increases the efficiency of electricity transmission.
9. Draw a labelled diagram of a transformer.
10. Explain why there is always a transformer between a generator and the National Grid.
11. Do transformers operate from a.c. or d.c.?
12. 1000 J of electricity enters the primary coil of a transformer. 20 J of heat energy appears in the transformer. Calculate the efficiency of the transformer.
13. The primary and secondary coils of a transformer have 920 and 48 turns of wire. If the primary coil is connected to a 230 V a.c. supply, what voltage appears at the secondary coil?

Gravity

Terminal speed

Jo drops a ball over the edge of a high cliff. As it falls, the ball picks up speed until it reaches its **terminal speed**. The ball stays at that speed until it hits the ground.

Gravity tugs the ball downwards, towards the centre of the Earth. So the ball speeds up. But as it speeds up, **friction** increases. At the terminal speed, the friction force has the same size as the gravity force.

The two forces become **balanced** – they have the same strength, but act in opposite directions.

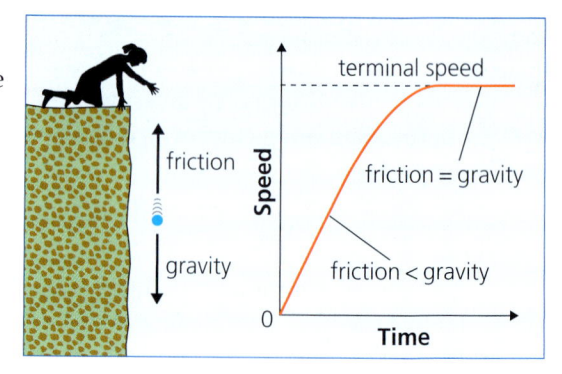

Free fall

In the absence of friction, all objects in free fall near the surface of the Earth have the same acceleration. The value of this acceleration g is about 10 m/s^2. So the speed increases by 10 m/s for every second that an object falls, if the friction is negligible.

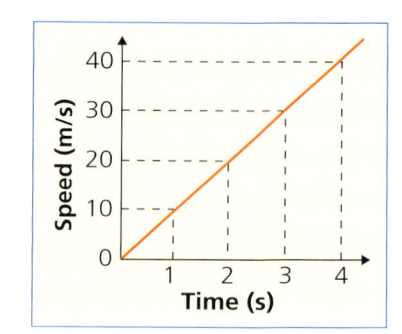

Gravity and weight

The force of gravity on an object is **weight**. It depends on the mass of the object and the acceleration of free fall, g.

weight	=	mass	×	g
(in newtons)		(in kilograms)		(in metres per second squared or newtons/kilogram)

The **mass** of an object does not depend on where it is. This is because mass is fixed by the number and type of atoms. However, the weight of an object changes as it moves from one place to another. This is because the value of g depends on the size and density of the planet. g is sometimes called the **gravitational field strength**.

Circular motion

The **velocity** of an object tells you two things about it:

- how fast it is moving, in m/s
- the direction in which it is moving.

The size of the velocity is given in m/s. An arrow gives the direction of velocity.

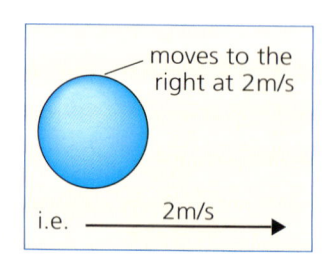

These objects have the same speed, but different velocities.

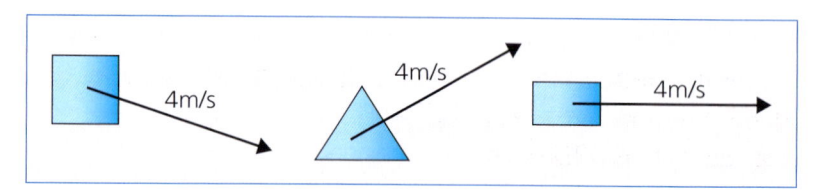

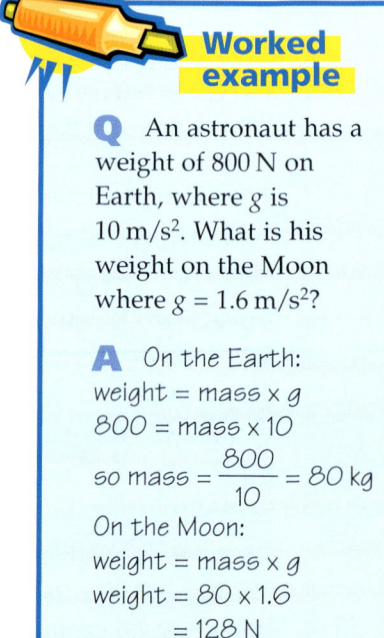

Worked example

Q An astronaut has a weight of 800 N on Earth, where g is 10 m/s^2. What is his weight on the Moon where g = 1.6 m/s^2?

A On the Earth:
weight = mass × g
800 = mass × 10
so mass = $\frac{800}{10}$ = 80 kg

On the Moon:
weight = mass × g
weight = 80 × 1.6
       = 128 N

Changing velocity

The velocity of an object does not change if the resultant force is zero. If all the forces balance out (or there are none in the first place), an object moves in a straight line with a constant speed.

If there is a non-zero resultant force, it will **accelerate** the object by changing its velocity.

Sometimes the velocity can be changed just by changing the direction of motion. If the force always acts towards the same point, the object may end up moving in a circle centred on that point. Although the speed of the object does not change, it keeps on changing its direction as it moves. So it is being accelerated by the **centripetal force**.

Gravity provides the centripetal force which keeps a planet in orbit around a star. The star pulls on the planet, continually accelerating it by changing its direction. The **orbit** of a planet can be circular or elliptical.

The planet pulls on the star with the same force as the star pulls on the planet. The acceleration of the star is very small because it has a very large mass.

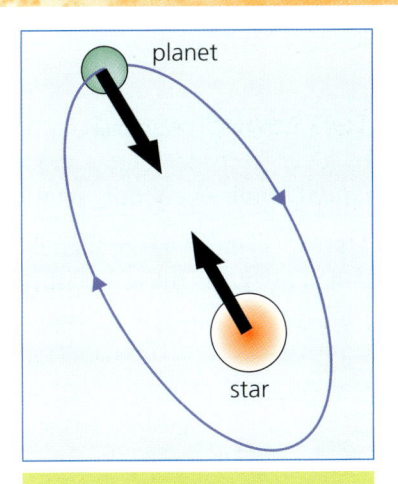

force = mass × acceleration

Gravity pulls everything towards everything else.

Questions

1. Name the two forces on a falling object. In which direction do they act?

2. Copy and complete the following sentences.
   When an object is released _____ acts on it, so its _____ increases. The motion through the air produces the force _____ which acts _____. The friction _____ as the speed increases. At the terminal speed, the forces are _____ and the speed _____.

3. A ball is dropped down a deep well. It is released from rest and hits the bottom after 3 s. If there is no friction with the air, calculate
   a the speed of the ball after 3 s
   b the average speed of the ball during its flight
   c the depth of the well.

4. State the formula for calculating weight from mass. What are the units of weight and mass?

5. Explain why the weight of an object depends on its location but its mass does not.

6. Anita weighs 500 N on Earth. What are her mass and weight when she goes to Mars ($g = 4$ m/s^2)?

7. What is the difference between speed and velocity?

8. An object moves in a circle at a constant speed. Which way must the force act on the object?

9. The force of gravity on Joe from the Earth is 750 N towards the centre of the Earth. What is the size and direction of the force of gravity on the Earth from Joe?

10. Name **two** things that a force can do to an object.

Space

The Earth we live on is a **planet**. It is a sphere of rock, surrounded by a very thin skin of gas and liquid (the atmosphere and oceans). Gravity pulls everything on the Earth towards its centre.

The **Sun** is much larger than the Earth. The Sun is our nearest **star**, a ball of hot gases (mostly hydrogen) which radiates a lot of light and heat energy. That energy comes from **fusion reactions** at the hot centre of the star. These reactions convert hydrogen into helium.

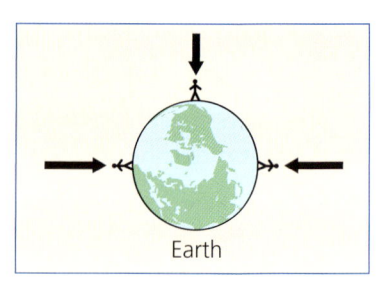

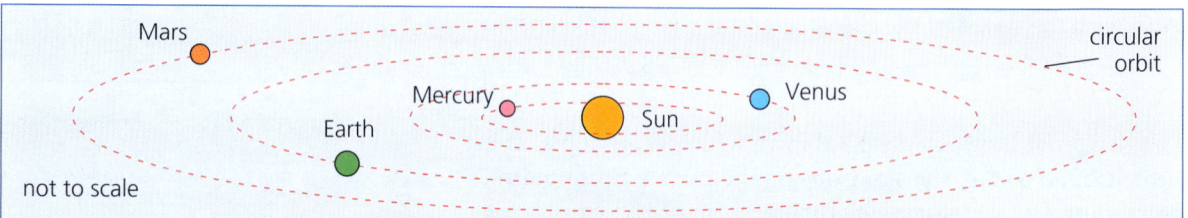

The Earth is only one of several planets which orbit the Sun. Gravity tugs each planet towards the Sun. This force keeps each planet moving in either a **circle** or an **ellipse** around the Sun.

There is no friction in space, so planets can stay in their orbits for billions of years.

Earth has just one **moon**. It goes once around the Earth in a month. A moon is a smaller lump of rock which orbits around a planet. Many planets have more than one moon.

You must know the order of these planets in our solar system.

The Universe

The Sun, its planets and their moons make up a **solar system**. There are billions of solar systems clumped together in our local **galaxy**, the Milky Way. The **Universe** contains billions of different galaxies, separated by empty space.

Life

The temperature and pressure on the surface of the Earth are just right for life, because they allow water to be a liquid. The atmosphere is also just right for life, with both carbon dioxide and oxygen.

There may be life on other planets with the same conditions. Robot spacecraft have travelled to other planets around our Sun to search for life on them. Astronomers search for life on planets around other stars by listening to signals coming from them with radio telescopes.

Evolution of the Universe

The Universe is about 15 billion years old. At the start of the Universe, all of its matter and energy was at one point. It just appeared suddenly. This event is called the **Big Bang**. The early Universe was very small and very hot. It immediately expanded rapidly, getting cooler. Eventually it was cold enough to form stable atoms of hydrogen and helium.

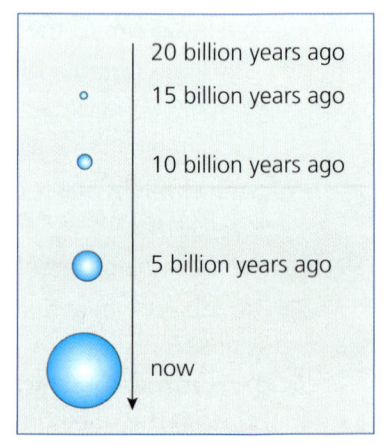

How the Universe has grown since the Big Bang

Stars

Shortly after the Big Bang, the Universe was just clouds of hydrogen gas. It was invisible. Then gravity made the clouds shrink and heat up until they formed **stars**. Stars are so hot that they emit huge amounts of light, making the Universe visible. The energy for this light comes from the **fusion** of hydrogen into helium deep inside the star.

Star fates

Stars do not last for ever. As they run out of hydrogen fuel, they become unstable. Their fate depends on how large they are. Large stars explode at the end of their life, briefly forming a bright **supernova**. The material left behind after the explosion forms a small super-dense **neutron star**.

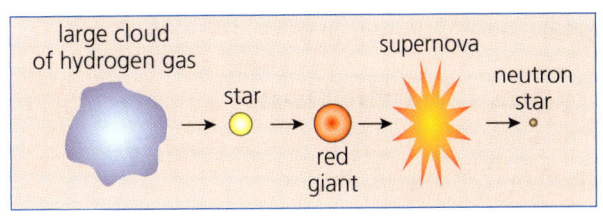

The life of a heavy star

If there is enough material, the object will collapse in on itself to form a **black hole**, with gravity so strong that not even light can escape from it.

Our own star, the Sun, is medium-sized. It will eventually swell up and change colour from white to red, turning into a **red giant**. Then it will shed its outer layers into space, forming a **planetary nebula**. Finally, the material left will shrink and cool to form a **white dwarf**.

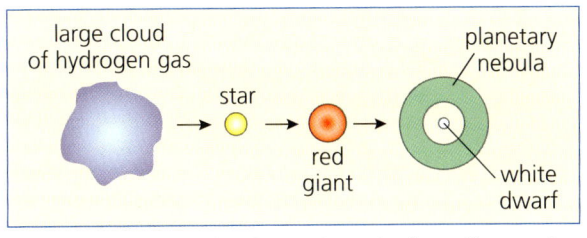

The life of a medium-sized star like our Sun

The Sun will last for a long time. It will be another 5 billion years before it turns into a red giant.

We know that the Universe is expanding because of the **red shift** of the light from other galaxies. When light is emitted by a galaxy moving away from us, its wavelength becomes longer so we see the light as red. The increase in wavelength can be used to measure the speed of the galaxy. Galaxies which are far away from us have a greater red shift than those which are close by.

Red shift and distance measurements provide evidence that all of the galaxies started off in the same place about 15 billion years ago. If there is enough material in the Universe, gravity will eventually stop its expansion and force it to shrink down into a single point – the big crunch! Otherwise, the Universe will carry on expanding for ever.

Questions

1. **a** Describe a planet. **b** How is it different from a star?
2. Describe the motion of a planet around a star. Why does it move this way?
3. Here is a list of objects. Write it out in order of size. Start with the smallest.
   galaxy   moon   star   solar system   Universe   planet
4. What is the difference between a planet and a moon?
5. **a** What is the Big Bang? **b** What happened to the Universe after the Big Bang?
6. Describe the stages in the life of the Sun.
7. Explain how a cloud of hydrogen gas can turn into a black hole.

Radioactivity

Some atoms have a nucleus which is unstable. It can break up, spitting out fragments which have a lot of energy. This process is called **radioactivity**.

All atoms contain a small **nucleus** at their centre. Most of the **mass** and all of the **positive charge** of an atom are in this nucleus. The rest of the mass and all of the **negative charge** are in the **electrons** which move around the rest of the atom.

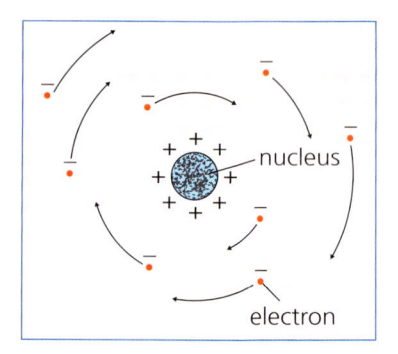

Types of radiation

There are three different **nuclear radiations** from radioactive substances:

- **alpha (α) particle**, which is a heavy, positive helium nucleus
- **beta (β) particle**, which is a light, negative electron
- **gamma (γ) ray**, which is an electromagnetic wave with no charge.

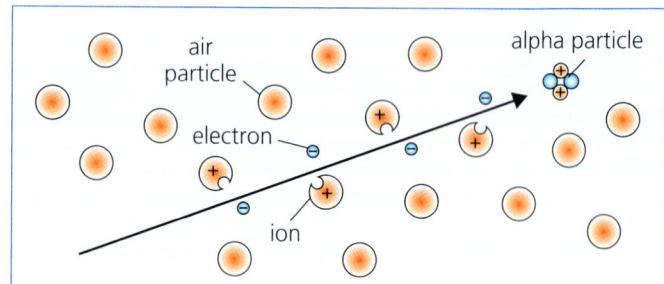

All three radiations cause **ionisation** of the matter they pass through. They do this by knocking electrons out of the atoms which they pass through, leaving **ions**. The ions are positively charged.

Alpha particles are the least penetrating radiation. They can be stopped by a sheet of paper. Beta particles are stopped by a few millimetres of aluminium. Gamma rays can pass through several centimetres of lead, so they are the most penetrating.

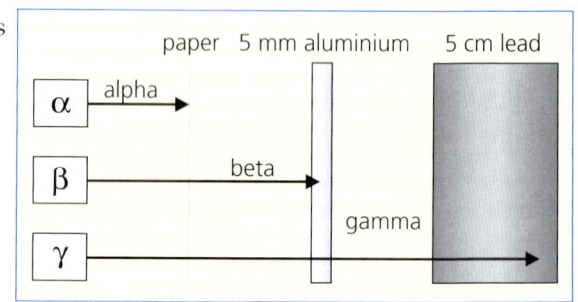

Dangers of radiation

Nuclear radiations are dangerous to living things. The ionisation that they cause can kill cells or change their genetic structure. Too much exposure to nuclear radiation can result in cancer.

Background radiation

We are exposed to radiation all the time. There are several causes of this background nuclear radiation:

- radioactive atoms, such as uranium, in rocks
- radioactive gases, such as radon, from the soil
- fallout from nuclear bomb tests and nuclear power stations
- cosmic rays from space.

Radioactive decay

The **activity** of a radioactive material goes down as time goes on. When the last unstable nucleus has split, the material is no longer radioactive. Some materials take a long time to decay, others are only radioactive for a short while.

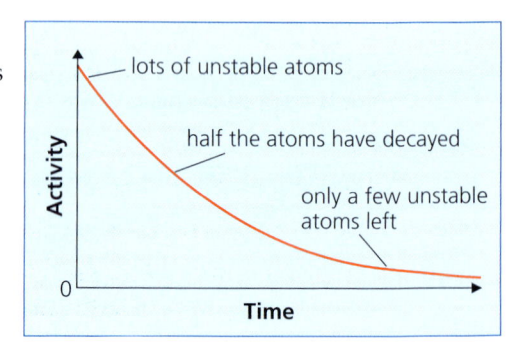

Activity is measured in **becquerels** (**Bq**). It tells you the rate at which atoms are changing. So if the activity is 365 Bq, there are, on average 365 atoms decaying in one second.

The **half-life** of an element is the amount of time it takes for half of the atoms to decay. Each element has its own half-life.

Uses of radioactivity

Here are some uses of nuclear radiation and radioactive substances.

- Uranium can be used to boil water in a nuclear power station.
- Gamma rays can be used to sterilise surgical instruments.
- Alpha particle sources are used in smoke alarms.
- Beta particle sources can be used to measure the thickness of sheets of material.
- Gamma rays can be used to kill cancer tumours.
- Radioactive materials make good tracers in plants and people.
- The age of a rock can be estimated by measuring how much of its uranium has turned into lead.

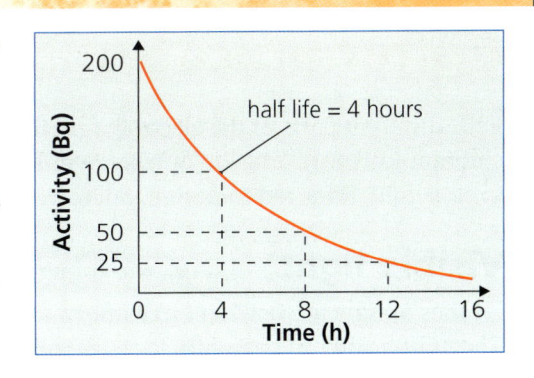

Worked example

Q A radioactive source has a half-life of 3 hours. If its activity is 400 Bq now, what will it be in 12 hours time?

A

Time (hours)	0	3	6	9	12
Activity (Bq)	400	200	100	50	25

so the final activity will be 25 Bq

Questions

1. Describe the structure of an atom.
2. What is the charge of a nucleus?
3. What is the charge of an electron?
4. What is radioactivity?
5. Name the three different nuclear radiations.
6. Which part of an atom does nuclear radiation come from?
7. State the charge of each of the nuclear radiations.
8. Name the radiation which   **a** has the greatest mass   **c** is a nucleus
   b is a wave   **d** is an electron.
9. Here is a list of radiations. Write them down in order of ability to penetrate solids. Start with the least penetrating power.
   beta   gamma   alpha
10. Name the **four** sources of background radiation.
11. A radioactive source has an activity of 100 Bq. How many atoms in it decay in a minute?
12. How does the activity of a radioactive material change with time? Explain why.
13. State one use for   **a** alpha particles   **c** gamma rays
    b beta particles   **d** uranium.

Communications

Four different parts of the electromagnetic spectrum allow us to communicate **information** quickly over long distances. They are visible light, infra-red radiation, microwaves and radio waves.

Visible light

Flashes of light are used to carry information between ships at sea. The light beam can be tightly focussed onto its target, but it is easily absorbed by bad weather. The light beam is either **on** or **off**, so the information it carries has to be coded as a series of pulses, giving a digital signal.

Infra-red

Infra-red radiation travels a lot further through an optical fibre than light does, so it is used for long-distance telephone communications. Telephones transmit sound information. Sound is an **analogue signal** as it can have many different values, so its information needs to be coded into a **digital signal** of infra-red pulses.

Digital signals are useful because:
- they can be easily coded, increasing security
- many messages can be sent along a link at the same time by interleaving their pulses
- they are difficult to destroy with background noise and outside interference.

The drawback of digital transmission is that special circuits are needed at either end of the link to convert the information between analogue and digital forms.

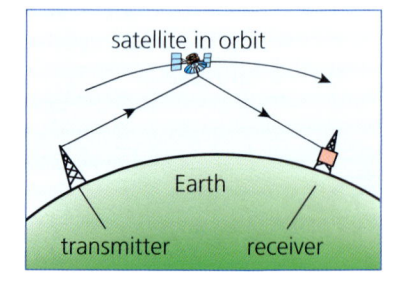

Microwaves

Mobile telephones use microwaves to communicate with the rest of the telephone system. Microwaves also carry information to and from **satellites** in orbit around the Earth. Communication satellites allow information to be sent rapidly all around the world. The ground station beams the microwaves up to the receiver dish on the satellite. The satellite amplifies the signal and uses another dish to beam microwaves to a receiving station on the ground.

Questions

1. Which parts of the electromagnetic spectrum carry information for us?
2. What is the difference between analogue and digital signals?
3. Which waves go down optical fibres?
4. Which waves are used to communicate with satellites?
5. Sort these items into digital or analogue:

   on-off switch   dimmer switch   thermometer   electronic watch   wind-up watch.

Concept map

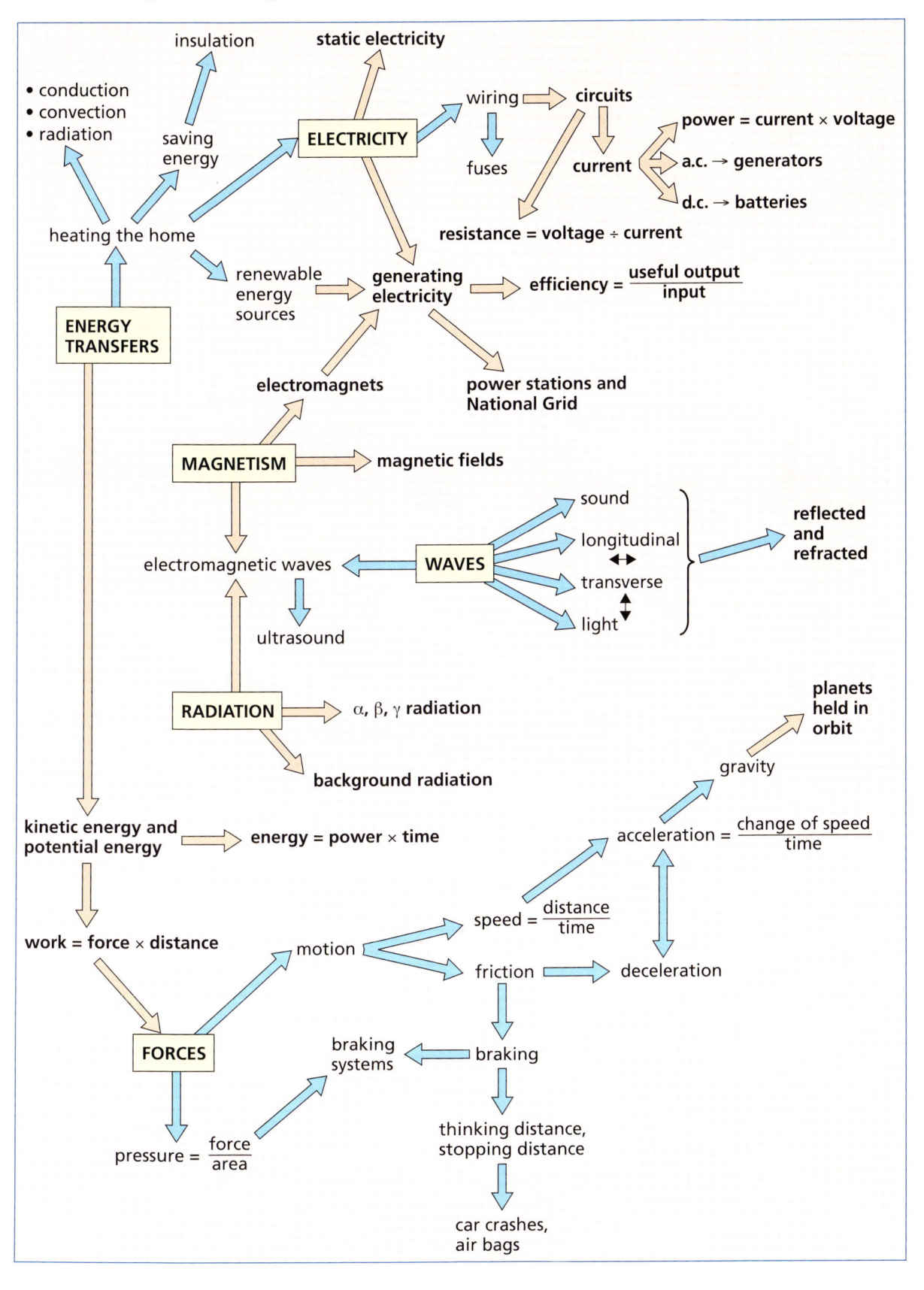

- conduction
- convection
- radiation

insulation

static electricity

saving energy

heating the home

ENERGY TRANSFERS

ELECTRICITY

wiring → circuits

fuses

current

power = current × voltage

a.c. → generators

d.c. → batteries

resistance = voltage ÷ current

renewable energy sources → generating electricity → efficiency = useful output / input

MAGNETISM

electromagnets

magnetic fields

power stations and National Grid

electromagnetic waves ← **WAVES** → sound, longitudinal, transverse, light → reflected and refracted

ultrasound

RADIATION → α, β, γ radiation

background radiation

planets held in orbit

gravity

acceleration = change of speed / time

kinetic energy and potential energy → **energy = power × time**

work = force × distance

motion → speed = distance / time

friction → deceleration

FORCES

braking systems ← braking

thinking distance, stopping distance

car crashes, air bags

pressure = force / area

Exam questions

1 Mel measures the power of a motor connected to a cell.

a She uses a voltmeter and an ammeter. Draw a circuit to show this. [2]
b The voltmeter reads 1.2 V. The ammeter reads 0.6 A.
  i Calculate the power of the motor. [3]
  ii Calculate the resistance of the motor. [3]
c Mel puts a rheostat in series with the motor. This allows her to change its speed. Use your idea of resistance to explain this. [3]

[11 marks]

2 Sam combs his hair. His hair becomes positively charged.
a Use your idea of electrons to explain why his hair becomes charged. [3]
b Sam's hair stands on end after it is combed. Explain why. [2]
c Sam uses a plastic comb. Julie uses a metal comb. Her hair does not get charged. Why? [2]

[7 marks]

3 a Jane is driving a car. She puts on the brakes.

  i Complete the sentence.
  The brakes transfer the _____ energy of the car into _____ energy. [2]
  The brakes exert a force of 500 N on the car. It stops in a distance of 20 m.
  ii Calculate the work done on the car by the brakes. [3]
  iii The car can stop in less than 20 m when it goes uphill. Use your idea of energy to explain why. [3]
b Jane pushes hard on the accelerator for 10 s. The engine transfers 50 000 J of kinetic energy to the car.
  i Calculate the power of the engine. [3]
  ii 200 000 J of chemical energy was transferred into the engine during the 10 s. Calculate the efficiency of the engine. [3]

[14 marks]

4 A power station burns coal to make electricity.

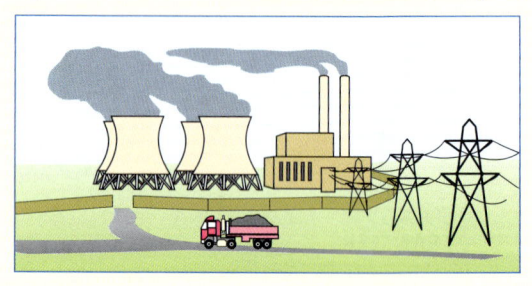

a Complete the sentences, choosing from:
**generator   turbine   furnace
transformer   boiler**
The coal is burnt in the _____. The heat energy turns water into steam in the _____. The steam passes through the _____ to make kinetic energy. This is transferred to electrical energy by the _____. The voltage of the electricity is raised by a _____. [5]
b The station uses 250 MJ of chemical energy in the coal to make 75 MJ of electrical energy. Calculate the efficiency of the power station. [2]
c Useless heat energy appears at various places in the power station.
  i Describe **three** of the places. [3]
  ii Explain why the heat energy is useless [1]

[11 marks]

5 Earth and Venus are planets in the Solar System. Look at the diagram. It is not drawn to scale. There is a star at the centre.

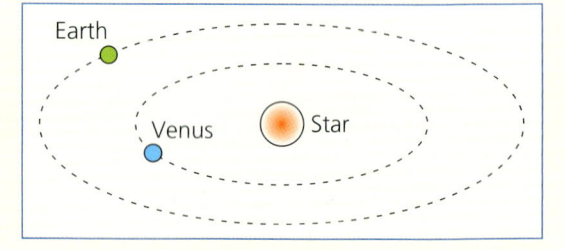

a What is the difference between a planet and a star? [1]
b Stars are kept hot by fusion. Describe the fusion reaction. [3]

c Stars start off as a large cloud of dust and gas. Explain how this can become a star. [4]

d Suggest what will happen to a star when its fusion reactions stop. Give an explanation. [2]

[10 marks]

6 Radioactivity is dangerous.
  a Why is radioactivity dangerous? [2]
  b Explain why a piece of radioactive material becomes less dangerous as time goes on. [3]
  c A radioactive source has an activity of 500 Bq now. Its half-life is 10 days. Calculate the activity of the source in 30 days time. [3]

[8 marks]

7 An LED is connected in series with a 3 V battery and a resistor.
  a Draw the circuit diagram [1]
  b Complete the sentences.
  Choose from:
  heat   light   sound   chemical   electrical
  _____ energy in the battery becomes _____ energy in the wires. The LED transfers _____ energy into _____ energy [4]
  c The voltage across the LED is 2 V when the current in it is 0.05 A.
    i Explain why the voltage across the resistor is 1 V. [1]
    ii Calculate the resistance of the resistor. [3]

[9 marks]

8 Complete the sentences.
Radioactivity is caused by the breakup of the _____ of an atom. Two of the radiations from radioactive materials are particles. These radiations are called _____ and _____ . The radiation which is a wave is called _____ .

[4 marks]

9 Avril is going to install central heating in her home. She can choose gas or electricity.
  a Write down **one** advantage and **one** disadvantage of using electrical central heating. [2]

b It costs Avril £2000 to keep the inside of her house at 25 °C all winter.
  i State one thing that Avril could do to reduce her heating bill. [1]
  ii Explain why it would reduce the heating bill. [2]
c Avril loses a lot of heat energy through the roof of her house. Complete the sentences. Choose from:
conduction, radiation, diffusion, convection.
Heat energy passes through the tiles of the roof by _____ . Heat energy is transferred from the surface of the roof by _____ and _____ . [3]

[8 marks]

10 A transformer has 1150 turns in its primary coil and 30 turns in its secondary coil. Both coils are wound on a metal core.
  a Suggest the best material for the core. Explain why it is the best. [2]
  b If the primary coil is connected to a 230 V supply, calculate the voltage across the secondary coil. [2]
  c Use the idea of changing magnetic fields to explain how a transformer works. [3]

[7 marks]

11 Julie throws a ball high into the air. The ball has a mass of 0.3 kg. The ball leaves Julie's hand with 60 J of kinetic energy and 30 J of potential energy.
  a Show that the ball leaves Julie's hand with a speed of 20 m/s. [2]
  b At the top of its flight, the ball has 80 J of potential energy.
    i How much kinetic energy does it have? [1]
    ii How high above the ground does the ball rise? [3]
  c If the ball stays on the ground when it hits it, what happens to its energy? [1]

[7 marks]

Answers

Answers to end of spread questions

PAGE 3

1. **a** chloroplasts **b** cell membrane **c** cell wall.
2. To allow more room to take up oxygen.

PAGE 5

1. Digestion is the breakdown of large food molecules into small soluble ones.
2. Bile is produced in the liver. It is released into the intestine to emulsify fats.
3. Enzymes speed up the breakdown of food.
4. Stomach acid provides the right conditions for stomach enzymes to work; kills microbes on food.
5. Stomach, pancreas.
6. If it is too cold enzymes do not move around very quickly and therefore they do not work very efficiently; too hot, and they are destroyed (denatured).
7. The small intestine is long, with lots of thin-walled villi to increase the surface area for absorption.
8. Peristalsis is the muscular contractions which squeeze food through the digestive system. It is so important because it ensures that food does not normally get stuck in the digestive system.

PAGE 7

1. We need oxygen to release energy from food in respiration.
2. In the alveoli there is a higher concentration of oxygen than in the blood. Therefore oxygen moves down the diffusion gradient into the blood.
3. Any three from: large surface area; thin walls; moist surface to aid diffusion; good transport system to carry the gases away.
4. Inhalation – diaphragm contracts and flattens, rib cage lifts, moving out and up; this increases the volume of the chest cavity and sucks air in. Exhalation – the diaphragm domes upwards, the ribs are lowered, the volume of the chest cavity decreases; therefore air is forced out.
5. The bronchi and larger bronchioles have cartilage to support them so that they do not collapse when the air pressure changes during exhalation.
6. Some of the chemicals in cigarette smoke are corrosive and attack the delicate lining of the alveoli, others stop the cilia beating; this causes mucus and trapped bacteria and dirt to accumulate in the lungs and set up infections.

PAGE 9

1. Any three from: water, digested food (e.g. glucose), hormones, waste products, urea, carbon dioxide.
2. They contain the oxygen carrier haemoglobin; they have no nucleus, therefore more room for haemoglobin, and they have a large surface area to take up more oxygen.
3. Oxygen enters in the lungs and leaves at respiring cells; carbon dioxide enters at respiring cells and leaves at the lungs; food enters at the small intestine and leaves at respiring cells.
4. It allows oxygen to be given up easily when the oxyhaemoglobin arrives at respiring cells.
5. Any two from: arteries have a narrow lumen; thick, elastic, muscular walls; contain blood at high pressure; do not contain valves. Veins have a wide lumen; thin, muscular walls; walls lack elastic fibres; blood at low pressure; contain valves.
6. It allows oxygenated blood to be sent from the heart at a higher pressure, giving a greater rate of flow to the tissues.
7. Right ventricle, left ventricle.
8. **a** To prevent blood flowing backwards when the heart contracts.
   b There are valves in veins, to prevent the backflow of blood.

PAGE 12

1. Retina contains the light-sensitive cells to respond to the different patterns of light; iris controls the amount of light entering the eye; optic nerve carries messages to the brain; lens bends the light so that it can come to a focus on the retina.
2. Circular muscles in the iris contract and the radial muscles relax to make the pupil small.
3. Motor neurones are very long, enabling them to cover long distances in the body; often insulated to speed up transmission of the message; end at effectors such as muscles or glands.
4. Synapse is the tiny gap between two different neurones. Synapses ensure that messages can only pass in one direction along a neurone.
5. Stimulus, pain of dog bite → pain receptor in skin → sensory neurone → central nervous system → motor neurone → arm muscle → hand moves away from the dog.

Answers

PAGE 12

1. Any three from: start their menstrual cycle (have periods); develop breasts; grow pubic and underarm hair; grow taller.
2. Hormones are released into the blood and travel to their target sites in the blood as it travels around the body, whereas nervous messages travel in a direct route.

PAGE 13

1. A pregnant woman maintains a high level of progesterone to keep the uterus lining in place for the baby to develop in, therefore the uterus lining cannot come away as menstruation.
2. They prevent the ovaries releasing eggs.
3. Oestrogen helps to repair and build up the lining of the uterus.

PAGE 14

1. Any two from: regulate plant shoot and root growth; control ripening of fruits; control flowering.
2. Auxins dissolve in water to move around the plant.
3. Light and gravity. Light is needed so that the plants can photosynthesise and produce the materials needed for them to grow; gravity ensures that whichever way a seed is planted, the roots will always grow down into the soil to obtain water and minerals.
4. The shoot is negatively geotropic and grows up towards the light; the root grows down towards gravity.

PAGE 15

1. Two from: rooting compound to ensure cuttings start to produce roots and shoots; selective weedkiller because it can accelerate the growth of certain plants to such an extent that they become too weak and die; enables farmers to pick fruit before fully ripe and then to complete ripening when required.; to break dormancy in seeds
2. A selective weedkiller is one which kills only certain types of plants, and leaves others unharmed.

PAGE 17

1. a Insects and other very small creatures.
   b Plants.   c Small nocturnal animals.

PAGE 19

1. a Producer – heather; primary consumer – rabbit, grouse, bees, deer; predator – fox, eagle.
   b Any two starting with heather, e.g. heather → grouse → fox.
   c Should show a normal pyramid shape.
2. Light energy.
3. A food chain shows only one feeding relationship, whereas a food web is more realistic and shows many more feeding relationships.
4. In a pyramid of numbers, one oak tree is represented as the same as one grass plant, or one mouse. If you use the mass of each, you take account of their relative sizes.
5. Energy is lost at each trophic level, therefore there is insufficient energy to sustain more than four or five trophic levels.

PAGE 21

1. Fungi and bacteria.
2. Decomposers recycle nutrients which would otherwise be locked away inside dead things.
3. a Mould grows faster in a warm environment than in a cold one.
   b i No mould.   ii Covered with mould.
4. Deforestation involves removal of trees, which would otherwise be removing carbon dioxide from the atmosphere for photosynthesis; burning these trees, or increased burning of fossil fuels, is increasing carbon dioxide in the atmosphere; increase in population leading to increased demand for cars, higher standard of living, etc. leading to more fossil fuels being burnt and more carbon dioxide in the atmosphere.
5. Photosynthesis.
6. Nitrogen-fixing bacteria change nitrogen into nitrates; denitrifying bacteria convert nitrates into nitrogen; nitrifying bacteria convert ammonia into nitrates.
7. Beans have root nodules with nitrogen-fixing bacteria in. They therefore put a lot of nitrates back into the soil when ploughed in.

PAGE 23

1. Use pesticides to reduce crop damage and loss; herbicides to reduce losses caused by competition.
2. Small birds ate the seed and were in turn eaten by brids of prey, where the poison accumulated to a toxic level.
3. Regular replanting and careful management of a woodland will preserve the habitats and food webs which are vital to the resident population of endangered red squirrels.

PAGE 29

1. Hydrogen sulphide, sugar, nitric acid.

Answers

2

Formula	No. of atoms in formula	No. of different elements
HCl	2	2
H_2O	3	2
CH_4	5	2
$AlCl_3$	4	2
H_2SO_4	7	3
$Cu(NO_3)_2$	9	3
$(NH_4)_2Cr_2O_7$	19	4

3 H_2S **4** NH_3

PAGE 30

1 a hydrogen + oxygen → hydrogen oxide
(reactant) (reactant)   (product)
b carbon + iron oxide → carbon dioxide + iron
(reactant) (reactant)   (product)   (product)
c propane → hydrogen + propene
(reactant) (product)   (product)
2 sodium + water → sodium hydroxide + hydrogen

PAGE 31

1 $Mg + O_2 \rightarrow 2MgO$
Reactant side: 1 atom of Mg, 2 atoms of O.
Product side: 2 atoms of Mg, 2 atoms of O.
Equation doesn't balance
$CH_4 + 2O_2 \rightarrow CO_2 + 2H_2O$
Reactant side: 1 atom of C, 4 atoms of H and 4 atoms of O. Product side: 1 atom of C, 4 atoms of O and 4 atoms of H.
Equation balances
2 a 2 **b** 2 **c** 3, 4 **d** 3, 2, 2 **e** 2, 2.

PAGE 32

1 Increase temperature, increase concentration of acid, increase surface area of the carbonate (use smaller pieces).
2 Increase temperature and concentration.

PAGE 33

1 a A. The slope is the steepest. **b** C

PAGE 34

1 A.
2 a X. **b** Y.
c There was a greater amount of reactants in Y which allowed more product to be formed eventually.
3 a The reaction goes more quickly.
b The rate of the reaction goes on increasing, then drops suddenly.

PAGE 35

1 Carbon dioxide and alcohol.
2 20–55 °C (about 40 °C).

PAGE 37

1 Broken: 4 × C—H, 1 × Cl—Cl.
Made: 3 × C—H, 1 × C—Cl, 1 × H—Cl.
2 400 × 4.5 × 4.2 = 7560 J

PAGE 38

1 Because it has a lower boiling point.
2 Because it has more carbon atoms.

PAGE 39

1 propane + oxygen → carbon dioxide + water
2 $C_3H_8 + 5O_2 \rightarrow 3CO_2 + 4H_2O$
3 $C_5H_{12} + 8O_2 \rightarrow 5CO_2 + 6H_2O$

PAGE 41

1 Respiration, combustion.
2 Photosynthesis.
3 78%, 21%, 0.035%, oxygen, carbon dioxide, respiration, combustion.

PAGE 43

1 a, b The majority of volcanoes lie close to the edges of the plates.
c The earthquake zones are very close.
2 a Underneath, into the mantle **b** They melt.
3 They get older.

PAGE 45

1 Large, igneous, metamorphic.
2 Sedimentary, metamorphic.

PAGE 46

1 zinc + copper oxide → zinc oxide + copper
2 Copper oxide, silver oxide, the metal and water will be formed.
3 CABD

PAGE 47

1 Reduced – iron oxide, oxidised – aluminium.
2 Reduction.
3 carbon + copper oxide → carbon dioxide + copper
4 a Zinc. **b** Zinc is more reactive than iron.

PAGE 49

1 Positive. **2** Negative. **3** Mg^{2+}
4 The ions can't move through the solid.
5 Negative electrode (cathode).
6 a Positive **b** negative.
7 a Reduced. **c** It has lost oxygen.

PAGE 53

1 2000 Hz **2** 4 m
3 Vibrations, compressions, rarefactions, frequency, hertz or Hz, wavelength, metres, longitudinal, energy flow.

4 a 3, 4 m, 25 cm
    b The energy flows from left to right but the wiggles are up and down.
5 $v = fL$ 6 24 m/s   7 50 m, 600 000 Hz

PAGE 55

1 60°, 60°; 40°, 40°   2 60°, 30°
3 See page 54.
4 To make endoscopes – medical instruments to look inside people's stomachs and other organs; for transmitting infra-red signals in telecommunications.
5 Binoculars, periscopes, cameras, bicycle reflectors.

PAGE 56

1 p-waves are longitudinal, s-waves are transverse.
2 47 Hz, 900 Hz, 12 000 Hz, 24 kHz, 50 000 Hz. The last two.
3 37.5 m   4 Looking inside people.

PAGE 57

1 Gamma rays, X-rays, ultraviolet, visible, infra-red, microwaves, radio waves.

PAGE 59

1 –20°C. Conduction, convection and radiation.
2 Kinetic, vibrate, energy, conduction.
3 Lose energy. Air at the top cools, shrinks and falls. It is replaced by a flow of hot air from the base of the fridge.
4 Bad, bad, good, good.   5 Gets smaller.
6 Wall cavities, double glazing and roof insulation reduce conduction. White walls and special window glass reduce radiation. Sheltered location and small surface area reduces convection.

PAGE 61

1 Chemical energy in gas → heat energy in the air duct → heat energy in the room.
2 Cheap to install, no waste gases.
3 Electricity is expensive.
4 Coal, oil, natural gas. Less pollution, can be made from renewable sources.
5 Wood (from plants).
6 Solar energy, using solar cells to make electricity directly.
Wind energy, to turn wind turbines which turn electrical generators to produce electricity.
Wave energy has potential energy that can be transferred to mechanical or electrical energy.
Plants use energy from the Sun to transfer light energy into chemical energy.
Hydroelectric energy transfers the potential energy of water stored in dams to kinetic energy to turn turbines transferring the energy to electrical energy.
7 5 years.
8 Insulator, air, conductor, metal.

PAGE 63

1 7p   2 60p
3 0.1p
4 Live (brown), neutral (blue), earth (green and yellow).
5 Thin wires get hot, thick wires stay cool.
6 Live and neutral transfer electrical energy. Earth protects against electric shock.
7 Cuts off current before the wires get too hot.
8 Melts if the live wire touches the outer casing of an appliance.
9 In the live wire.   10 Double insulated.
11 Outer metal casing. To prevent electric shocks.

PAGE 65

1 v (m/s), s (m), t (s); $v = s/t$ 2 20 m/s
3 1.67 m/s   4 3000 m   5 5 s
6 1 = c, 2 = d, 3 = b   7 1 = c, 2 = a, 3 = b
8 a 25 m   b 100 m   c 50 m
9 a 2 m/s   b 0 m/s   c 2 m/s

PAGE 67

1 Acceleration = change of speed/time taken, m/s^2
2 $10 \, m/s^2$ 3 6 s   4 10 m/s
5 Air resistance, contact between tyres and road, moving parts in the wheels.
6 Steady speed, getting faster, slowing down.
7 6000 N   8 65 000 N   9 $2 \, m/s^2$
10 Distance moved before the brakes start to slow the car down. Lack of concentration, tiredness, intoxication.
11 Distance moved while the brakes are on. Incorrect adjustment, rain, bald tyres, badly inflated tyres.
12 21 m   13 a 5 s   b 75 m
14 10.5 m, 2.5 s, 18.8 m

PAGE 68

1 Any five from: turning taps on or off, bicycle pedals, screwdrivers, spanners, door handles, steering wheels, unscrewing or screwing up bottle tops.
2 Moment = force x distance to pivot.
3 6 Nm
4 Increase the force, increase the distance from point of force to pivot.

PAGE 69

1 $x = 1$ m; $x = 2$ m.

Answers

PAGE 75

1. Growth needs the production of identical cells, all carrying all the chromosomes. Only mitosis does this.

2.
Mitosis	Meiosis
Occurs in growth asexual reproduction	Occurs in gamete formation
Produces two identical cells	Produces four non-identical cells
Same number of chromosomes as parent cell	Half the number of chromosomes as parent cell

PAGE 77

1. 50% blue, 50% brown; Bb ¥ bb = Bb, Bb (both brown), bb, bb (both blue).

2. 50% rollers, 50% non-rollers. Ratio 1 : 1.

3.
Gametes
	X	X^c
X^c	XX^c	X^cX^c — colour-blind girl
Y	XY	X^cY

or Gametes
	X^c	X^c
X^c	X^cX^c	X^cX^c — all girls colour blind
Y	X^cY	X^cY

PAGE 78

1. Some body parts not fossilised; not many organisms die in the right conditions to form fossils; may not have found all the fossils formed.
2. Individuals best adapted to their environment survive and breed therefore are more likely to increase in number.
3. The soot-covered bark camouflaged the black version of the moth. Therefore they were less likely to be seen and eaten, and so survived and increased in number. Black moths were fitter because they were better adapted to their environment than the pale moths.
4. Species poorly adapted to their environments are likely to become extinct. If the environment changes and a species cannot adapt to the new conditions, it will become extinct.

PAGE 79

1. a speed.
   b Selective breeding – pick two speedy parents, breed them and pick the fastest foal, repeat.
2. Similarities: both involve 'survival of the fittest'; in both cases the selected characteristics are inherited by later generations. Differences: in artificial selection the selection force is humans, in natural selection the selection force in the environment; artificial selection takes a fairly short time, but natural selection takes a very long time.

3. Two or more genetically identical individuals.
4. Mitosis.
5.
Selective breeding	Genetic engineering
Advantages • Gradually produce living things with more and more desirable characteristics.	Advantages • Outcome is known. • Once set up it is quicker than selective breeding. • Can transfer genes from one species to another. • Can make large amounts of useful products, e.g. insulin.
Disadvantages • Time consuming. • Outcome not predictable.	Disadvantages • Expensive to set up. • Worries about transferred gene escaping into other species. • Worries about effects of eating genetically altered individuals. • Ethical worries, including how it might be applied to human beings.

PAGE 81

1. Green plants use light energy to change carbon dioxide and water into sugars (food).
   carbon dioxide + water Æ glucose + oxygen
   chlorophyll and light energy
2. Carbon dioxide comes from the atmosphere; water from the soil via the root hairs.
3. Any three from: broad; thin; lots of chlorophyll; good transport system; stomata.
4. Oxygen and water vapour.
5. No, because they need light to photosynthesise.
6. Plants appear green because they reflect green light. Light that they reflect cannot be used for photosynthesis, therefore green light is not very good for photosynthesis and plants do not grow well.

PAGE 83

1. Any three from: changed into sucrose for transport; changed into cellulose; changed into proteins; respired to release energy; changed into starch for storage.
2. It allows some materials to pass through it, but not others.
3. There is more water inside the chips than there is in the concentrated sugar solution around them, therefore water will move from a high concentration to a low concentration, leaving the cells and making them smaller; in the dilute sugar solution, the osmotic

Answers

gradient is the other way round, with water moving into the cells and causing the chip to become longer.

4 The xylem, to transport absorbed water and minerals; the phloem to transport dissolved sucrose.
5 Magnesium is used to make chlorophyll, which makes plants look green. Chlorophyll is essential for photosynthesis, which makes the materials necessary for the plant to grow.
6 One crop will rapidly use up certain minerals in the soil, and if the crop is harvested rather than ploughed back into the soil, the minerals are removed as well. Farmers have to use fertilisers to replenish the lost minerals.
7 To absorb water and dissolved minerals.

PAGE 85

1 A vascular bundle is a group of tissues concerned with transport, therefore it contains xylem and phloem.
2 Prevents the plant losing too much water by evaporation.
3 Transpiration is the evaporation of water from the leaves of a plant and its replacement by water from the xylem.
4 Any three from: provides water for photosynthesis; cools the plant down; helps to move minerals up the plant; provides support because the cells are stiff when full of water.
5 a Carbon dioxide diffuses in through open stomata.
   b Oxygen diffuses out through the stomata from a high concentration to a relatively lower concentration in the atmosphere.

PAGE 87

1 Respiration is the release of energy from glucose (food).
2 a glucose + oxygen → carbon dioxide + water + energy
   b glucose → lactic acid + some energy
3 Any two from: aerobic produces more energy; aerobic produces carbon dioxide; anaerobic produces lactic acid; only aerobic uses oxygen.
4 Respiration occurs in all the cells in the body.
5 Any two from: breathing rate increases; heart beat increases; aerobic respiration increases.
6 Breathing rate, more oxygen; heart beat, faster delivery of oxygen and glucose to cells; more respiration, more energy to work the muscles.
7 During vigorous exercise the muscles have to respire anaerobically. This forms lactic acid. To get rid of lactic acid, oxygen is needed, therefore at the end of the exercise you have built up a lot of lactic acid which must be broken down. The oxygen needed to break it down is referred to as the oxygen debt.

PAGE 89

1 Homeostasis means maintaining conditions in your body at a steady state (optimum level).
2 Pancreas, liver.
3 Water, urea, and salt as urine.
4 Carbon dioxide dissolves in the blood to form carbonic acid. A change in the blood pH will affect enzyme activity around the body.
5 On a hot sunny day you lose water through sweating, therefore there is less water in the body to be lost in the urine, so you produce more concentrated urine.
6 Brain.
7 Sweat uses some of our body heat to evaporate it from the skin, therefore some of the body heat is used up.

PAGE 91

1 Tears contain antiseptic which destroys microbes.
2 Blood blocks the hole (platelets) and white blood cells launch a counter attack.
3 An antibody is a chemical produced to attack something our body recognises as foreign (antigen).
4 White blood cells leave the blood to reach any invading microbes so that they can launch an attack.
5 A drug is a substance that changes the way your body works.
6 Chemicals in cigarette smoke stop the cilia beating, therefore mucus and microbes lodge in the lungs rather than constantly being removed. In the lungs microbes can cause infections.
7 Depressant – slows down brain activity, e.g. alcohol.
   Stimulant – speeds up brain activity, e.g. caffeine.

PAGE 97

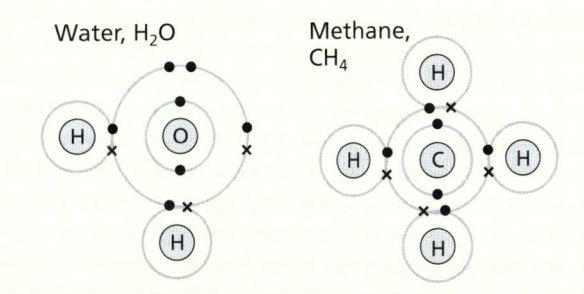

1 Water, H_2O Methane, CH_4

146 Answers

Carbon dioxide, CO_2

Ethene, C_2H_4

2

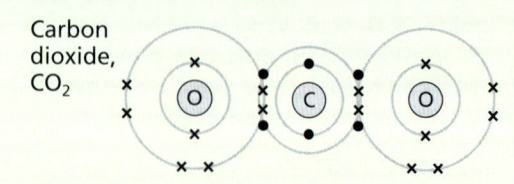

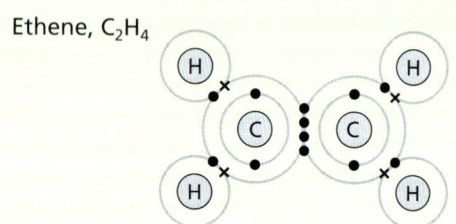

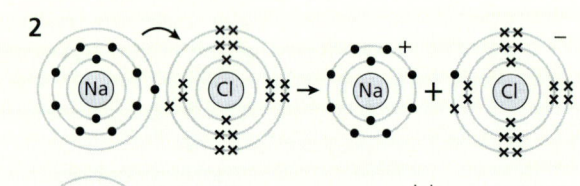

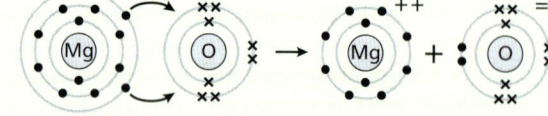

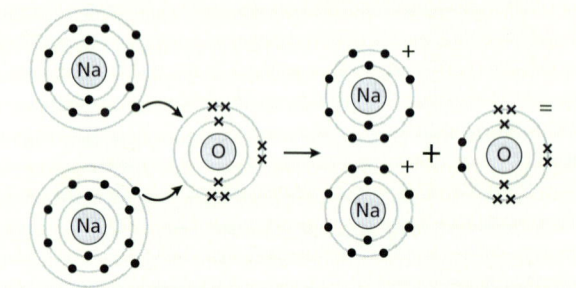

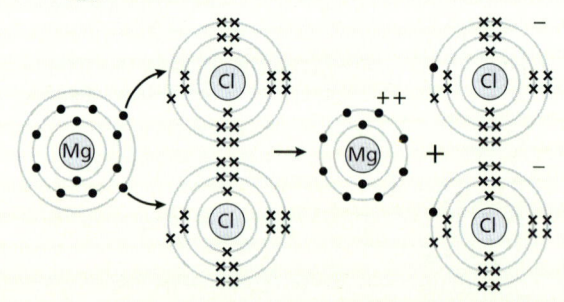

3 a Molecular structure
  b giant structure.

PAGE 99

1 1   2 6
3
4 It has many weak forces.

5 a CH_4, C_2H_6, C_3H_8.   b C_2H_4, C_3H_6.
6 a $C_3H_6 + Br_2 \rightarrow C_3H_6Br_2$
  b $C_3H_6 + H_2 \rightarrow C_3H_8$

PAGE 101

1 Poly(propene) is much stiffer and will support weight.
2 PVC will wear better out of doors and last longer.
3

4

PAGE 103

1 Falls.
2 a Sodium chloride
  b Potassium nitrate.
  c Ammonium sulphate.
  d Copper sulphate.
3 Iron sulphate.
4 a Copper nitrate and water.
  b $CuO + 2HNO_3 \rightarrow Cu(NO_3)_2 + H_2O$

PAGE 105

1 A reaction that will go in either direction.
2 Nitrogen and hydrogen.
3 Make the process automatic so that there are fewer operators needed.
4 a Make it quickly (use a catalyst), recycle any unused gases, make the process automatic.
  b Using a high temperature, high pressure.
5 a Yield increases.
  b It would be too expensive because of the extra costs required for extra-thick reaction vessels, pipes and heavy duty compressors.
  c Percentage yield at 300 atmospheres is 48%, as shown in graph.

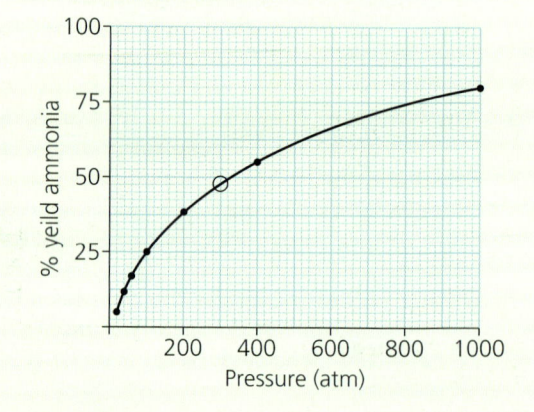

Answers

PAGE 107
1. **a** 24 g **b** 64 g
2. 64%   **3** Cu_2O

PAGE 109
1. Oxygen-18 has two more neutrons than oxygen-16.
2. 26   **3** 30
4. **a** 7 **b** 7
   c 2 in the first shell, 5 in the next.
5. 2,8,1   **6** 2,8,8,1

PAGE 110
1. They have two outer electrons, which they lose to leave a stable shell.
2. Group 8 elements have a stable outer electron shell.
3. **a** Atomic mass about 80; melting point about 7 °C.
   b Took the average between chlorine and iodine.

PAGE 111
1. sodium + water → sodium hydroxide + hydrogen
2. $2Na + 2H_2O → 2NaOH + H_2$

PAGE 112
1. hydrogen + chlorine → hydrogen chloride + hydrogen
2. $2Na + Cl_2 → 2NaCl$

PAGE 119
1. Electrons.
2. Glass and wool.
3. Iron and copper.
4. Insulator, electrons, comb, charged.
5. Fur, glass, negative, positive.
6. Glass is positive, silk is negative.
7. Attract, attract, repel.
8. Photocopier, paint sprayer.
9. Sparks can cause explosions.
10. The car is charged as it moves through the air, and the charge flows through you to earth.

PAGE 121
1. 15 C   **2** 20 A
3. See the table on page 120.
4. 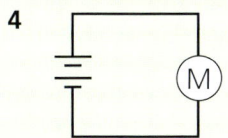
5. 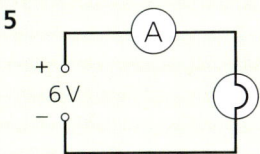
6. They all read 2 A
7. 2 A
8. 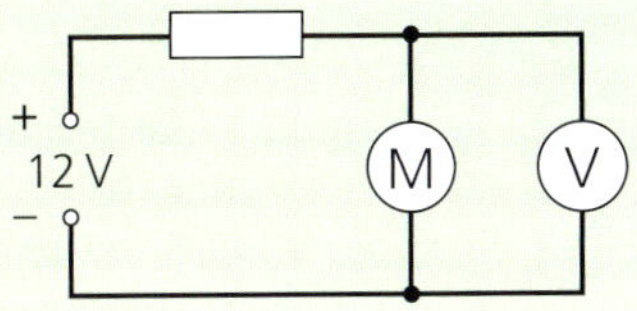
9. 96 J

PAGE 123
1. $P(W) = I(A) × V(V)$
2. 60 W
3. 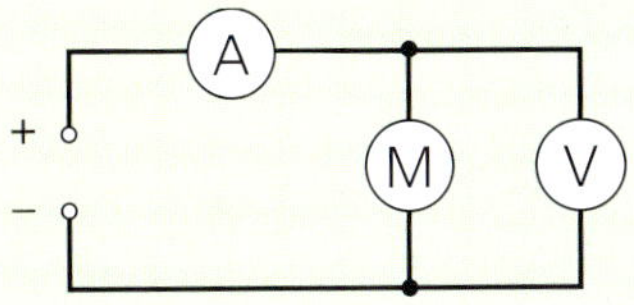
4. 0.4 A   **5** B
6. $R(Ω) = V(V)/I(A)$ **7** 48 Ω
8. 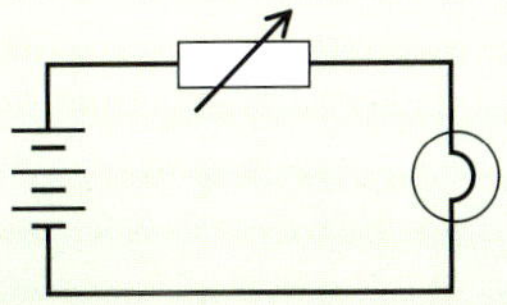
9. 4 A
10. 100 V
11. Increased temperature reduces the resistance of a thermistor. Increased light reduces the resistance of an LDR.

PAGE 125
1. $W(J) = F(N) × s(m)$
   W = work, J = joiles; F = force, N = newtons; s = distance, m = metres.
2. 75 J, 75 J.   **3** 20 m   **4** 2500 N
5. 500 J   **6** a, b
7. Chemical, potential, potential, kinetic, heat.
8. 3500 J   **9** 2500 J
10. 200 W

PAGE 127
1. Right, right, left.
2. Steel for the magnet; copper for the wire in the coil.
3. See page 126.
4. The commutator carries current to and from the coil.
5. Stronger magnet; more turns in the coil; increased current.
6. **a** −0.1 V   **b** 0.0 V.
7. Move faster; stronger magnet.
8. ero, negative.
9. Any four from: faster motion; more coils of wire; increase area of coil; use soft iron core in coil; use stronger magnet.
10. Steel magnet, copper coil wound on soft iron.
11. Twice as many cycles, double the amplitude.

Answers

PAGE 129

1. Burning oil heats water to make steam. Steam rotates turbine. Turbine turns generator.
2. Chemical energy in the fuel → heat energy in the steam → kinetic energy in the turbine → electrical energy in the generator.
3. Heat energy is lost up the chimney from the combustion of gases, from pipes carrying steam and friction in the turbine and generator.
4. efficiency = $\dfrac{\text{output}}{\text{input}} \times 100$
5. 25%, heat energy.
6. High-voltage wires which transport electricity over long distances.
7. Heat energy, 95%.
8. Reduces current in wires.
9. See page 129.
10. To raise and lower the voltage.
11. a.c.
12. 98%
13. 12 V.

PAGE 131

1. Gravity downwards, friction upwards.
2. Gravity, speed, friction, upwards, increases, balanced, stays the same.
3. a 30 m/s   b 15 m/s   c 45 m
4. Weight (N) = mass (kg) × gravity (N/kg or m/s²)
5. Mass is fixed by number of atoms, g is fixed by planet.
6. 50 kg, 200 N
7. Velocity is both speed and direction.
8. Towards the centre of the circle.
9. 750 N from centre of Earth towards Joe.
10. Change its speed and its direction of motion.

PAGE 133

1. a A sphere of rock or gas which orbits a star.
   b A star is a ball of gases kept hot by fusion reactions.
2. The planet goes in a circle or ellipse around the star. Gravity pulls on it.
3. Moon, planet, star, solar system, galaxy, universe.
4. A moon is lighter than the planet which it orbits.
5. a The beginning of the Universe.
   b Expanded and cooled.
6. Clouds of hydrogen gas condensed by gravity to form the white, hot Sun. It will expand to become a red giant star and shed its outer layers to form a planetary nebula. Finally, it will shrink to form a white dwarf.
7. A cloud of hydrogen gas condenses by gravity to a large hot star. At the end of its life it becomes unstable and explodes becoming a supernova. The material left behind after the explosion forms a small super-dense neutron star. If there is enough material, it will collapse in onto itself to form a black hole.

PAGE 135

1. A small central nucleus with electrons moving around it.
2. Positive.
3. Negative.
4. The breakup of a nucleus.
5. Alpha, beta and gamma.
6. Nucleus.
7. Alpha is positive, beta is negative and gamma has no charge.
8. a Alpha
   b Gamma
   c Alpha
   d Beta.
9. Alpha, beta, gamma.
10. Uranium in rocks; radon in the air; nuclear fallout from bomb tests; cosmic rays from space.
11. 6000
12. Goes down, as the number of unstable atoms decreases.
13. a Smoke alarms
    b Thickness measurement
    c Sterilising instruments, killing cancers
    d Generating electricity.

PAGE 136

1. Visible light, infra-red radiation, microwaves and radio waves.
2. Digital signals are either on or off. Analogue signals can have many different values.
3. Infra-red and visible.
4. Microwaves.
5. Digital, analogue, analogue, digital, analogue.

Answers

AT2 – Year 10

Question	Answer	Marks	Total

1 a
  c
  d
	Break it down into small, soluble bits. b Lipids or fats.
	Emulsifies fats; providing a larger surface area for enzymes to work on.
	Any two of: very long; large surface area or lots of villi; permeable surface; good blood supply.
		1 1
		2
		
		2
			6 marks

2 a b	Any three of: permeable; moist; large surface area; good blood supply. Support the bronchioles/bronchi; to prevent collapsing when pressure changes during inhalation and exhalation.	3 2	5 marks

3 a   i
     iii
  b
	Haemoglobin ii oxygen + haemoglobin → oxyhaemoglobin
	Actively respiring; cells /body tissues.
	Artery; small lumen with thick, elastic walls. To allow materials to be exchanged. Vein; valves.
		1 1
		2
		
		5
			9 marks

4 a b	Hormones. Any four from: increases heart rate; increases breathing rate; therefore more blood with oxygen and glucose delivered to the muscles; converts glycogen to glucose to increase glucose availability; diverts blood to muscles and brain away from gut and other less important areas.	1 4	5 marks

5 a
  b
  c
	Phototropism.
	Enables them to take up light; needed for photosynthesis.
	Produced at the tip and diffuses back down the shoot; on light side auxin is destroyed; on shaded side auxin causes the cells to elongate; this side therefore grows whereas the side in the light stops growing.
		1
		2
		
		3
			6 marks

6 a
  b
  c
	Receptor; sensory neurone; motor neurone; effector.
	Two of: blinking; sneezing; swallowing; suckling.
	Two of: long; insulating sheath; branched endings.
		3
		2
		2
			7 marks

7	Any four of: nitrates encourage growth of surface algae; these cut off light to plants below; plants cannot photosynthesise so die; decomposers rot the dead plants; they use up oxygen in the water; all other living things suffocate; waterway becomes largely uninhabited.	4	4 marks

8 a
  b
  c   i
  d   e
  f
	Nucleus; contains genetic information to control activities of the cell.
	To leave more room to transport oxygen.
	To release energy by respiration ii To release the energy for it to swim.
	Oxygen. e Water (can accept a named mineral)
	A and D. Both have cell walls/both have a large vacuole.
		2
		1
		1 1
		1 1
		3
			10 marks

9 a
 	
  b
 	
  c
  d
  e
	They break down food (or break down large insoluble food molecules) into small soluble ones.
	The enzyme has broken down the starch into glucose; which has passed through the semi-permeable membrane.
	Blood.
	Starch is too big a substance to pass through the membrane.
	Nothing; boiling has destroyed the enzyme; therefore no glucose can be produced.
		2
		
		2
		
		1
		1	

10 a
   b
 	
   c
 	
   d
   e
	Correctly labelled parts – check back to diagram in the text.
	Cornea starts to bend the light. Retina contains the light-sensitive cells. Lens completes bending of light to focus image on the retina.
	In dim light the circular muscles are relaxed; the radial muscles are contracted; making the pupil large; to allow in lots of light; reverse for bright light.
	Reflex action.
	Prevents excess light getting into the retina and damaging it.
	3 9 marks
		3
		3
		
		4
		
		1
		1
			12 marks

Answers

Question	Answer	Marks	Total
11 a	Lining of the uterus comes away/menstruation.	1	
b	Causes the lining of the uterus to thicken. c 14	1 1	
d	Level will stay high; because the yellow body stays active.	2	
e	Other things may cause the body temperature to increase, for example a fever or 'flu'.	1	6 marks
12 a	Randomly; place the quadrat on the ground and count; the number and types of plant species.	3	
b	Collect insects; sweeping net a set number of times through undergrowth; use pooter to collect insects for counting and identification.	3	
c	Collects nocturnal animals; add a bait; count and identify regularly.	3	9 marks
13 a	Must start with water lily, duckweed, pondweed or reeds; next level must contain insects, tadpoles or small fish. Arrows must point in the right direction.	3	
b	Energy flow.	1	
c	At each level there is energy loss; as respiration; death and decay; therefore less energy available to support next level.	2	
d	Pondweed, small fish, larger fish, heron, fox or larger fish, human.	3	9 marks
14 a	To make into proteins/nucleic acids.	1	
b	Nitrogen is unreactive; most living things need soluble nitrates.	2	
c	Conversion of nitrogen to nitrates.	1	
d	Add a fertiliser; plant a crop with root nodules.	2	6 marks

AT3 – Year 10

Question	Answer	Marks	Total
1 a	calcium + oxygen → calcium oxide *One mark for the reactants, one mark for the product.*	2	
c	$2Ca + O_2 \rightarrow 2CaO$ One mark for the reactants, one mark for the product.	2	4 marks
2 a	Any two of: larger hydrocarbons; have more intermolecular forces; which makes the molecules harder to separate.	2	
b i	Oxidation. ii Carbon dioxide and water.	1 2	
iii	$CH_4 + 2O_2 \rightarrow CO_2 + 2H_2O$ *One mark for correct formulae, one mark for correct balancing.*	2	
iv	Carbon monoxide and water.	2	
v	$CH_4 + 1.5O_2 \rightarrow CO + 2H_2O$ or $2CH_4 + 3O_2 \rightarrow 2CO + 4H_2O$ *One mark for correct formulae, one mark for correct balancing.*	2	11 marks
3 a	Igneous. b Interlocking crystals.	1 2	
c	Rock A. It has small crystals.	1	
d	The plate split, and the two halves moved apart.	2	6 marks
4 a	Ions.	1	
b	Ions can travel through the liquid but not the solid.	1	
c i	Anode. ii Cathode.	1 1	
iii	They go to the cathode and turn into atoms (they are neutralised).	2	6 Marks

Answers

AT4 – Year 10

Question			Answer	Marks	Total
1	a	i	Transverse. Energy flow at right angles to displacement.	2	
		ii	A iii 3 Hz iv 1.5 m/s	1 2 2	
	b		Jill's voice vibrates her cup. This sends a longitudinal wave along the string. This vibrates Tom's cup, creating a sound wave.	3	10 marks
2	a		(diagram of reflection off mirror)	1	
	b		All the reflected rays appear to come from a single point behind the mirror.	2	3 marks
3	a		i Ultrasound. ii Radio. iii X-rays	1 1 1	
			iv Microwaves. v X-rays and ultrasound.	1 2	
	b		i It is refracted into the glass, towards the normal.	2	
			ii It is reflected.	1	9 marks
4	a		Heat energy increases vibration of particles in the wall. Particles in solids touch each other, so the energy of vibration is passed from one particle to another.	2	
	b	i	Fibre wool ii It contains air, which is a poor conductor.	1 2	
	c	i	Block up gaps in windows and doors. ii 8 months	1 2	
	d		Double glaze windows to reduce heat conducting through. Reduce the temperature of the house to reduce heat flow to the cold outside.	4	12 marks
5	a	i	1.2 kWh ii 9.6p b Live, neutral, earth.	1 1 3	5 marks
6	a	i	3 m/s^2 ii 60 kg b 300 m	2 2 2	
	c		Friction is the only horizontal force, acting against her velocity. So she has a negative acceleration.	3	
	d		When Melissa falls off she will stop moving very suddenly. This means a large force has acted, producing a large (negative) acceleration. The helmet reduces the acceleration of Melissa's head by increasing the time in which it has to stop moving	3	12 marks
7	a		Rise to room temperature.	1	
	b		Heat energy makes particles in solids vibrate. Particles are connected to each other. So the vibration is passed from particle to particle through the solid.	3	
	c		Heat radiation is reflected from a shiny material, so the rate at which heat energy enters the ice cream is reduced.	2	
	d		Wrap the ice cream in a material which contains trapped air. Air is a poor conductor of heat.	2	
	e		Cold air falls, so that all of the freezer gets cold.	1	9 marks
8	a	i	The distance moved before the car starts to slow down. ii 0.67 s	1 2	
		iii	Tiredness, inebriation.	2	
	b	i	–5.4 m/s^2 ii 933 kg	3 3	11 marks

Answers

AT2 – Year 11

Question	Answer	Marks	Total
1 a c d	Nucleus. b 46, or 23 pairs. Any four of: caused by exposure to radiation; mutagens; ultraviolet light; results in changed genetic code which may cause cancers; birth defects or developmental defects. Mutations; not inherited the same combination of genes from the mother and father.	1 1 4 2	8 marks
2 a c d	B, A, D, C E b 8 Any two of: asexual reproduction; growth; repair. Any two of: cells formed only contain half the number of chromosomes; the cells formed are not identical genetically; 4 daughter cells are formed rather than 2.	4 1 2 2	9 marks
3 a b	Any four of: selecting plant for required characteristics; chopping it into a large number of pieces of tissue; keeping aseptic technique; transferring pieces of tissue to suitable culture medium; growing them under suitable conditions. Advantages – genetic outcome guaranteed; lots produced relatively cheaply. Disadvantages – genetically identical therefore no variation to help overcome adverse environmental conditions; all susceptible to the same microbes and diseases.	4 4	8 marks
4 a b c 	Smooth regular-shaped petals. Will only show in the phenotype if homozygous. Use any letter – e.g. R for regular, r for jagged d RR × rr Gametes: R R / r Rr Rr / r Rr Rr Gametes: R r / R RR rR / r Rr rr all will be regular, because R is dominant three will be regular but one will be jagged Jagged are recessive homozygous; therefore if she breeds jagged with jagged, all the offspring should be jagged.	1 1 4 4 3	13 marks
5	Any five of: grey squirrels have out-competed red ones; because they are better suited to the environment; they can live in a variety of habitats, not just pine woods; they can eat a wider range of foods; they are bigger and can therefore beat red ones if they do end up in the same habitat; they have a greater reproductive potential than red ones; therefore there will be more of them each year; this is an example of survival of the fittest.	5	5 marks
6 a b	Any three of: transparent epidermis; long thin palisade cells tightly packed; lots of chloroplasts; air spaces in the mesophyll; stomata to allow the gases in and out; internal surface area to volume ratio very large. Carbon dioxide concentration.	3 1	4 marks
7 a b c	All the cells of the body. $C_6H_{12}O_6 + 6O_2 \rightarrow 6CO_2 + 6H_2O$ (+ energy) The water on Max's skin is using his body heat; to evaporate it.	1 3 2	6 marks

Answers

Question			Answer	Marks	Total
8	a		Stimulants increase the transmission of impulses across synapses in the brain.	1	
	b	i	Addiction is when the drug produces a dependence within the drug taker, so that they then have to keep taking the drug; withdrawal symptoms are unpleasant effects which the person experiences if they stop or are prevented from taking the drug.	2	
		ii	When the body gets used to a level of the drug and requires more and more to be able to experience the same effect; this leads to the user having to obtain greater amounts of the drug with associated cost implications.	2	5 marks
9	a		+ 1; –2; –4; –5.	4	
	b		If graph plotted correctly, the point at which the length remains unchanged is the answer to c, which is 1.3 mol/dm^3 sugar solution (+ or – 0.1).		
	c			5	
	d		Water moves out of the cells; due to osmosis; down the concentration gradient; therefore all the cells are a little smaller and the cylinder seems to shrink.	4	13 marks
10	a		Homeostasis.	1	
	b		Water; salt; pH; temperature; glucose; carbon dioxide; urea.	3	
	c		Blood is filtered; useful molecules, such as glucose, are reabsorbed; urea and leftover water remain in the kidney tubule to form urine.	4	
	d		On a hot day you would sweat; therefore less water needs to be lost from the body in urine; small volume of concentrated urine; reverse argument for cold day.	3	11 marks

AT3 – Year 11

Question			Answer	Marks	Total
1	a	i	Crude oil. ii To make nitric acid or fertiliser or explosives.	1 2	
		iii	Wages, raw materials, energy, building the factory, etc.	3	
	b	i	A substance which speeds up a reaction and can be recovered.	2	
		ii	Iron. c The reaction will go in either (and both) direction.	1 1	
	d	i	43% ii Cost of compressors or need for thicker walled reaction vessel.	1 1	12 marks
2	a	i	38 ii The number of neutrons. b i Two	1 1 1	
		ii	Strontium and calcium are in the same group/have the same number of outer electrons, so will have very similar properties.	2	
	c	i	14 ii 2, 8, 3	1 1	7 marks
3	a		They have a stable outer shell or they have eight electrons in the outer shell.	1	
	b		i 2 ii 6 c Double positive.	1 1 2	5 marks

Answers

Question			Answer	Marks	Total
4	a		Salt. b i Three ii Three iii 98	1 1 1 1	
	c	i	Eutrophication	1	
		ii	Any three from: algae grow on the surface; this cuts the light to the lower plants; plants die and rot; using up oxygen from the water; killing animals such as fish.	3	8 marks
5	a		Two. b i They are shared.	1 1	
			ii Two electrons in the first shell, four in the second.	2	
	c	i	Alkene group. ii Bromine water. iii Goes colourless.	1 1 1	
		iv	Stays orange/brown.	1	
	d	i	–E–E–E–E–E–E–E–E–E–E– ii Use high pressure and a catalyst.	1 2	
	e	i	PVC. ii Acrylic. iii Polythene. iv Polycarbonate.	1 1 1 1	15 marks
6	a	i	Sugar, moisture, warmth. ii Alcohol (ethanol).	3 1	
	b	i	Speeds up the reaction. ii It can be recovered.	1 1	
	c		Carbon dioxide gas.	1	
	d		Speeds up, to reach its maximum rate at 37 °C, then slows down as the yeast is killed and stops.	4	11 marks
7	a	i	One. ii Seven. iii Ionic.	1 1 1	
		iv	The outer electron is given from the sodium to the chlorine so that each ends up with eight outer electrons.	2	
	b		High. c i Insulator. ii Conductor.	1 1 1	8 marks
8	a		Exothermic b Joules or kilojoules	1 1	
	c		500 × 4.18 × 26 = 54 340 J or 54.340 kJ	2	4 marks
9	a		Collisions: greater surface area/more places for collision.	2	
	b		Particles move faster, collide more often. Particles have more energy so can break bonds more easily.	4	
	c		Increase the concentration, use a catalyst.	2	8 marks

AT4 – Year 11

Question		Answer	Marks	Total
1	a	(circuit diagram with A, M, V) b i 0.72 W ii 2 Ω	2 3 3	
	c	As the resistance of the rheostat increases the current decreases, lowering the power of the motor, so reducing its speed.	3	11 marks
2	a	The comb pulls electrons off his hair. Electrons are negative, leaving the hair positive.	3	
	b	Like charges repel. Each hair is repelled by all the other hairs, forcing it upright.	2	
	c	Plastic is an insulator, so carries the electrons away from the hair. Electrons removed from hair by a metal comb can flow through it back to the hair.	2	7 marks

Answers

Question			Answer	Marks	Total
3	a	i	Kinetic, heat. ii 10 000 J	2 3	
		iii	Some of the KE can become PE as the car moves up, so the brakes need to do less work.	3	
	b	i	5000 W ii 25%	3 3	14 marks
4	a		Furnace, boiler, turbine, generator, transformer. b 30%	5 2	
	c	i	Waste gas from the furnace, from the cooling tower where the steam condenses, heat radiated from the hot boiler.	3	
		ii	Because it is too spread out to be converted into electricity.	1	11 marks
5	a		Stars generate heat energy within them.	1	
	b		Hydrogen atoms collide and join to form helium atoms.	3	
	c		Gravity pulls the particles towards each other, giving them kinetic energy. So the cloud collapses and heats up. Eventually, the pressure and temperature are high enough for fusion to start.	4	
	d		The heat of the star will radiate into space, so it will cool down.	2	10 marks
6	a		The emissions can break up molecules in living cells, killing them or damaging their DNA.	2	
	b		Each nucleus can only decay once. As time goes on, there are fewer and fewer nuclei left to decay.	3	
	c		63 Bq	3	8 marks
7	a			1	
	b		Chemical, electrical, electrical, light	4	
	c	i	3V from battery is shared between LED and resistor. ii 20 Ω	1 3	9 marks
8			Nucleus, alpha, beta, gamma.	4	4 marks
9	a		Cheap to install, but expensive to run.	2	
	b	i	Install double glazing.	1	
		ii	Reduce conduction of heat through the windows by having a layer of trapped air in the window.	2	
	c		Conduction, radiation, convection	3	8 marks
10	a		Iron, because it is easily magnetised. b 6 V	2 2	
	c		Alternating current in the primary creates a changing magnetic field in the secondary, which induces an alternating voltage in the secondary coil.	3	7 marks
11	a		Use KE = $\frac{1}{2} mv^2$	2	
	b	i	10 J ii 27 m c Heat energy.	1 3 1	7 marks

Index

A

acceleration 32, 66, 131
acids 4–5, 29, 102–3
    pH 34, 102
active site 34
active transport 82
adaptations 16–17
addiction reaction 99
addition polymerisation 100, 101
adrenaline and adrenal glands 13
aerobic respiration 86
air 40–1
alcohol 91
algal bloom 103
alkali 102–3
alkali metals 111
    see also potassium; sodium
alkanes 39, 98
    see also methane
alkenes 98–9
alleles 76
alpha particle/radiation 134
alternating current 121
aluminium 46, 49
alveoli 6
ammeter 120
ammonia 29, 104–5
ammonium compounds 103
amplitude 52, 53
anaerobic respiration 86
analogue signal 136
angles of reflection, refraction and incidence 54
animals see life
anode 48–9, 123
antibodies 90
anticlockwise moment 69
arteries 8
artificial selection 79
aseptic technique 79
asexual reproduction 74
atomic mass 106, 134
atomic number 108
atoms 28, 48, 108–9, 134
atria, right and left 9
attraction 118
auxins 14–15

B

bacteria 20, 21
balanced forces 130
balancing levers 69
bases 102–3
batteries 120, 121
beta particle/radiation 134
bicuspid valves 9
bicycle reflectors 55
Big Bang 132

bile 4
binoculars 55
biodegrading 101
biological control 22
biomass, pyramid of 19
black hole 133
blast furnace 47
blood 8, 89
    cells, red and white 3, 8, 90
bond making and breaking 28, 37, 48, 96–7
    see also compounds
braking distance in car 67
breathing see respiration
bromine 99, 112
bronchi and bronchioles 6, 7
Buckminster Fullerene 96
burning 20, 37, 39
butane 39

C

caffeine 91
calcium 46, 48, 107
    compounds 29, 106
calculations, chemical 106–7
camouflage 17
capillaries 8
carbon 46, 47, 49
    compounds 98–101
    cycle 20
    electrons 109
    moles 106, 107
    three forms of 97
carbon dioxide 29, 40, 113
    from burning 20
    as greenhouse gas 23
    molecule 28
    and photosynthesis 80, 81
    and reactions 33, 39
    and respiration 6, 40, 86, 87
carbon monoxide 39, 47
carbonates 29, 113
carnivores 18
catalysts and reactions 32, 104
    see also enzymes
cathode 48–9, 123
cells 2–9
cellulose 2
central nervous system 10
centripetal force 131
CFCs 23
charge 48–9, 118, 119, 134
    see also current; ions
chemical bonds 28
chemical energy 60, 128
chemical reactions see reactions
chlorides 28, 29, 30, 31, 48, 102
chlorine 30, 31, 96, 107, 108, 112
chloroethene 100
chlorophyll 80, 81

chloroplasts 2
chromosomes 74–5, 77
cilia 7
circuits 120
    breaker 63
circular motion 130
circulation 8–9
clockwise moment 69
cloning 79
communications 136
competition 16
compounds 28, 37
    carbon 98–101
    covalent 96, 97
    formulae 28–9
    ionic 48
    transition metals 113
compressions 52
concentration gradient 82
concentration and reactions 32
conduction (electrical) 48, 118
conduction (heat) 58, 61
consumers 18
continental crust 42
contraception 13
control, animal and plant 10–15
convection 42, 58
cooling mechanisms in body 89
copper 46, 47, 49, 107, 113, 129
    compounds 29, 103, 106, 113
copper oxide 103, 113
copper sulphate 106
core of Earth 42
covalent bonding 96
covalent giant structures 97
covalent molecules 97
cramp 86
crust of Earth 42
current 120–1, 122, 123
cycles, natural 13, 20–1
cytoplasm 2

D

danger see safety and danger
decay 20
    radioactive 134–5
decomposers 20
denatured enzymes 5
depressant drugs 91
diabetes 12
diamond 97
diffraction 55
diffusion 3, 5, 6, 82
digestion/digestive system 4–5
digital signal 136
diode 123
direct current 121
discharge 118

diseases see under medicine
displacement reactions 46, 112
distance 67
    –time graphs 64–5
distillation of oil 38, 98
dominant alleles 76
dormancy, control of 15
double circulatory system 9
drugs (addictive) 91
drugs (medicines) 35, 90
dwarfism 13

E

earthing electricity 62–3
earthquakes 42, 56
echoes 56
ecology see under environment
effector 11
electricity 60–3, 118–23
    generating 126–9
    off-peak 61
    sources of 60
    static 118–19
    transporting 128–9
    wiring 62–3
    see also charge; electromagnetism; voltage
electrodes 48–9, 123
electrolysis 48–9
electrolyte 48
electromagnetism 126–7
    waves/spectrum 57
electrons (and shells) 48, 108, 109, 110, 118
elements 28, 110–13
    Periodic Table 110–13
ellipse/circular orbit 132
emulsifying 4
endangered species 23
endoscope 55
endothermic reactions 36, 37, 40
energy 36–41
    chemical 60, 128
    in home 58–63
    kinetic 58, 124–5, 128
    loss in food chain 19
    and reactions 32, 36–7
    renewable 60
    from respiration 86
    transfer 52–3, 58–9, 128–9
    see also electricity; heat; light; power
environment
    ecology 16–23
    pollution 23, 60, 103
    variation and 75
enzymes 4–5, 34–5
equations, chemical 30–1
ethane 39, 98
eutrophication 103

Index

evolution 75, 78
exercise 86
exothermic reactions 36, 37, 40
expansions 52
eye 10

F

families (Periodic Table) 110–13
farming 22
fermentation 35
fertilisation 75
fertilisers 22, 103
fight or flight 13
fluorine 109, 112
food
    chains and webs 18–19, 22
    digestion 4–5
    for plants
        see photosynthesis
    production 22, 35
forces 68–9, 124–5
formulae 28–9, 98–9, 106–7
fossil fuels, burning 20, 37, 60
fossils 44, 78
fractional distillation 38, 98
free fall 130
frequency 52, 53
friction 66
fuels 36, 37, 38–9
    see also fossil fuels
fungi 20
fuses 63
fusion reactions 132

G

gall bladder 4
gamma rays 57, 134
gases 38
    exchange 6
    noble 48, 113
    see also carbon dioxide; hydrogen; nitrogen; oxygen
genes and genetics 74, 75
    genetic engineering 35, 79
genotype 76
geotropism 14–15
giant structures 28, 96, 97
glands 12–13
global warming 23
glucose *see* sugars
glycogen 12
gold 46, 113
graphite 97
gravity 130–1
greenhouse gas 23
groups (Periodic Table) 110–13
growth hormones 13

H

Haber process 104–5
half-life 135
halogens and halides 112
    see also chlorine
health *see* medicine
heart 8, 9
heat and heat energy
    in body 89
    and Haber process 104
    for houses 59–60
    and photosynthesis 80, 81
    and reactions 36, 37, 40
    transfer 58–9, 60, 61, 128
    and transition metals 113
helium 28, 109
herbicides 22
herbivores 18
heterozygous 76
homeostasis 88–9
homozygous 76
hormones 12–15
hydrocarbons 38–9, 98–9
hydrochloric acid 29, 30, 102, 103
hydroelectric energy 60
hydrogen 29
    and alkenes 99
    electrons 109
    in equations 30, 31
    molecule 96, 106
    moles 106, 107
    reactivity 46
    and stars 133
hydrogen chloride 28, 31
hydrogen peroxide 32

I

igneous rocks 44, 45
image 54
immunity and immunisation 90
induction of electricity 126
information 136
infra-red radiation 57, 58, 59, 136
inheritance 76–7
insulation (electrical) 63, 118, 129
insulation (heat) 59, 61
insulin 12
intensive farming 22
inter/intramolecular forces 101
intrusions 45
iodine 112
ionic bonding/compounds 48, 96
ions 48, 109
iron 107, 113
    compounds 29, 46
    reduction and extraction 46, 47
    soft 129
isotopes 108

K

kidneys 88
kinetic energy 58, 124–5, 128

L

lactic acid 86
leaves 3, 81, 84–5
leguminous plants 17, 21
lenses 54, 55
levers, balancing 69
life and living things (mainly animals) 1–27, 74–95, 132
    see also plants
light
    communicating with 136
    and photosynthesis 60, 80, 81
    refraction and reflection 54, 56
    and resistance 123
    waves 54–5
limiting factors 81
lithium 109, 111
lithosphere 42
live wire 62–3
liver 12, 88
longitudinal waves 52
lungs 7, 88

M

magnesium 46
    compounds 29, 30, 109
magnetism/magnetic field 126–7
mantle of Earth 42
mass
    and acceleration 66
    atomic 106, 134
    formulae 106–7
    and gravity 130
    number 108
materials 28–51, 118–23
medicine/medical procedures
    diseases and disorders 76, 77, 90
    drugs 35, 90
    and radiation 55, 56, 57, 135
meiosis 74–5
membrane, cell 2
menstrual cycle 13
metals
    as conductors 61
    and halogens 112
    from minerals 46–7
    reactivity 19, 46, 111
    transition 113
    see also alkali metals
metamorphic rocks 44, 45
methane 37, 38, 98, 106
micropropagation 79
microwaves 57, 59, 136
minerals
    metals from 46–7
    and plants 83
    in rocks 44, 45
mitochondria 2
mitosis 74, 79
molecules 28, 96–7, 98, 106–7
moles 106–7
moment (turning effect) 68–9
monohybrid 77
monomers 100
moons 132
motion 64–9, 130
motor 125
motor neurones 10–11
mucus 7
muscle fatigue 86
mutation 75
mutualism 17

N

National Grid 128
natural selection 75, 78
negative charge 48–9, 118, 123, 134
negative feedback 89
nervous system 10–11
neurones 10–11
neutral wire 62–3
neutralisation 102–3
neutron 48, 108
neutron star 133
nicotine 91
nitrates 102
nitric acid 29, 102
nitrogen 6, 107, 109
    cycle 21
    and plants 83, 103
noble gases 48, 113
non-renewable energy
    see fossil fuels
normal, the 54
nucleus of atom 48, 108, 134
nucleus of cell 2

O

oceanic crust and plates 42, 43
oceans 41
oestrogen 12, 13
oil and uses 38–9, 98–101
omnivores 18
optimum temperature 34
orbits 131
ore 45
osmosis 82–3
oxidation 39, 111
oxides 29, 46, 48, 103, 113
oxygen 29, 40, 109
    debt 86
    molecule 28, 96, 106, 107
    and photosynthesis 80
    in reactions 32, 39
    and respiration 6, 8, 40, 86

Index

P

palisade cells 3
parallel, circuit in 120–1
parasites 17
partially permeable
    membrane 82
pentane 39
percentage yields 107
Periodic Table 110–13
    period in 110
peripheral nervous system 10
periscope 55
peristalsis 5
pests and pesticides 22
pH *see under* acids
phenotype 76
phloem 82, 84–5
phosphorus 83, 103
photosynthesis 40, 60, 80–1, 83
phototropism 14
pitfall traps 16
pituitary gland 15
pivot 68
planetary nebula 133
planets 131, 132
plants 80–5
    adaptations 17
    cell 2
    control in 14–15
    cuttings 15, 79
    minerals 83
    see also leaves
plasma 8
plastics 99, 100–1
plate tectonics 42–3
platelets 8
pollution 23, 60, 103
poly(e)thene 100
polymers 100–1
pooter 16
populations 16–17
positive charge 48–9, 118, 123, 134
potassium 29, 83, 103, 111
potassium hydroxide 103
potential difference 121
potential energy 124–5
power
    calculating 122
    nuclear 135
    rating 62
    see also electricity; energy
predators and prey 17, 22
pregnancy 13
primary coil 129
producers 18
products 30–1, 33, 80
progesterone 13
propane 39, 98, 99
proton 48, 108
    number 108
pulses 56
p-waves 56
pyramids of biomass and
    numbers 18–19

Q

quadrat 16

R

radiation 57, 58, 59, 134–5
    radioactivity 134–5
radio waves 57
rarefactions 52
reactions/reactivity 30–1, 36–7
    fusion 132
    metals 19, 46, 111
    rates of 32–3
    reactants 30–1, 80
    reversible 104–5
receptors 10–11
recessive alleles 76
recycling 101
red giant 133
red shift 133
reduction 46–7
reflection 54, 56
reflex actions 11
refraction 54
relative atomic mass 106
renewable energy 60
reproduction 74–5
repulsion 118
resistance 122, 123
respiration/breathing 6–7, 40, 86–7
reversible reactions 104–5
rheostat 122
rocks 44–5, 78
    see also metals
root hair cells 83, 84

S

safety and danger
    electric 62–3, 119
    radioactive 134
    road 67
salts 102, 112
    see also sodium chloride
satellites 136
saturated molecules 98
saving energy 59
sea floor spreading 43
secondary coil 129
secondary sexual
    characteristics 12
sedimentary rocks 44, 45
seismic waves 56
selection 79
semiconductor 123
senses/sense organs 10–11
series, circuit in 120
sex linkage 77
sexual development 12
sexual reproduction 74–5
skin 88
smoking 7, 91
sodium 46, 48, 107, 109, 111, 112
sodium chloride 29, 30, 96, 102, 106, 112
sodium hydroxide 29, 102, 103, 113
solar energy 60
solar system 132
solvents 91
sound 52, 56
space 131–3
speed
    acceleration 32, 66
    and gravity 130
    –time graphs 65
    of waves 53
spring 52
stars 132–3
steam turbine 128
stimulant drugs 91
stimuli and reactions to 10–11
stomata 81, 85
subduction 43
sugars (glucose and sucrose)
    in body, controlling 12
    and fermentation 35
    and plants 80, 82
    and respiration 40, 86
sulphates 102
sulphur 107
sulphur dioxide 23
sulphuric acid 29, 103
supernova 133
surface area and reactions 32
survival of fittest 79
sustainable development 23
s-waves 56
switch 63
symbols 28
synapse 11

T

target cells 12
temperature 34, 89, 123
    high *see* heat
    and reactions 32, 36, 37
terminal speed 130
testosterone 12
thermal decomposition 113
thinking distance in car 67
thrust 66
time graphs 64–5
tissue culture 92
tolerance, drug 91
total internal reflection 54
transformers 129
transition metals 113
translocation 82
transpiration 84–5
transport
    in body 8–9
    electricity 128–9
    in plants 81–3
transverse waves 52
tricuspid valves 9
trophic levels 18–19
turbine 128
turning forces 68

U

ultrasound 56
ultraviolet waves 57
Universe 132
unsaturated alkene 99

V

vacuole, cell 2
valves in heart 9
variation 75
veins 8
velocity 130–1
ventricles, right and left 9
vibration 52, 58
villi 5
volcanoes 41, 42
voltage 62, 120, 121, 122
    -current curves 123
    induced 126
    very high 129
voltmeter 121

W

warming mechanisms in body 89
water
    in body 86, 88
    fish in 16
    formula 28, 29
    oceans 41
    in plants 83–5
    in reactions 32, 111
    and respiration 40, 86
wave energy 60
wavelength 52, 53
waves 52–72, 136
weedkillers, selective 15
weight 130
white dwarf 133
wind energy 60
withdrawal symptoms 91
work and energy 124–5

X

X-rays 57
xylem 83, 84–5

Y

yields 107

Z

zinc 29, 46